INTERNATIONAL
GCSE
(9–1)

GRAHAM HILL
ROBERT WENSLEY

Chemistry
for Edexcel International GCSE

SECOND
EDITION

D1335974

HODDER
EDUCATION
AN HACHETTE UK COMPANY

The Acknowledgments are listed on page viii.

Although every effort has been made to ensure that website addresses are correct at time of going to press, Hodder Education cannot be held responsible for the content of any website mentioned. It is sometimes possible to find a relocated web page by typing in the address of the home page for a website in the URL window of your browser.

Orders: please contact Bookpoint Ltd, 130 Milton Park, Abingdon, Oxon OX14 4SB.
Telephone: (44) 01235 827720. Fax: (44) 01235 400454. Lines are open 9.00–17.00, Monday to Saturday, with a 24-hour message answering service. Visit our website at www.hoddereducation.co.uk

© Graham Hill, Robert Wensley 2017

First published in 2017 by

Hodder Education

An Hachette UK Company,

338 Euston Road

London NW1 3BH

Impression number   5 4 3 2 1

Year   2021   2020   2019   2018   2017

Cover photo © Andrew Brookes/Corbis

Typeset in ITC Legacy Serif by Elektra Media Ltd.

Printed in Italy

Project managed by Elektra Media Ltd.

A catalogue record for this title is available from the British Library.

ISBN 978 151 040 5202

Contents

Contents

Section 4 Organic Chemistry

Getting the most from this book

Welcome to the Edexcel International GCSE (9–1) Chemistry Student Book. This book has been divided into four Sections, following the structure and order of the Edexcel Specification, which you can find on the Edexcel website for reference. Section 1 has been divided into two parts to help you structure your learning.

Each Section has been divided into a number of smaller Chapters to help you manage your learning.

The following features have been included to help you get the most from this book.

PRACTICAL

Practical boxes tell you whether the practical work is required or suggested by the exam board, and include links to the specification.

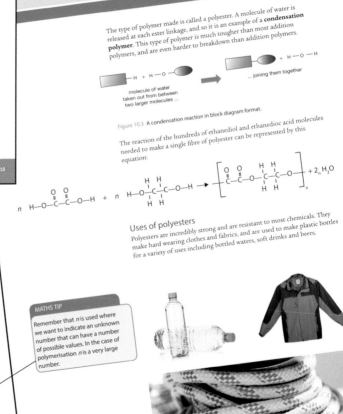

RESEARCH • CALCULATE

Try the activity before you start, and then have a look at it again once you have completed the Section to see if your responses are different before and after learning more about the topics.

MATHS TIP

Maths tips give you additional help with the maths in the book so you can avoid losing valuable marks in the exam.

EXAM TIP

Exam tips throughout the book will guide you in your learning process.

STUDY QUESTIONS

At the end of each Chapter you will find Study Questions. Work through these in class or on your own for homework. Answers are available online.

Summary

I am confident that:

✓ I can describe how the mixture of hydrocarbons in crude oil is separated using fractional distillation, and can name the main fractions and state the number of carbon atoms in each fraction

✓ I can describe the trend in boiling points and viscosity of the main fractions of crude oil
  • As the number of carbon atoms increases, the boiling point increases.
  • As the number of carbon atoms increases, the viscosity increases.

✓ I know that fractional distillation of crude oil provides insufficient short-chain hydrocarbons such as gasoline
  • The process of cracking makes long-chain hydrocarbons into alkenes and useful shorter-chain hydrocarbons.

✓ I understand the complete and incomplete combustion of carbon-based fuels
  • Incomplete combustion produces carbon monoxide
  • Inhalation of carbon monoxide is dangerous as it prevents absorption of oxygen in the body.

✓ I know that nitrogen in the air at high temperatures inside car engines can be converted to nitrogen oxides
  • Nitrogen oxides as well sulfur oxides contribute to acid rain.

✓ I know the products of complete and incomplete combustion of hydrocarbons
  • Complete combustion produces only water and carbon dioxide.
  • Partial combustion produces water and carbon monoxide.
  • Incomplete combustion produces water and carbon (soot).

✓ I can explain the terms
  • homologous series
  • hydrocarbon

• saturated
• unsaturated
• general formula
• displayed formula
• isomerism
• functional group.

✓ I know that alkanes are made from only carbon and hydrogen
  • Alkanes have the general formula C_nH_{2n+2}
  • They have only single bonds.
  • They are fairly unreactive.

✓ I know that alkenes are made from only carbon and hydrogen
  • Alkenes have the general formula C_nH_{2n}
  • They have at least one double carbon-carbon bond.
  • They are very reactive.

✓ I can draw displayed formulae for straight-chain alkanes with up to six carbon atoms and name them
  • These are named according to the longest straight chain of carbon atoms, methane(1C), ethane (2C), propane (3C), butane (4C), pentane (5C), and hexane (6C).

✓ I can draw displayed formulae for the alkenes ethene and propene

✓ I can describe the UV light-initiated substitution reaction of methane with bromine
  • I can write a balanced equation using displayed formulae.

✓ I can describe the addition reaction of alkenes with bromine
  • The decolorisation of bromine water is a test for alkenes.

✓ I can describe how ethanol can be manufactured, by:
  • the reaction of ethene with steam
  • the fermentation of sugars such as glucose by yeast.

✓ I can describe how ethanol may be oxidised by:
  • air in combustion
  • microbial oxidation
  • potassium dichromate(VI).

Sample answers and expert's comments

1 Methane is the simplest hydrocarbon. The table below shows some information about methane molecules.

	Methane	Ethane
molecular formula	CH_4	
displayed formula		
dot and cross diagram of bonding		
state at room temperature	gas	

a) Copy and complete the table to show the same information for ethane as is shown for methane. (4)

b) What is a hydrocarbon? (1)

c) Methane and ethane are part of a homologous series. What is a homologous series? (1)

d) Methane burns to produce water vapour. Name the other three possible products of the combustion of methane, and state the conditions necessary for each product to be made. (3)

(Total for question = 9 marks)

Student response			Expert comments and tips for success
a)		Ethane	Full marks. The formula is correct and so are the displayed formula and dot and cross diagram. The answer shows a clear understanding of carbon's need for four bonds, and hydrogen's one bond.
molecular formula		C_2H_6 ✓	
displayed formula			
dot and cross diagram of bonding			
state at room temperature		gas ✓	
b) A compound containing only carbon and hydrogen ✓			Correctly explains the elements present in a hydrocarbon.

At the end of each Section, you will find a summary checklist highlighting the key facts that you need to know and understand, and key skills that you learnt in the Section.

Before you try the Exam-style questions, look at the sample answers and expert's comments to see how marks are awarded and common mistakes to avoid.

Biopolyesters

Polyesters are very resistant to chemical and microbial attack. This means that they can pose a significant environmental hazard as they are hard to biodegrade. To overcome this problem chemists have designed biopolyesters. These are polyesters that on prolonged contact with oxygen break down into carbon dioxide, water, sometimes methane, and biomass. This means that the residue from the polyester is non-toxic and can be subject to natural decay processes.

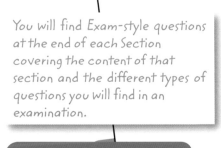

propanediol(HOCH$_2$CH$_2$CH$_2$OH).

4 Evaluate the benefits of using a biopolyester thread against an ordinary polyester thread for making surgical stitches inside a person's body.

...tween ethanol and

...t of the homologous series
...plain why methanedioc acid

...r can be made
...OOCCOOH) and

EXTEND AND CHALLENGE

When you have completed all the Exam-style questions for the Section, try the extension activity.

You will find Exam-style questions at the end of each Section covering the content of that section and the different types of questions you will find in an examination.

ANSWERS

Answers for all questions and activities in this book can be found online at www.hoddereducation.co.uk/igcsechemistry

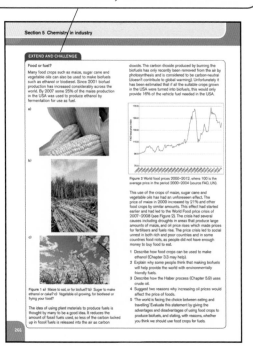

Section 5 Chemistry in industry

EXTEND AND CHALLENGE

Food or fuel?

Many food crops such as maize, sugar cane and vegetable oils can also be used to make biofuels such as ethanol or biodiesel. Since 2001 biofuel production has increased considerably across the world. By 2007 some 25% of the maize production in the USA was used to produce ethanol by fermentation for use as fuel.

Figure 1 a) Maize to eat, or for biofuel? b) Sugar to make ethanol or cake? c) Vegetable oil growing, for biodiesel or frying your food?

The idea of using plant materials to produce fuels is thought by many to be a good idea. It reduces the amount of fossil fuels used, so less of the carbon locked up in fossil fuels is released into the air as carbon

dioxide. The carbon dioxide produced by burning the biofuels has only recently been removed from the air by photosynthesis and is considered to be carbon-neutral (doesn't contribute to global warming). Unfortunately it has been estimated that if all the suitable crops grown in the USA were turned into biofuels, this would only provide 16% of the vehicle fuel needed in the USA.

Figure 2 World food prices 2000-2012, where 100 is the average price in the period 2000-2004 (source FAO, UN).

This use of the crops of maize, sugar cane and vegetable oils has had an unforeseen effect. The price of maize in 2009 increased by 21% and other food crops by similar amounts. This effect had started earlier and had led to the World Food price crisis of 2007-2008 (see Figure 2). The crisis had several causes including droughts in areas that produce large amounts of maize, and oil price rises which made prices for fertilisers and fuels rise. The price crisis led to social unrest in both rich and poor countries and in some countries food riots, as people did not have enough money to buy food to eat.

1 Describe how food crops can be used to make ethanol (Chapter 33 may help).

2 Explain why some people think that making biofuels will help provide the world with environmentally friendly fuels.

3 Describe how the Haber process (Chapter 5.9) uses crude oil.

4 Suggest two reasons why increasing oil prices would affect the price of foods.

5 'The world is facing the choice between eating and travelling.' Evaluate this statement by giving the advantages and disadvantages of using food crops to produce biofuels, and stating, with reasons, whether you think we should use food crops for fuels.

266

Acknowledgments

The Publisher would like to thank the following for permission to reproduce copyright photographs:

p.1 © EcoView – Fotolia.com; p.2 l © jubax – Fotolia.com, r © Wissmann Design – Fotolia.com; p.6 t © pixelbliss / 123RF, b © Sinisa Botas – Fotolia.com; p.9 t © GRAHAM J. HILLS / SCIENCE PHOTO LIBRARY, b © Science Museum / Science & Society Picture Library; p.10 © Science Photo Library; p.12 © lucielang – Fotolia.com; p.13 © boonsom – Fotolia.com; p.14 © Lance Bellers – Fotolia.com; p.15 © Geoff Tompkinson / Science Photo Library; p.18 t © Image Source / Getty Images, b © A. Barrington Brown, Gonville and Caius College / Science Photo Library; p.19 © Mark Physsas – Fotolia.com; p.21 © Alexandra Karamyshev – Fotolia.com; p.23 © Marco Desscouleurs – Fotolia.com; p.26 © ewg3D / iStockphoto; p.29 © .shock – Fotolia.com; p.30 © buntworthy – Fotolia.com; p.33 © nickolae – Fotolia.com; p.34 Courtesy of Wikipedia Commons; p.36 © Mikael Damkier – Fotolia.com; p.41 t © George Steinmetz / Getty Images, b © John Foxx / Getty Images; p.48 l © rabbit75_fot – Fotolia.com, r © Steven Puetzer / Getty Images; p.49 © 2012 IGN France; p.50 l © Schlierner – Fotolia.com, r © Konstantin Sh – Fotolia.com; p.51 tl © Gabriel Gonzalez G. – Fotolia.com, tr © Chris Leachman – Fotolia.com, bl © Lev – Fotolia.com, br © Kayros Studio – Fotolia.com; p.54 © MARTYN F CHILLMAID / SCIENCE PHOTO LIBRARY; p.55 © J.M. – Fotolia.com; p.57 © Ingram Publishing Limited / Alamy; p.58 © Africa Studio – Fotolia.com; p.60 l © think4photop – Fotolia.com, r © nickos – Fotolia.com; p.61 © Björn Wylezich – Fotolia.com; p.62 © Martyn F. Chillmaid; p.65 © morchella – Fotolia.com; p.67 © Mary Perry / 123RF; p.72 © Larry Brownstein / Getty Images; p.73 t © Olga Lipatova / 123RF, t © Claudio Divizia – Fotolia.com; p.75 © Martyn F. Chillmaid; p.77 © RIA NOVOSTI / SCIENCE PHOTO LIBRARY; p.78 tl © Unclesam – Fotolia.com, tr © Vasiliy Timofeev – Fotolia.com, b © Becky Stares – Fotolia.com; p.81 © kyrien – Fotolia.com; p.82 t © FomaA – Fotolia.com, b © pedrolieb – Fotolia.com; p.83 l © Gary Ombler / Getty Images, r © merial – Fotolia.com; p.84 © Rafael Ben-Ari / 123RF; p.87 © Leonid Andronov – Fotolia.com; p.88 © Magalice – Fotolia.com; p.89 © Anne Wanjie; p.90 © terex – Fotolia.com; p.91 © Adwo / Shutterstock; p.92 t © John Henderson / Alamy, b © ellenamani – Fotolia.com; p.95 Courtesy of Wikipedia Commons; p.106 l © Tlex – Fotolia.com, r © Vincenzo Lombardo / Getty Images; p.107 © zimmytws – Fotolia.com; p.108 © sciencephotos / Alamy; p.110 t © Bettmann / Getty Images, b @ jeffrey waibel / iStockphoto; p.112 l © ANDREW LAMBERT PHOTOGRAPHY / SCIENCE PHOTO LIBRARY, c © MARTYN F. CHILLMAID / SCIENCE PHOTO LIBRARY, r © CHARLES D. WINTERS / SCIENCE PHOTO LIBRARY; p.113 tl © zirconicusso – Fotolia.com, tc © agnadevi – Fotolia.com, tr © tlorna – Fotolia.com, bl © Ivaylo Ivanov / 123RF, bc © razorpix / Alamy, br © Metta image / Alamy; p.114 © Martyn F Chillmaid; p.116 t © PhotoAlto / 27 Objects; b © Herbivore – Fotolia.com; p.117 © Thermit Welding; p.119 © Imagestate Media (John Foxx) / Deep V3052; p.123 © Scanrail – Fotolia.com; p.126 t © davis – Fotolia.com, b © GIPhotoStock/SCIENCE PHOTO LIBRARY; p.129 t © DEA / G. DAGLI ORTI / Getty Images, a © photocrew – Fotolia.com, b © atoss – Fotolia.com, c © Viktar Malyshchyts / 123RF, d © Roman Ivaschenko – Fotolia.com, e © yakovlev – Fotolia.com, f © M.Studio – Fotolia.com; p.131 © Anna Ivanova / 123RF; p.136 © Ingram Publishing Limited / Lifestyle Platinum Vol 1 CD 3; p.137 © Graham Corney / Alamy; p.138 t © DIRK WIERSMA/SCIENCE PHOTO LIBRARY, b © ARNO MASSEE/SCIENCE PHOTO LIBRARY; p.139 © MeanTeam – Fotolia.com; p.140 © Howard Davies / Alamy; p.141 © Universal Images Group / DeAgostini / Alamy; p.143 © Laurentiu Iordache / 123RF; p.144 t © kenzo – Fotolia.com, bl © dell – Fotolia.com, bc © EpicStockMedia – Fotolia.com, br © alma_sacra – Fotolia.com; p.146 © gabe123 / 123RF; p.147 © CHARLES D. WINTERS / SCIENCE PHOTO LIBRARY; p.150 l © timolina– Fotolia.com, r © brulove – Fotolia.com; p.152 © jayfish – Fotolia.com; p.156 © Anne Wanjie; p.157 © Jeff J Daly / Alamy; p.160 © Martyn F Chillmaid; p.163 t © akeeris – Fotolia.com, b © Rémi BORNET – Fotolia.com; p.167 © Ronald Hudson – Fotolia.com; p.171 t © Alexander Gospodinov – Fotolia.com, b © SCIENCE PHOTO LIBRARY; p.172 © Colin Edwards – Fotolia.com; p.188 © chiakto – Fotolia.com; p.189 © Konstantin Kulikov – Fotolia.com; p.190 © SCIENCE PHOTO LIBRARY; p.193 © MARTYN F. CHILLMAID/ SCIENCE PHOTO LIBRARY; p.196 © www.takenbychris.co.uk; p.198 a © niranjancreatnz – Fotolia.com, b © megasquib – Fotolia.com, c © megasquib – Fotolia.com, d © Stanislav Khomutovsky / 123RF; p.200 © smileus / 123RF; p.201 © Ingus Evertovskis – Fotolia.com; p.206 © Carolyn Franks / 123RF; p.209 © Anne Wanjie; p.213 © wrangler – Fotolia.com; p.216 t © Owen Price – iStockphoto, b © Imagestate Media (John Foxx) / Spirit V3070; p.221 l © EMILIO SEGRE VISUAL ARCHIVES / AMERICAN INSTITUTE OF PHYSICS / SCIENCE PHOTO LIBRARY, p.230 © alexandre zveiger – Fotolia.com; p.231 t © imagebroker / Alamy, b © Brooke Becker – Fotolia.com; p.234 © Leung Cho Pan / 123RF; p.235 © Mark Richardson – Fotolia.com; p.237 © mmmx – Fotolia.com; p.239 © DAVID HALPERN/SCIENCE PHOTO LIBRARY; p.240 © Yaroslavna Kulinkina – Fotolia.com; p.242 © BSANI – Fotolia.com; p.243 © Lenscap / Alamy; p.246 t © MChillmaid, b © maxriesgo / 123RF; p.248 © Africa Studio – Fotolia.com; p.249 © Cultura Creative / Alamy; p.251 © cantor pannatto – Fotolia.com; p.252 © Mohamed Asama / 123RF; p.255 © Maitree Laipitaksin / 123RF; p.257 © tobi / 123RF; p.258 © Evgeny Litvinov – Fotolia.com; p.259 © JAMES HOLMES / ZEDCOR / SCIENCE PHOTO LIBRARY; p.260 © Global Warming Images / Alamy; p.261 © serezniy / 123RF; p.262 tl © karandaev / 123RF, tr © Viktor Nikitin / 123RF, b © shopartgallerycom / 123RF; p.272 t © © OpenStreetMap contributors.

1
Principles of chemistry 1

DISCUSS · PRESENT

1 Make a list of 20 items you have used today. Separate them into two groups: those that are good conductors of electricity and those that are poor conductors. Can you suggest why some materials conduct electricity and others do not?

2 Find out what a shorthand typist used to do. Suggest what use 'shorthand' might be in chemistry.

3 There are two methods for making a chemical fertiliser. One method turns 60% of the raw materials into the fertiliser. The other method converts 90% of the raw materials into the fertiliser, but uses four times as much energy. Suggest the economic and environmental advantages of each process.

Everything around us, everything we use, and even our bodies, depend on taking raw materials like this iron ore and transforming it into useful substances. The cars we ride in depend on the chemical processes that turn the iron ore into steel.

Why are some substances solids, others liquids and some gases?

What are the rules governing chemical reactions? How can we predict what will happen in different reactions? How can we describe to other people easily in a universal language what is happening when two substances react together?

To understand all of these we need to know the science of substances – the principles of chemistry.

By the end of this section you should:
- be familiar with the states of matter
- know how to obtain pure substances
- understand the Periodic Table, what it is and how it is useful in chemistry (this is on p. 273)
- be able to describe the structure of an atom using information from the Periodic Table of elements
- be able to describe the electronic configuration of the first 20 elements of the Periodic Table
- be able to calculate the relative formula mass of a compound.

1.1 Particles and solubility

How does the liquid get through the filter paper when filter coffee is made? The coffee grains don't get through the paper. Why is this?

When sugar is added to hot tea or coffee, it dissolves quickly. The sugar seems to disappear. What happens to the sugar when it dissolves? Where does the sugar go?

Figure 1.1 Everyday evidence for particles.

■ Dissolving is evidence

Look at the photos in Figure 1.1 and try to answer the questions above. In order to answer these questions, you will need to use the idea that:

> All materials are made up of particles.

We can explain how the sugar dissolves and disappears using the idea of particles. Both sugar and water are made up of very small particles. These particles are much too small to see, even under a microscope. When sugar dissolves, tiny particles break off each solid granule. These tiny invisible sugar particles mix with the water particles in the liquid. The solution tastes sweet even though you cannot see the sugar.

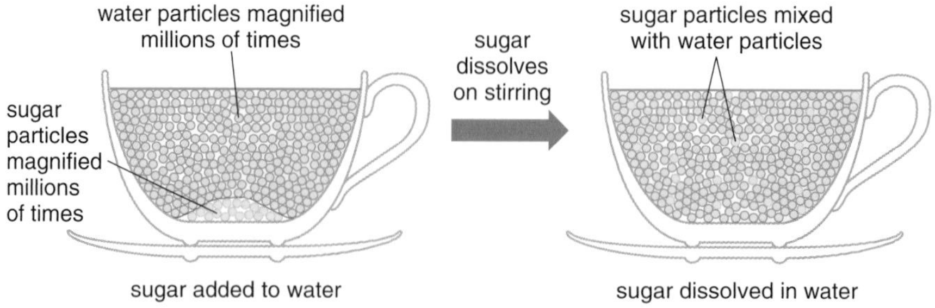

PRACTICAL

If possible, get some sugar and stir it into a cup of warm water (Figure 1.2). Watch the sugar disappear as you stir the water. Sugar dissolving is practical evidence for particles.
Do not eat or taste the sugar solution if it has been made in the laboratory.

water particles magnified millions of times

sugar particles mixed with water particles

sugar dissolves on stirring

sugar particles magnified millions of times

sugar added to water

sugar dissolved in water

Figure 1.2 Explaining what happens when sugar dissolves in water.

The sugar is the substance that dissolves. We call a substance that dissolves the **solute.** The water that the sugar dissolves in is called the **solvent**. The mixture of dissolved sugar and water is called a **solution**.

This experiment will enable you to discover the maximum mass of salt that can dissolve in water at a specific temperature. Make sure eye protection is worn for this experiment.

1. Measure 100 cm³ of water into a beaker. This will have a mass of 100 g.
2. Record the temperature of the water.
3. Add 5 g of salt to the water and stir. Look to see if there is any undissolved salt left in the bottom of the beaker.
4. If all the salt has dissolved add another 5 g of salt and stir again.
5. Keep adding 5 g of salt at a time and stirring until there is some undissolved salt left in the bottom of the beaker. Make a note of how many grams of salt you have added in total.

When no more salt will dissolve in the water you have a saturated solution. Your experimental results will be the solubility of salt in grams per 100 g of water.

Solvents, solutes and solutions

Not all substances dissolve in water. Different masses of different substances (solutes) dissolve in water. There is a maximum mass of a solute that can dissolve in the solvent. When no more solute can dissolve in the solution we say the solution is **saturated**.

Solubilities are often measured in g of solute per 100 g of solvent.

For many substances the temperature of the solvent affects the maximum mass of solute you can dissolve in 100 g of solution. Increasing the solvent's temperature usually increases the mass of solute that dissolves. If you repeat the experiment above at five different temperatures you can plot a graph of solubility in g per 100 g of solvent against temperature. Figure 1.3 shows a graph for the solubility of sodium chloride (salt) at different temperatures.

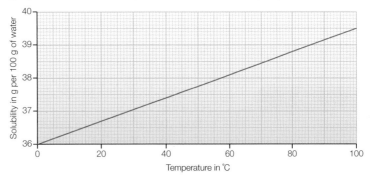

Figure 1.3 A graph of the solubility of sodium chloride at different temperatures.

Solubility curves

Not all graphs of solubility against temperature are linear relationships. Often they are curves. Figure 1.4 shows solubility curves for four different substances.

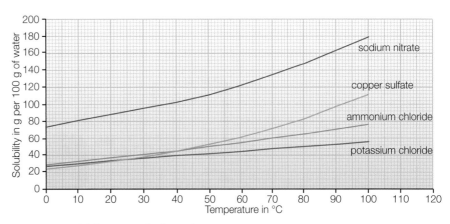

Figure 1.4 Solubility curves for four substances.

A straight line graph like the one in Figure 1.3 shows a relationship of $y = mx + c$. It is a linear relationship between two variables, x and y. This means that the value on the vertical or y-axis is always equal to the value on the horizontal x-axis multiplied by a constant m plus another constant c.

The solubility of each of these substances can be found from the graph at any temperature between 0 °C and 100 °C. If you need to know the mass of sodium nitrate needed to make a saturated solution at 80 °C you should:

- find the temperature you want on the horizontal x-axis, 80 °C
- look up the line at 80 °C until you find the curve for sodium nitrate
- look across at the y-axis to read off the mass needed to make a saturated solution in 100 g of water.

Finding solubilities by evaporation

If you make a saturated solution of anhydrous sodium sulfate using 100 cm³ of water you can find out the mass of sodium sulfate dissolved by heating the solution in an evaporating basin. Weigh the basin empty, add the solution, heat and evaporate the water. When the basin is dry re-weigh the basin. The difference between the two mass readings is the mass of sodium sulfate dissolved in 100 g of water.

■ How large are the particles of substances?

Anyone who cooks knows that a small amount of pepper, ginger or curry powder will give food a really strong taste. Too much spice can spoil the whole meal. This suggests that tiny particles in the spice can spread throughout the whole meal.

Figure 1.5 shows an experiment that will help to give you some idea about the size of particles.

1 Dissolve 1 g of dark purple potassium manganate(VII) crystals in 1000 cm³ of water.
2 Take 100 cm³ of this solution and dilute it to 1000 cm³ with water.
3 Now take 100 cm³ of the once-diluted solution and dilute this to 1000 cm³ with more water.
4 Carry out further dilutions until you get a solution in which you can only *just* see the pink colour. It is possible to make six dilutions before the pink colour is so faint that it is only just noticeable.

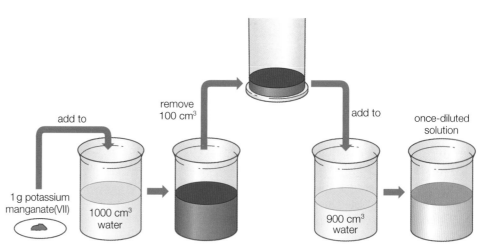

add to

remove 100 cm³

add to

once-diluted solution

1 g potassium manganate(VII)

1000 cm³ water

900 cm³ water

Figure 1.5 Estimating the size of particles in potassium manganate(VII). **If you try this experiment, wear eye protection.**

When potassium manganate(VII) dissolves, its particles spread throughout the water making a dark purple solution. When this solution is diluted, the particles spread further apart.

This experiment shows that the tiny particles in only 1 g of potassium manganate(VII) can colour 1 000 000 000 (one thousand million) cm^3 of water. This suggests that there must be millions and millions of tiny particles in only 1 g of potassium manganate(VII).

Similar experiments show that the particles in all substances are extremely small. For example, there are more air particles in a tea cup than grains of sand on a large beach.

STUDY QUESTIONS

1 Krisnan and Christine were talking about dissolving sugar in tea. Krisnan thought that the sugar would weigh less when it had dissolved because it would be floating in the tea.
   a) What do you think happens to the mass of a substance when it dissolves?
   b) Plan an experiment to test your suggestions in part (a).
   c) If possible, carry out your suggested experiment. Explain your results.

2 Get into groups of two or three. Use the idea of particles to discuss and explain what happens when:
   a) water in a kettle boils to produce steam
   b) you add water to a clay flower pot and the outside of the pot becomes wet
   c) puddles disappear on a fine day
   d) tightly tied balloons go down after some time.

3 Explain the following terms:
   a) solute
   b) solvent
   c) solution
   d) saturated
   e) solubility
   f) $y = mx + c$

4 Use Figure 1.4 to help you answer these questions.
   a) In what unit is solubility measured?
   b) Which substance's solubility has a linear relationship?
   c) Name a substance with a non-linear solubility graph.
   d) Calculate the solubility of sodium nitrate at 80 °C

5 Look back at Figure 1.5 and the experiment involved. Suppose that 1 g of potassium manganate(VII) has a volume of cm^3 and that there is one particle of potassium manganate(VII) in every drop of the final 1 000 000 000 cm^3 of faint pink solution.
   a) Estimate the number of drops in 1 cm^3 of the faint pink solution.
   b) How many particles of potassium manganate(VII) are there in 1 000 000 000 cm^3 of the faint pink solution?
   c) Calculate the volume of one particle of potassium manganate(VII) in the crystal.

1.2 Particles in motion

Fish and chips have a delicious smell. How does the smell get from the fish and chips to your nose?

Figure 2.1 Fish and chips.

■ Diffusion

The way that smells travel from their source suggests that particles, whether from fish and chips or from perfume, move through the air. This movement of particles is called **diffusion**.

Gases consist of tiny particles moving at high speeds. The particles collide with each other and with the walls of their container. Sooner or later, gases like those from the fish and chips will diffuse into all the space they can find.

Diffusion also occurs in liquids, but it takes place much more slowly than in gases (Figure 2.3). This means that liquid particles move around more slowly than gas particles. Diffusion does not happen in solids.

Figure 2.2 Why is it possible to smell the perfume that someone is wearing from several metres away?

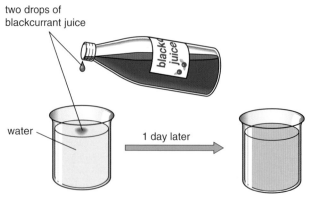

two drops of blackcurrant juice

water

1 day later

Figure 2.3 Demonstrating diffusion in a liquid.

You can investigate diffusion in liquids using blackcurrant juice.

1   Add two drops of blackcurrant juice very carefully to a glass of water. The juice colours a small part of the water purple.
2   Leave the glass in a safe place where it cannot be disturbed. The purple juice moves away from the top of the water.
3   Check the glass again after one day. All the water is now a pale lilac colour. Particles in the purple juice have moved about and mixed with the water particles.

Do not drink the juice or its solution if it has been made in a laboratory.

Diffusion is very important in living things. It explains how the food you eat gets into your bloodstream, where it is carried by your blood to different parts of your body. After a meal, food passes into your stomach. Here, large particles are broken down into smaller particles. These smaller particles can diffuse through the walls of the intestines into the bloodstream.

Particle motion and temperature

As the temperature rises, particles have more energy and they move about faster. This means that gases and liquids diffuse faster when the temperature rises.

■ The kinetic theory of matter

The idea that all substances contain incredibly small moving particles is called **the kinetic theory of matter**. The word 'kinetic' comes from a Greek word meaning moving.

The main points of the kinetic theory are:

■   All matter is made up of tiny, invisible, moving particles. These particles are atoms, molecules and ions.
■   Particles of different substances have different sizes. Particles of elements, like iron, copper and sulfur, are very small. Particles of compounds, like petrol and sugar, are larger, but still very small.
■   Small particles move faster than larger particles at the same temperature.
■   As the temperature rises, the particles have more energy and move around faster.
■   In a solid, the particles are very close and arranged in a regular pattern. They can only vibrate about fixed positions (Figure 2.4).
■   In a liquid, the particles are not in a regular arrangement. They have more energy and they can slide past each other (Figure 2.5).
■   In a gas, the particles are far apart. They move very fast and randomly in all the space they can find (Figure 2.6).

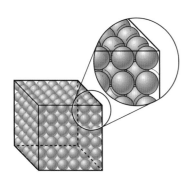

Figure 2.4 Particles in a solid.

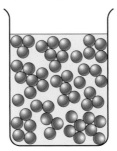

Figure 2.5 Particles in a liquid.

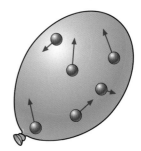

Figure 2.6 Particles in a gas.

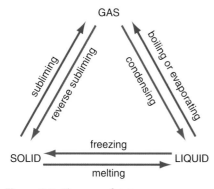

Figure 2.7 Changes of state.

■ Changes of state

The kinetic theory can be used to explain how a substance changes from one state to another. A summary of the different changes of state is shown in Figure 2.7. These changes are usually caused by heating or cooling.

Melting and freezing

When a solid is heated, its particles gain energy. The particles vibrate faster and faster until eventually they break away from their fixed positions. The particles begin to move around each other and the solid has melted to form a liquid.

> The temperature at which the solid melts is called the **melting point**.

The temperature at which a solid melts tells us how strongly its particles are held together. Substances with high melting points have strong forces of attraction between their particles. Substances with low melting points have weak forces of attraction between their particles. Metals and alloys, like iron and steel, have high melting points. This suggests that there are strong forces of attraction between their particles. This is why metals can be used as girders and supports.

Evaporating and boiling

The particles in a liquid can move around each other. Some particles near the surface of the liquid may have enough energy to escape from the liquid into the air. When this happens, the liquid evaporates to form a gas.

If the liquid is heated, its particles move faster. This gives more of them sufficient energy to escape from the surface. So, evaporation increases as the temperature of the liquid rises.

On further heating, the liquid particles are moving so rapidly that bubbles of gas form inside the liquid.

> The temperature at which a liquid boils is called its **boiling point**.

Boiling points tell us how strongly the particles are held together in liquids. Volatile liquids, like petrol, evaporate easily and boil at low temperatures. They have weak forces of attraction between their particles.

STUDY QUESTIONS

1 What do you understand by the following terms: *diffusion, kinetic theory, states of matter, melting point, boiling point?*

2 What happens to the particles of a liquid:
   i) as it cools down;
   ii) as it freezes?

3 Use the kinetic theory to explain why:
   i) gases exert a pressure on the walls of their container;
   ii) you can smell hot, sizzling onion several metres away, but you have to be near cold onion to smell it;
   iii) liquids have a fixed size but not a fixed shape;
   iv) solid blocks of air freshener disappear without leaving any solid;
   v) you can smell some cheeses even when they are wrapped in clingfilm.

1.3 Atoms and molecules

In ancient times the Greeks thought that everything was made from just four substances: earth, fire, air and water. The Greeks called these the four 'elements'.

Chemists now know that none of these are elements – two are mixtures, one a compound and fire is a chemical reaction taking place. We now recognise 118 different elements, the simplest types of substances that all other substances are made from. They are all listed in the Periodic Table. The smallest particle of an element is an atom.

■ What is an atom?

An **atom** is the smallest particle of an element. The word 'atom' comes from a Greek word meaning 'indivisible' or 'unsplittable'. At one time, scientists thought that atoms could not be split. We now know that atoms can be split. But, if an atom of one element is split, it becomes a different element.

Copper contains only copper atoms and carbon contains only carbon atoms.

So far we have learnt that all substances and all materials are made of particles. There are only three different particles in all substances – atoms, molecules (see the next page) and ions. **Ions** are atoms or molecules that are electrically charged. There is more about ions in Chapters 1.8, 1.14 and 1.17.

Electron microscopes can magnify objects more than a million times. In 1958, scientists in Russia identified individual atoms for the first time using an electron microscope. The atoms they identified were those of barium and oxygen. Figure 3.1 shows an electron microscope photo of a gold crystal. The magnification is 40 000 000 times. Each yellow blob is an individual gold atom.

■ Representing atoms with symbols

The word 'atom' was first used by John Dalton in 1807 when he put forward his 'Atomic Theory of Matter'. Dalton suggested the name atom for the smallest particle of an element and he also suggested a method of representing atoms with **symbols**. Figure 3.3 shows some of Dalton's symbols. The modern symbols that we use for different elements are based on Dalton's suggestions.

Table 1 gives a list of the symbols for some of the common elements. (A longer list of symbols appears on page 280). Notice that most elements have two letters in their symbol. The first letter is *always* a capital, the second letter is *always* small. These symbols come from either the English name (O for oxygen, C for carbon) or from the Latin name (Au for gold – Latin: aurum; Cu for copper – Latin: cuprum).

Figure 3.1 This photo of a gold crystal was taken through an electron microscope. What do you think the yellow blobs are?

Figure 3.2 John Dalton, who called the smallest particle of an element an 'atom'. He was born in 1766 in the village of Eaglesfield in Cumbria. His father was a weaver. For most of his life, Dalton taught at the Presbyterian College in Manchester.

Figure 3.3 Dalton's symbols for some common elements.

Table 1 The modern symbols for some elements.

Element	Symbol	Element	Symbol	Element	Symbol
aluminium	Al	hydrogen	H	oxygen	O
argon	Ar	iodine	I	phosphorus	P
bromine	Br	iron	Fe	potassium	K
calcium	Ca	krypton	Kr	silicon	Si
carbon	C	lead	Pb	silver	Ag
chlorine	Cl	magnesium	Mg	sodium	Na
chromium	Cr	mercury	Hg	sulfur	S
copper	Cu	neon	Ne	tin	Sn
gold	Au	nickel	Ni	uranium	U
helium	He	nitrogen	N	zinc	Zn

■ Compounds and atoms

A **compound** is a substance that contains atoms of two or more elements combined together chemically.

Water contains both hydrogen and oxygen atoms combined together chemically, and carbon dioxide contains both carbon and oxygen. Compounds always contain atoms from more than one element.

Mixtures are different from compounds as the different substances are not combined together chemically.

Pure substances have fixed melting and boiling points. Pure water melts at 0 °C and boils at 100 °C. If ethanol is mixed with the water the liquid freezes over a range of temperatures near to 0 °C, and boils over a range of temperatures from around the boiling point of ethanol (78 °C) up to the boiling point of water at 100 °C.

A substance that melts or boils over a range of temperatures will be a mixture, not a pure compound or element.

■ What is a molecule?

A **molecule** is the smallest particle that can have a separate, independent existence.

When atoms of the same element join together the result is a molecule of an element. When atoms of different elements join together the result is a molecule of a compound.

For example, a molecule of water contains two atoms of hydrogen combined with one atom of oxygen. A molecule of carbon dioxide contains one atom of carbon combined with two atoms of oxygen (Figure 3.4).

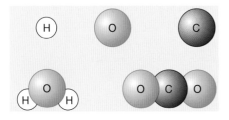

Figure 3.4 Atoms of hydrogen, oxygen and carbon above molecules of water and carbon dioxide.

Molecular formulae

The symbols for elements can also be used to represent molecules and compounds. So, water is represented as H_2O – two hydrogen atoms (H) and one oxygen atom (O). Carbon dioxide is written as CO_2 – one carbon atom (C) and two oxygen atoms (O).

'H_2O' and 'CO_2' are called molecular formulae or just formulae, for short. Numbers are written after symbols as subscripts if there are two or more atoms of the same element in a molecule.

> A **molecular formula** shows the numbers of atoms of the different elements in one molecule of a substance.

Some other diagrams of molecules and their chemical formulae are shown in Figure 3.5.

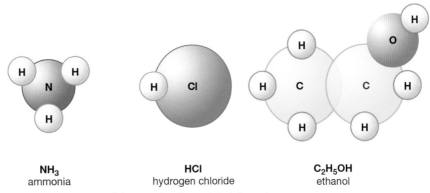

| NH_3 | HCl | C_2H_5OH |
| ammonia | hydrogen chloride | ethanol |

Figure 3.5 Diagrams of three molecules and their formulae.

Some molecules are very simple, such as hydrogen chloride (HCl) and water (H_2O). Others are more complex, such as ethanol (C_2H_5OH). Others, such as chlorophyll, are very complex ($C_{51}H_{72}O_4N_4Mg$).

Atoms and molecules of elements

Almost all elements, for example iron (Fe), aluminium (Al) and copper (Cu), can be represented simply by their symbols, because they contain single atoms. But, this is not the case with oxygen, hydrogen, nitrogen or chlorine. These elements exist as molecules containing two atoms combined together.

So, oxygen is best represented as O_2 and not O, hydrogen as H_2 not H, nitrogen as N_2 and chlorine as Cl_2 (Figure 3.6). These molecules of elements containing two atoms are described as **diatomic molecules**.

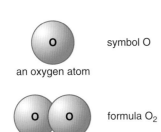

symbol O

an oxygen atom

formula O_2

an oxygen molecule

Figure 3.6 An atom and a molecule of oxygen.

1.4 Separating materials

How much money has been saved in the jar in Figure 4.1? It is hard to count the money when it is all mixed up together. You need to separate the mixture. If you did this by hand you would put coins of the same value in piles of ten and count them up. Suggest how the coin-counting machine separates the different coins.

Most naturally occurring materials are mixtures. Very often these mixtures have to be separated before we can use the materials in them. The methods that we choose to separate mixtures depend on the different properties of the substances in them.

■ Separating an insoluble solid from a liquid

Filtration

Usually, it's easy to separate an insoluble solid from a liquid by **filtering**. This method is used to make filter coffee by separating the **residue** (coffee grains) from the **filtrate** (filter coffee). Notice how the equipment used to make filter coffee in Figure 4.2 is similar to that which you would use for filtration in the lab.

Clean water for our homes

Filtration plays an important part in obtaining clean water for our homes. Figure 4.3 shows the main stages in the purification of our water supplies.

1 The water is first stored in a reservoir where most of the solid particles can settle out.
2 As the water is needed, it is filtered through clean sand and gravel which trap smaller particles of mud and suspended solids (Figure 4.4).
3 After filtering, the water is treated with small amounts of chlorine to kill harmful bacteria in the water.
4 The purified water is finally pumped to storage tanks and water towers from which it flows to our homes.

Filtration is also used to separate beer from its sediment (yeast) before bottling. The beer is filtered by forcing it through filter cloths to catch the sediment.

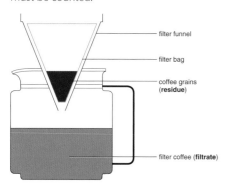

Figure 4.1 To find the value, the money must be counted.

filter funnel
filter bag
coffee grains (**residue**)
filter coffee (**filtrate**)

Figure 4.2 Filtering coffee. The filter bag is made of filter paper. It has tiny holes that let the liquid through, but are too small for the solid coffee grains to pass through.

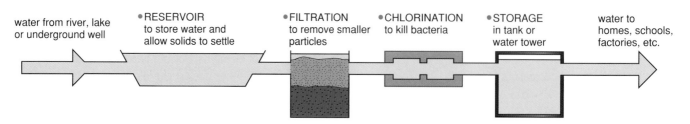

water from river, lake or underground well

●RESERVOIR to store water and allow solids to settle

●FILTRATION to remove smaller particles

●CHLORINATION to kill bacteria

●STORAGE in tank or water tower

water to homes, schools, factories, etc.

Figure 4.3 Stages in the purification of our water supplies.

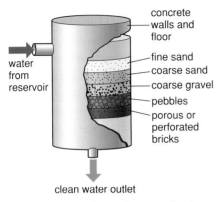

concrete
walls and
floor

fine sand
coarse sand
coarse gravel
pebbles
porous or
perforated
bricks

water
from
reservoir

clean water outlet

Figure 4.4 Water for our homes, schools and workplaces is filtered through layers of sand and gravel, which trap small particles.

Centrifuging

Sometimes, solid particles in a liquid are so small that they can pass through a filter paper, so filtration is useless. The tiny solid particles float in the liquid as a **suspension**. In this case, the solid can be separated by **centrifuging**. The mixture is poured into a tube and spun round very rapidly in a centrifuge. This forces the denser solid particles to the bottom of the tube and the liquid can be poured off easily. Centrifuging is used in hospitals to separate denser blood cells from blood plasma (liquid). It is also used in dairies to separate milk from cream.

■ Separating a soluble solid from a solution

Tap water is clean but *not* pure. It contains dissolved gases including oxygen from the air and dissolved solids from the soil and river beds over which it flowed. Tap water is a **solution**. Seawater (brine) is another example of a solution. It contains salt and many other substances dissolved in water. You can't see the salt in clear seawater, but it must be there because you can taste it. The salt has been broken up into tiny particles which are too small to be seen even with a microscope. These particles are so small that they can pass through the holes in filter paper during filtration.

The mixture of dissolved salt and water forms a **solution**.
The substance that dissolves is called the **solute**.
The liquid in which the solute dissolves is the **solvent**.

Solids, such as salt and sugar, which dissolve are described as **soluble**.
Solids, such as sand, which do not dissolve are **insoluble**.
The easiest way to obtain a soluble solid from its solution (such as the salt in seawater) is by allowing the solvent, which is water in this case, to evaporate.

Extracting salt from seawater

When seawater is left in a bowl, white salt is left behind as the water evaporates. Next time you are at the seaside, look for white rings of salt around the edges of rock pools.

The process during which a liquid turns to a vapour is called **evaporation**.

If the solvent evaporates slowly from a solution, the solute is often left behind as large, well-shaped crystals.

Usually, evaporation is carried out more rapidly by boiling the solution. In this case, the solute is left behind as small, poorly shaped crystals.

In some hot countries, salt is obtained from seawater on a large scale by crystallisation. The sea is allowed to flood flat areas in shallow ponds called salt pans. As the water evaporates, sea salt is left behind as white crystals.

Figure 4.5 Crystallisation is used to obtain large quantities of sea salt from seawater in hot countries.

PRACTICAL

It is very important to be able to separate a pure substance from a mixture. Make sure you know these techniques and can use them.

Separating a solvent from a solution

Sometimes, the part of a solution that you want is the liquid solvent and *not* the solute. In this case, **distillation** can be used to collect the solvent. Distillation can be used to separate pure water from seawater (Figure 4.6). When the seawater is boiled, water evaporates off as steam. The steam then passes into a water-cooled sloping tube called a **condenser**. Here the steam turns back to water. This pure water is called the **distillate**.

The process during which vapour changes to liquid is called **condensation**.

Notice from the process of distillation in Figure 4.6 that:

distillation = evaporation + condensation

Distillation is an important process in:

- obtaining pure drinking water from seawater in parts of the Middle East where fuel is cheap
- making 'spirits' such as whisky, gin and vodka from diluted alcoholic solutions.

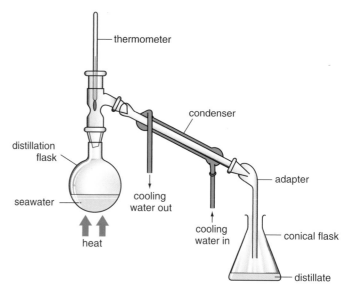

Figure 4.6 Separating pure water from seawater by distillation.

Figure 4.7 Whisky is made by distilling a liquid called wort in large copper vessels. Wort is like weak beer. It is made by fermenting barley.

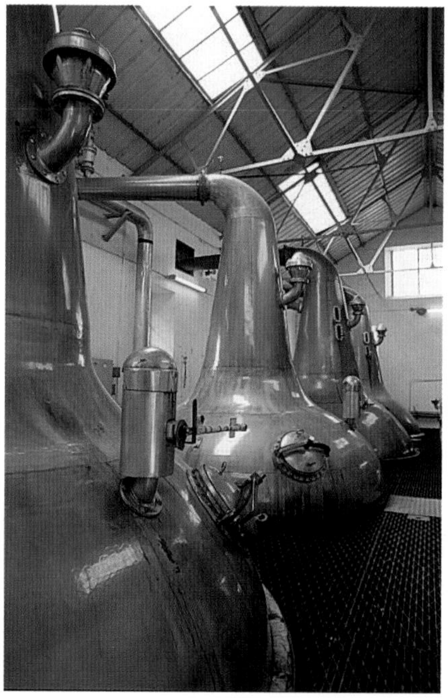

Separating liquids which mix completely

If alcohol is added to water, the two liquids mix completely to form a single layer. Liquids like these which mix completely are described as **miscible**. Miscible liquids can be separated by a special form of distillation called **fractional distillation**. The method works because the different liquids have different boiling points. When the mixture is heated, different liquids boil off at different temperatures as each one reaches its boiling point. The liquid with the lowest boiling point is collected first, then the one with the next lowest boiling point, and so on.

Fractional distillation is important in separating the different fractions in crude oil (Chapter 4.1). It can also be used to separate a mixture such as

ethanol and water. The apparatus shown in Figure 4.8 has a fractionating column which allows the vapour to condense and re-vaporise several times. When the vapour reaches the top of the fractionating column and condenses the distillate is nearly pure ethanol. If the mixture was distilled using a simple distillation apparatus, then the distillate would be a mixture of ethanol and water.

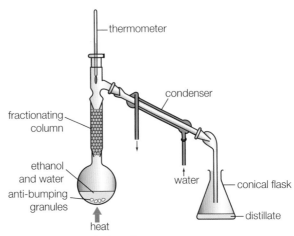

Figure 4.8 Fractional distillation of ethanol.

■ Separating similar substances

Chromatography can sometimes be used to separate very similar substances. For example, it is used to separate dyes in ink, different sugars in urine, and drugs in the blood.

Figure 4.10 shows how dyes in ink can be separated by chromatography. A spot of ink is applied to a piece of chromatography paper. This is then placed in a solvent. As the solvent moves up the paper, the dyes in the ink spot separate. The dyes that dissolve more readily in the solvent will travel further up the paper.

Figure 4.9 This scientist is using chromatography to study new dyes.

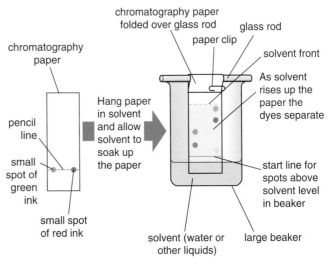

Figure 4.10 Separating the dyes in inks by chromatography. How many dyes are there in (i) the green ink; (ii) the red ink?

This method was initially used to separate mixtures of coloured substances. It was called chromatography from the Greek word 'khroma' meaning colour.

Chromatography is also used to separate colourless substances. After the solvent has soaked up the paper, it is dried and then sprayed with a **locating agent**. The locating agent reacts with each of the colourless substances to form a coloured product that can be seen.

R_f values and chromatograms

Figure 4.11 shows two chromatograms. They were made at different times, but the results need to be interpreted together. You cannot just compare the dots. Scientists discovered that if you use the same solvent and the same type of paper, then the relative distance moved by the chemical when compared to the solvent front (the distance moved up the paper by the solvent) is always the same. They called this the R_f **value**. You can calculate it using this equation:

$$R_f = \frac{\text{distance moved by chemical}}{\text{distance moved by solvent front}}$$

The R_f value is always less than 1.

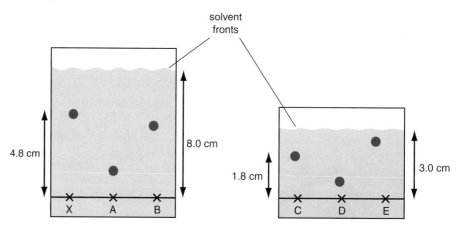

Figure 4.11 Comparing two chromatograms. X has an R_f value of 4.8/8.0 = 0.6 and C has an R_f value of 1.8/3.0 = 0.6. So X is the same substance as C.

STUDY QUESTIONS

1 What are the main stages in the purification of water for our homes?

2 Your younger brother and sister are playing at cooking. They decide to mix sugar with sand. Fortunately, you have a good chemistry set. Describe how you would separate dry sand and sugar crystals from their mixture.

3 You are given a yoghurt pot, some pebbles and some sand.
   a) Design a small-scale filtration plant which you could use to clean muddy river water. Draw a diagram of your design.
   b) How could you check how well your model works?

4 How would you obtain dry, well-shaped crystals from a solution of salt water?

5 How would you prepare a jug of filter coffee? In your answer, use the words: *solution, solvent, solute, dissolve, soluble, insoluble, filtrate*.

6 Whisky is obtained by distilling a solution made from fermented grains such as barley. The solution contains ethanol (boiling point 78 °C) and water (boiling point 100 °C).
   a) Which liquid boils at the lower temperature: ethanol or water?
   b) Which of these liquids evaporates more easily?
   c) If beer is distilled, will the distillate contain a larger or smaller percentage of ethanol?
   d) Why is whisky more alcoholic than beer?

7 Some students investigated the pigments used in six different inks. They did some paper chromatography of the inks. The chromatogram shows their results.

   a) How many pigments were present in the six inks?
   b) Which of the inks A-F are identical? Explain your answer.
   c) Calculate the R$_f$ value of the red pigment.

1.5 Atomic structure

Figure 5.1 In the 19th century atoms were thought to be like pool balls.

During the 19th century atoms were thought to be solid particles that were all identical. At the end of the 19th century (1896), a scientist called J.J. Thomson found evidence of a smaller particle. He called it an electron. The electron was found to be negatively charged, and could be produced out of neutral atoms. This led to the suggestion of the existence of a small positively charged particle as part of the atom.

■ Discovering atomic structure

In 1909 two scientists, Hans Geiger and Ernest Marsden, discovered that radioactive particles called alpha particles fired at thin sheets of gold foil could travel straight through but were sometimes deflected. These results were explained in 1911 by Ernest Rutherford, who suggested that an atom had a small central positive **nucleus** that was very heavy, and a cloud of negative electrons round it. Most of the atom was an empty space!

The model was very successful in explaining atomic structure but there was still one problem, the mass of an atom. Only for hydrogen did the number of protons in the nucleus add up to the mass of the atom. This problem was solved in 1932 when James Chadwick discovered a neutral particle, the neutron, with the same mass as a proton that was also in the nucleus.

Most hydrogen atoms have one proton, no neutrons and one electron. Since the mass of the electron is almost zero compared to the mass of the proton and neutron, a hydrogen atom has a 'relative mass' of one unit (one proton mass). Most helium atoms have two protons, two neutrons and two electrons. The two protons and two neutrons give a helium atom a relative mass of four units.

Figure 5.2 James Chadwick discovered neutrons in 1932 when he was working with Rutherford in Cambridge. In 1935, he won a Nobel Prize for this achievement.

Table 1 The relative masses of hydrogen and helium.

	Hydrogen atom	Helium atom
number of protons	1	2
number of neutrons	0	2
relative mass	1	4

■ Protons, neutrons and electrons

Scientists now know that:

- all atoms are made up from three basic particles – protons, neutrons and electrons
- the nuclei of atoms contain protons and neutrons
- the mass of a proton is almost the same as that of a neutron
- protons have a positive charge, but neutrons have no charge
- electrons move in the space around the nucleus, in 'shells'
- the mass of an electron is negligible compared to that of a proton
- electrons have a negative charge
- the negative charge on an electron is equal in size, but opposite in sign, to the positive charge on a proton
- in any atom, the number of electrons is equal to the number of protons
- all atoms of a particular element have the same number of protons
- atoms of different elements have different numbers of protons.

The positions, relative masses and relative charges of protons, neutrons and electrons are summarised in Table 2.

Figure 5.3 If the nucleus of an atom was enlarged to the size of a pea and put on top of a pyramid, the electrons furthest away would be on the sand below.

Table 2 Properties of the three sub-atomic particles.

Particle	Position	Mass (relative to a proton)	Charge
proton	nucleus	1	+1
neutron	nucleus	1	0
electron	shells	1/1840	–1

Explaining elements

Different atoms have different numbers of protons, neutrons and electrons. The hydrogen atom is the simplest of all atoms. It has one proton in the nucleus, no neutrons and one electron (Figure 5.4). The next simplest atom is that of helium, with two protons, two neutrons and two electrons. The next, lithium, has three protons, four neutrons and three electrons. Heavier atoms can have large numbers of protons, neutrons and electrons. For example, atoms of uranium have 92 protons, 92 electrons and 143 neutrons.

Notice that hydrogen, the first element in the Periodic Table, has one proton. Helium, the second element in the Periodic Table, has two protons. Lithium, the third element in the Periodic Table has three protons and so on. So, the position of an element in the Periodic Table tells us how many protons it has. This is shown on all Periodic Tables as the **atomic number**, or **proton number**.

Remember that atoms have equal numbers of protons and electrons, so that the positive charges (on the protons) balance the negative charges (on the electrons).

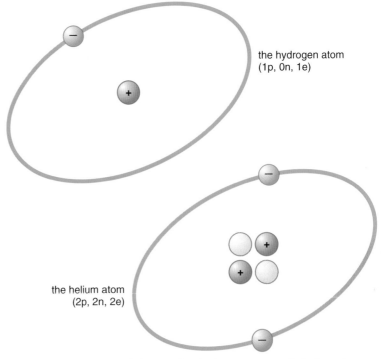

the hydrogen atom
(1p, 0n, 1e)

the helium atom
(2p, 2n, 2e)

Figure 5.4 Protons, neutrons and electrons in a hydrogen atom and a helium atom (⊕ = proton, O = neutron, ⊖ = electron).

STUDY QUESTIONS

1 What are the charges, relative masses and positions in an atom of protons, neutrons and electrons?
2 How many protons, neutrons and electrons are there in one:
   a) H atom
   b) N atom
   c) Li atom
   d) Ar atom?
      (Refer to a Periodic Table. There is one on page 273.)

3 Oxygen is the eighth element in the Periodic Table. How many protons and electrons are there in one:
   a) O atom
   b) O_2 molecule
   c) H_2O molecule?
4 Make a timeline of important dates, scientists, and facts in the development of our ideas about atomic structure.

1.6 Atomic number and mass number

Atoms are like trousers. There are two numbers that must be used to adequately describe each one. For atoms, these numbers are the atomic number or proton number and the mass number. Like trouser measurements, these numbers refer to different features of each atom, in this case the number of protons (and electrons) in the atom and how heavy the atom is. The atomic number (or number of protons) decides the type of the atom; the mass number how much it weighs.

■ Atomic number

Hydrogen atoms are the only atoms with one proton. Helium atoms are the only atoms with two protons. Lithium atoms are the only atoms with three protons, and so on. It is the number of protons in the nucleus of an atom that decides which element it is.

Chemists refer to the number of protons in the nucleus of an atom as the **atomic number**. So, hydrogen has atomic number 1, helium has atomic number 2, and so on.

> atomic number = number of protons

Aluminium has 13 protons so its atomic number is 13. In the Periodic Table the elements are arranged in order of atomic number, so aluminium is the thirteenth element in the Periodic Table (there is more about the Periodic Table in Chapter 1.11).

Using the Periodic Table, we can find the atomic number of any element. The sixth element in the Periodic Table has atomic number 6, the twentieth element has atomic number 20, and so on.

■ Mass number

Protons do not account for all the mass of an atom. Neutrons in the nucleus also contribute to the mass. Therefore, the mass of an atom depends on the number of protons plus the number of neutrons. This number is called the **mass number** of the atom.

> mass number = number of protons + number of neutrons

Hydrogen atoms (with one proton and no neutrons) have a mass number of 1. Helium atoms (two protons and two neutrons) have a mass number of 4 and lithium atoms (three protons and four neutrons) have a mass number of 7.

Figure 6.1 Two numbers can describe trousers – the waist measurement and the length of the legs.

MATHS TIP

mass number = number of protons + number of neutrons
This can be rearranged to:
number of protons = mass number – number of neutrons
How can it be re-arranged to work out the number of neutrons?

■ Atomic symbols

We can write the symbol ^7_3Li (Figure 6.2) to show the mass number and the atomic number of a lithium atom. The mass number is written at the top and to the left of the symbol. The atomic number is written at the bottom and to the left. A sodium atom (11 protons and 12 neutrons) is written as $^{23}_{11}Na$.

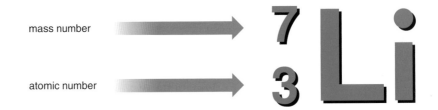

Figure 6.2 The atomic symbol for lithium.

■ Isotopes

If the mass number of an element is the sum of the number of protons and the number of neutrons in the nucleus, every relative atomic mass should be a whole number. Looking at the Periodic Table, this is not true. Some elements have relative atomic masses that are nowhere near whole numbers. For example, the relative atomic mass of chlorine is 35.5 and that of copper is 63.5. At one time, chemists could not understand why the relative atomic masses of these elements were not close to whole numbers. In 1919, F.W. Aston discovered the answer to this problem when he built the first **mass spectrometer**.

Using his mass spectrometer, Aston could compare the masses of atoms. He discovered that some elements had atoms with different masses. When atoms of these elements were ionised and passed through the mass spectrometer, the beam of ions separated into two or more paths. This suggested that one element could have atoms with different masses.

Atoms of the same element with different masses are called **isotopes**.

Isotopes have the same number of protons, but different numbers of neutrons. Each isotope has a relative mass close to a whole number, but the mean (average) atomic mass for the mixture of isotopes is not always close to a whole number. This is called the **relative atomic mass**.

STUDY QUESTIONS

1 Explain the following terms:
   i) atomic number;
   ii) mass number;
   iii) isotope.
2 a) What is the atomic number of fluorine? (Refer to a Periodic Table – see page 273.)
   b) How many protons, neutrons and electrons are there in one fluorine atom of mass number 19?

3 a) What do 16, 8 and O mean with reference to the symbol, $^{16}_8O$?
   b) How many protons, neutrons and electrons are there in one $^{23}_{11}Na$ atom?
4 Why do some elements have relative atomic masses which are not close to whole numbers?

1.7 Isotopes

The isotopes of some elements are radioactive. Some of them are relatively harmless if used with care and are used in medical imaging as in the photo of a pulmonary scan. They help doctors decide if a patient has a disease such as cancer, where the tumour is, and the possible treatment options. Some isotopes are also used in the treatment and cure of cancers and other illnesses.

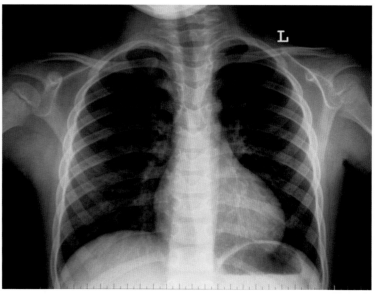

Figure 7.1 Some isotopes are radioactive. This can make them very useful. This patient has a bone cancer, identified by the scan of the lungs.

■ What is an isotope?

Isotopes are atoms of the same element with different masses. All the isotopes of one element have the same number of protons. Therefore, they have the same atomic number. As isotopes have the same number of protons, they must also have the same number of electrons. This gives them the same chemical properties because chemical properties depend upon the number of electrons in an atom.

Isotopes do, however, contain different numbers of neutrons. This means that:

Isotopes have the *same* **atomic number** but *different* **mass numbers**.

Isotopes of neon

Neon has two isotopes (Figure 7.2). Each isotope has 10 protons and 10 electrons and therefore an atomic number of 10. But one of these isotopes has 10 neutrons and the other has 12 neutrons. Their mass numbers are therefore 20 and 22. They are sometimes called neon-20 and neon-22.

$$^{20}_{10}\text{Ne} \qquad ^{22}_{10}\text{Ne}$$

	neon-20	neon-22
number of protons	10	10
number of electrons	10	10
atomic number	10	10
number of neutrons	10	12
mass number	20	22

Figure 7.2 The two isotopes of neon.

These two isotopes of neon have the same chemical properties because they have the same number of electrons. But they have different physical properties because they have different masses. Samples of $^{20}_{10}\text{Ne}$ and $^{22}_{10}\text{Ne}$ have different densities, different melting points and different boiling points.

Similarities and differences

We have mentioned the similarities and difference between the isotopes of neon. All isotopes have the following similarities and differences:

Isotopes have the same:
- number of protons
- number of electrons
- atomic number
- chemical properties.

Isotopes have different:
- numbers of neutrons
- mass numbers
- physical properties.

■ Relative atomic mass

Most elements contain a mixture of isotopes. This explains why the relative atomic masses of some elements are *not* whole numbers.

> The **relative atomic mass** of an element is the mean (average) mass of one atom, (taking account of its isotopes and their relative proportions), relative to $\frac{1}{12}$ of the mass of an atom of carbon-12.

MATHS TIP

Relative Atomic Mass is really a mean value. It is the arithmetic average of all isotopes of an element using the percentage of each isotope in a sample of the element.

Look at the mass spectrometer trace for chlorine in Figure 7.3. This shows that chlorine consists of two isotopes with mass numbers of 35 and 37. These isotopes can be written as $^{35}_{17}\text{Cl}$ and $^{37}_{17}\text{Cl}$.

If chlorine contained 100% $^{35}_{17}\text{Cl}$, its relative atomic mass would be 35. If it contained 100% $^{37}_{17}\text{Cl}$, its relative atomic mass would be 37. A 50:50 mixture of $^{35}_{17}\text{Cl}$ and $^{37}_{17}\text{Cl}$ would have a relative atomic mass of 36 (see Table 1).

Table 1 The relative atomic mass of chlorine for different mixtures of its isotopes.

	100	75	50	25	0
Percentage of $^{35}_{17}$Cl	100	75	50	25	0
Percentage of $^{37}_{17}$Cl	0	25	50	75	100
Relative atomic mass	35	35.5	36	36.5	37

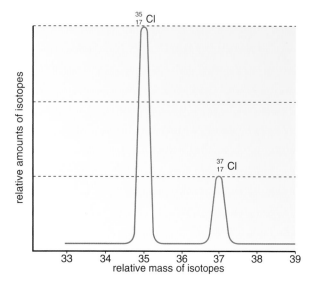

Figure 7.3 A mass spectrometer trace for chlorine.

Figure 7.3 shows that naturally occurring chlorine contains three times as much $^{35}_{17}$Cl as $^{37}_{17}$Cl, i.e. 75% to 25%. This gives a relative atomic mass of 35.5, as shown in Table 1.

The relative atomic mass can be calculated as:

75% chlorine-35 + 25% chlorine-37

$$= \frac{75}{100} \times 35 + \frac{25}{100} \times 37$$
$$= 26.25 + 9.25$$
$$= 35.5$$

STUDY QUESTIONS

1 There are three isotopes of hydrogen with mass numbers of 1, 2 and 3. (Naturally occurring hydrogen is almost 100% $^{1}_{1}$H.) How many protons, neutrons and electrons do each of the three isotopes have?

2 Neon has two isotopes, with mass numbers of 20 and 22.
   a) How do you think the boiling point of a sample of $^{20}_{10}$Ne will compare with a sample of $^{22}_{10}$Ne? Explain your answer.
   b) Suppose a sample of neon contains equal numbers of the two isotopes. What is the relative atomic mass of neon in this sample?

   c) Neon in the air contains 90% of $^{20}_{10}$Ne and 10% of $^{22}_{10}$Ne. What is the relative atomic mass of neon in the air?

3 Discuss the following questions with two or three others.
   a) Why do isotopes have the same chemical properties, but different physical properties?
   b) Why do samples of natural uranium from different parts of the world have slightly different relative atomic masses?
   c) Why can chlorine form molecules of Cl_2 with three different relative molecular masses?

1.8 The arrangement of electrons

Early ideas about the arrangement of electrons in the atom suggested they orbited the nucleus like planets orbiting the Sun. These ideas were quickly discovered to be too simple. The Danish scientist Niels Bohr suggested that orbiting electrons were grouped together in layers or *shells*. Each shell could only hold a limited number of electrons. The arrangement of electrons in the shells of the atom is called the *electronic configuration*.

Figure 8.1 Are atoms really like mini solar systems?

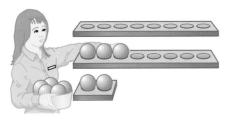

Figure 8.2 Filling shells with electrons is like filling shelves in a shop. The lowest shells (shelves) are filled first. Each shell (shelf) only holds a limited number of electrons (items).

■ Filling the shells

The first shell is nearest the nucleus. The electrons in it are strongly attracted to the nucleus. It can hold only two electrons. When the first shell contains two electrons, it is full (Figure 8.3).

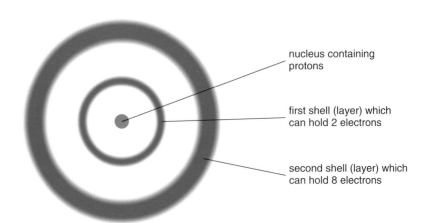

nucleus containing protons

first shell (layer) which can hold 2 electrons

second shell (layer) which can hold 8 electrons

Figure 8.3 A model for the arrangement of electrons in the first and second shells.

As the atomic number increases, when the first shell is full, the second shell starts to fill. This shell is further from the nucleus and the electrons in it have more energy. The second shell can hold a maximum of eight electrons.

For larger atoms again, once the second shell is full, the third shell starts filling. This shell is further from the nucleus again.

■ Electronic configurations of elements

Figure 8.4 shows the first 20 elements, in Periodic Table order. The atomic number of each element is written below its symbol, and the electronic configuration is shown below that. When the first shell is full at helium, further electrons go into the second shell. So the electronic configuration of lithium is 2, 1; beryllium is 2, 2; boron is 2, 3; etc. When the second shell is full at neon, electrons start to fill the third shell, and so on.

Electronic configuration helps us to explain why elements in the same group (columns in the Periodic Table) have similar properties.

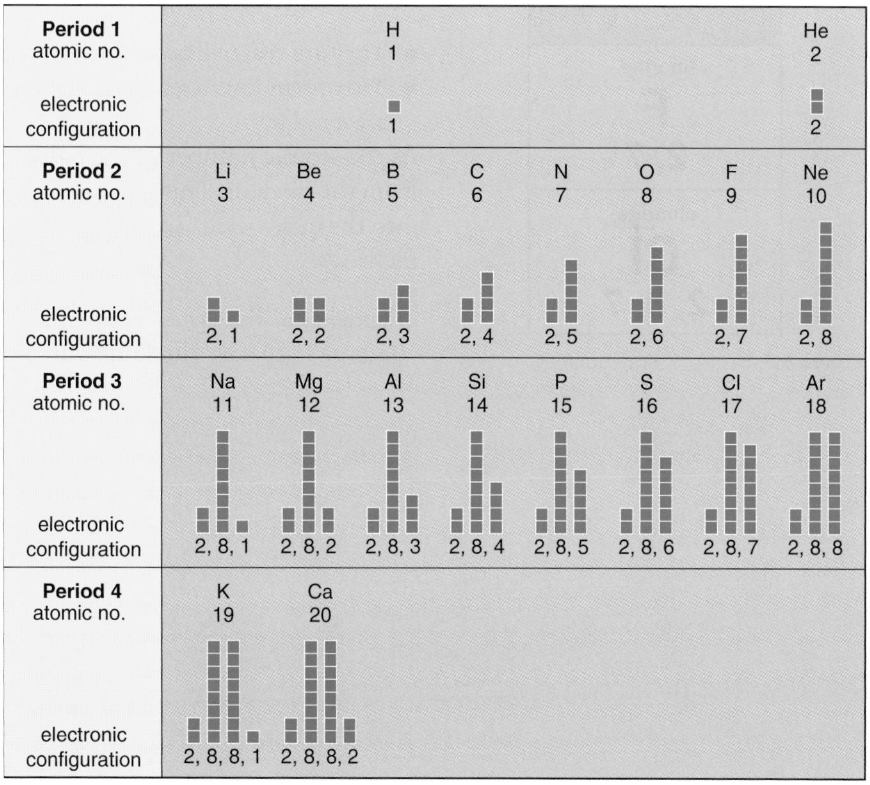

Period 1 atomic no.				H 1				He 2
electronic configuration				1				2
Period 2 atomic no.	Li 3	Be 4	B 5	C 6	N 7	O 8	F 9	Ne 10
electronic configuration	2, 1	2, 2	2, 3	2, 4	2, 5	2, 6	2, 7	2, 8
Period 3 atomic no.	Na 11	Mg 12	Al 13	Si 14	P 15	S 16	Cl 17	Ar 18
electronic configuration	2, 8, 1	2, 8, 2	2, 8, 3	2, 8, 4	2, 8, 5	2, 8, 6	2, 8, 7	2, 8, 8
Period 4 atomic no.	K 19	Ca 20						
electronic configuration	2, 8, 8, 1	2, 8, 8, 2						

Figure 8.4 The electronic configurations of the first 20 elements in the Periodic Table.

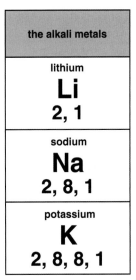

Figure 8.5 Electronic configurations of the first three alkali metals.

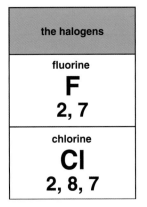

Figure 8.6 Electronic configurations of two halogens.

Group 1: the alkali metals

Look at Figure 8.5. Notice that atoms of the alkali metals lithium, sodium and potassium have one electron in the outer shell. Alkali metals can lose this outer electron very easily to form ions with one positive charge (Li^+, Na^+, K^+).

- They are very reactive because they lose their single outer electron so easily.
- They form ions with a charge of 1+, so the formulae of their compounds are similar.

As the atomic number of the alkali metals increases, the outer electron is further from the positive nucleus. This means that the electron is held less strongly by protons in the nucleus. So, the electron is lost more readily and this explains why the alkali metals become more reactive as their atomic number increases.

Group 7: the halogens

All halogen atoms, such as fluorine and chlorine, have seven electrons in their outer shell (Figure 8.6). By gaining one electron, they form negative ions (F^-, Cl^-).

Halogens have similar properties to one another because they have the same number of electrons in their outer shell.

- They are reactive because they easily gain one electron.
- They form ions with a charge of 1−, so the formulae of their compounds are similar.

As the atomic number of the halogens increases, the outer shell is further from the nucleus. This means that an electron is attracted less readily into the outer shell. So, halogens get less reactive as their atomic number increases.

Elements in the same group of the Periodic Table have similar properties because they have the same number of electrons in their outer shell.

Figure 8.7 Chlorine is the most useful and most common halogen. It is added in very small quantities to water in swimming pools to kill bacteria and other micro-organisms.

Group number and outer electrons

We have seen that all Group 1 elements have one electron in the outer shell, and all Group 7 elements have seven electrons in the outer shell. This is the case for all main group elements. You can therefore deduce the number of outer electrons in a main group element from the group to which it belongs.

So, for example, all the elements in Group 1 have one electron in the outer shell; all the elements in Group 2, including magnesium and calcium, have two electrons in their outer shell; all elements in Group 3 have three electrons in the outer shell, and so on.

■ Atoms, ions and the Periodic Table

Look at Table 1. This shows the electronic configurations of the atoms and ions of elements in Period 3 of the Periodic Table.

Table 1 Electronic configurations of the atoms and ions of elements in Period 3.

Group ➤	1	2	3	4	5	6	7	0
Elements in Period 3	Na	Mg	Al	Si	P	S	Cl	Ar
Electronic configuration	2,8,1	2,8,2	2,8,3	2,8,4	2,8,5	2,8,6	2,8,7	2,8,8
No. of electrons in outer shell	1	2	3	4	5	6	7	8
Common ion	Na^+	Mg^{2+}	Al^{3+}	–	–	S^{2-}	Cl^-	–
Electronic configuration of ion	2,8	2,8	2,8	–	–	2,8,8	2,8,8	–

EXAM TIP

Ions are atoms that have gained or lost one or more electrons. The charge on the ion is 1+, 2+ or 3+ if the atom has lost 1, 2 or 3 electrons. It is 1–, 2– or 3– if the atom has gained 1, 2 or 3 electrons.

■ Table 1 shows that for any element the group number is always the same as the number of outer electrons. Silicon in Group 4 has four outer electrons, sulfur in group 6 has six outer electrons.

■ The elements in Groups 1, 2 and 3, for example sodium, magnesium and aluminium, have only 1, 2 or 3 electrons in their outer shell. These elements at the beginning of the period *lose* electrons to form positive ions (Na^+, Mg^{2+}, Al^{3+}). Their ions have an electronic configuration the same as the previous noble gas.

■ The element sulfur in Group 6 gains two electrons and chlorine in Group 7 gains one electron.

■ The elements in Groups 4 and 5 do not form ions but make bonds by sharing electrons.

■ The atoms of the elements in Group 0, for example argon, do not easily lose or gain electrons. These elements, at the end of a period, do not usually form compounds.

Figure 8.8 Electric light bulbs are filled with argon or krypton. These inert gases are so unreactive that the metal filament can be above 1000 °C without reacting with them.

STUDY QUESTIONS

1 Why are the noble gases so unreactive?

2 a) Write down the electronic configurations of magnesium and calcium.
   b) How many electrons are there in the outer shell of an atom of an element in Group 2?
   c) What charge will ions of Group 2 elements have?

3 Write the electronic configuration for:
   a) Li
   b) Li^+
   c) O
   d) O^{2-}.

1.9 Measuring atoms

Atoms are so small it can be really difficult to understand their size. It's also difficult to measure them using simple apparatus. There are lots of problems to be overcome, such as how do you know when you have an atom? There have been some clever ideas about how to measure the size of atoms easily; today we use very expensive equipment to do this.

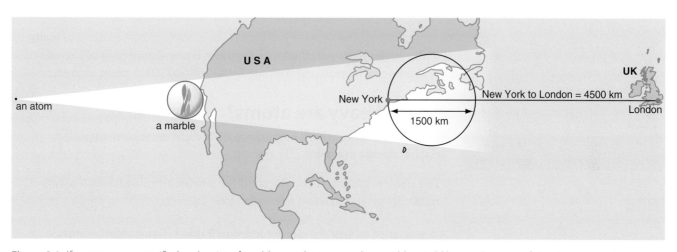

Figure 9.1 If atoms were magnified to the size of marbles, on the same scale a marble would have a diameter of about 1500 km – this is one-third the distance between New York and London.

■ How small are atoms?

Experiments with thin films of oil on water show that olive oil particles are about 1/10 000 000 cm thick. But olive oil particles are large molecules containing more than 50 atoms. If we estimate that one molecule of olive oil is about 10 atoms thick, how big is a single atom?

Electron microscope photos and X-ray diffraction studies suggest that atoms are about one hundred millionth (1/100 000 000) of a centimetre in diameter. So, if you put 100 million of them in a straight line, they would still only measure one centimetre. It's very difficult to imagine anything as small as this, but Figure 9.1 should give you some idea. If atoms were magnified to the size of marbles then, on the same scale, marbles would have a diameter of 1500 km – one-third of the distance between New York and London.

How small is small?

Figure 9.2 will also help you to appreciate just how small atoms are. It shows a step-by-step decrease in size from 1 cm to 1/100 000 000 cm. Each object is 100 times smaller than the one before it. The dice on the left is about 1 cm wide. In the next picture, the grain of sand is about 1/100 cm across. The bacterium in the middle is 100 times smaller again – about 1/10 000 (10^{-4}) cm from end to end. In the next picture, the molecule of haemoglobin is 100 times smaller than this – about 1/1 000 000 (10^{-6}) cm in diameter.

> **PRACTICAL**
>
> Using a drop of cooking oil is a clever method to try to estimate the size of an atom or molecule. Try to think of some sources of error in obtaining a thin layer of oil one molecule deep on the water.

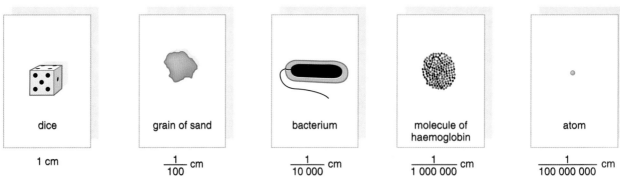

Figure 9.2 Step-by-step to the size of atoms.

Finally, in the right-hand picture, the atom is one-hundredth of the size of the haemoglobin molecule – about $1/100\,000\,000$ (10^{-8}) cm in diameter.

■ How heavy are atoms?

The relative masses which scientists use for different atoms are called **relative atomic masses**.

> The element carbon is the standard for relative atomic masses. Carbon-12 atoms are given a relative mass of exactly 12.

A few relative atomic masses are listed in Table 1. Other relative atomic masses are given on page 274.

The symbol for relative atomic mass is A_r. So, we can write A_r (C) = 12, A_r (Mg) = 24, or simply C = 12, Mg = 24, etc.

Table 1 The relative atomic masses of a few elements.

Element	Symbol	Relative atomic mass
carbon	C	12
hydrogen	H	1
chlorine	Cl	35.5
magnesium	Mg	24
oxygen	O	16
iron	Fe	56
copper	Cu	63.5
gold	Au	197

EXAM TIP

The values of relative atomic masses have no units because they are relative.

STUDY QUESTIONS

1 The radius of a potassium atom is $2/100\,000\,000$ cm. How many potassium atoms can be arranged next to each other to make a line 1 cm long?
2 Use the relative atomic masses on page 274 to answer the following questions.
   a) Which element has the lightest atoms?
   b) Which element has the next lightest atoms?
   c) On average how many times heavier are silicon atoms than nitrogen atoms?
   d) Which element has atoms that, on average, are four times as heavy as oxygen?
3 Put the following in order of size from the largest to the smallest:
   a bacterium, the thickness of a human hair, a molecule of sugar (which contains about 50 atoms), a smoke particle, a copper atom, a fine dust particle.

1.10 Patterns of elements

A shuffled deck of playing cards has absolutely no order or pattern. That is why card games are games of chance. Each card contains three pieces of information: colour, number and suit. You can sort the cards in a variety of ways that will allow you to predict the next card in the deck.

At the start of the 19th century the chemical elements were just like a deck of shuffled playing cards, except no one knew which pieces of information were important, some of the information was not accurate and some of the cards were missing. The question was how to bring order and a useful pattern to the elements.

Figure 10.1 There are many ways to organise a deck of playing cards. Which one would you choose, and why?

■ Early attempts at classifying the elements

As soon as chemists understood that elements were the simplest substances they began to classify them. One of the most useful ways of classifying elements is as metals and non-metals, but it is not easy to classify some elements this way.

Take, for example, silicon. It has a high melting and boiling point like metals, but a low density like non-metals. It conducts electricity better than non-metals, but not as well as metals. Elements with some properties like metals and other properties like non-metals are called **metalloids**.

By the mid-19th century, chemists realised that it was impossible to classify all elements neatly as metals and non-metals. They began to look for patterns in the properties of smaller groups of elements.

Newlands' octaves

In 1864, John Newlands, an English chemist, arranged all the known elements in order of their relative atomic masses. He found that one element often had properties like those of the element seven places in front of it in his list. Newlands called this the '**law of octaves**'. He said that 'the eighth element is a kind of repetition of the first, like the eighth note of an octave in music'.

Figure 10.2 shows the first three of Newlands' octaves. Notice that similar elements sometimes occur seven places on and in the same column. For example, the second column contains lithium, sodium and potassium.

> The regular periodic repetition of elements with similar properties led to the name **Periodic Table**.

Unfortunately, Newlands' classification grouped together some elements which were very different. For example, iron (Fe) was placed in the same family as oxygen (O) and sulfur (S). Because of this, Newlands was ridiculed. His ideas were criticised and rejected.

H	Li	Be	B	C	N	O
F	Na	Mg	Al	Si	P	S
Cl	K	Ca	Cr	Ti	Mn	Fe

Figure 10.2 Newlands' octaves.

Mendeléev's Periodic Table

In spite of the criticism of Newlands' ideas, chemists carried on searching for a pattern linking the properties and relative atomic masses of the elements.

In 1869, the Russian chemist, Dmitri Mendeléev, produced new ideas to support the theory that Newlands had suggested five years earlier.

Figure 10.4 shows part of Mendeléev's Periodic Table. Notice that elements with similar properties, such as lithium, sodium and potassium, fall in the same vertical column. Which other pairs or trios of similar elements appear in the same vertical column of Mendeléev's table?

Figure 10.3 Dmitri Mendeléev (1834–1907) was the first chemist to successfully arrange the elements into a pattern linking their properties and relative atomic masses.

	GROUP							
	I	II	III	IV	V	VI	VII	VIII
Period 1	H							
Period 2	Li	Be	B	C	N	O	F	
Period 3	Na	Mg	Al	Si	P	S	Cl	
Period 4	K / Cu	Ca / Zn	* / *	Ti / *	V / As	Cr / Se	Mn / Br	Fe Co Ni
Period 5	Rb / Ag	Sr / Cd	Y / In	Zr / Sn	Nb / Sb	Mo / Te	* / I	Ru Rh Pd

Figure 10.4 Part of Mendeléev's Periodic Table.

In Mendeléev's (and our modern) Periodic Table:

- The vertical columns of similar elements (i.e. the chemical families) are called **groups**.
- The horizontal rows are called **periods**.

Mendeléev was more successful than Newlands because of three brilliant steps he took with his Periodic Table.

- He left gaps in his table so that similar elements were in the same vertical group. Four of these gaps are shown as asterisks in Figure 10.4.
- He suggested that elements would be discovered to fill the gaps.
- He predicted the properties of the missing elements from the properties of elements above and below them in his table.

Why Mendeléev's Periodic Table was successful

Initially, Mendeléev's Periodic Table was nothing more than a *curiosity*. But it encouraged chemists to search for further patterns and look for more elements. Within 15 years of Mendeléev's predictions, three of the missing elements in his table had been discovered. They were named scandium, gallium and germanium, and their properties were very similar to Mendeléev's predictions.

The success of Mendeléev's predictions showed that his ideas were probably correct and this sparked off even more research. His Periodic Table was quickly accepted as an *important summary* of the properties of elements.

STUDY QUESTIONS

1 Explain the following terms in relation to the Periodic Table: *periodic properties, group, period*.

2 In 1871 Mendeléev made the following predictions for the missing element in Period 4 below silicon.
   - Grey metal with density 5.5 g/cm³.
   - Relative atomic mass = mean (average) of relative atomic masses of Si and Sn = $\frac{28 + 119}{2}$ = 73.5
   - Melting point higher than that of tin – perhaps 800 °C.
   - Formula of oxide will be XO_2 with a density of 4.7 g/cm³.
   This element was discovered in 1886.

   a) What is the name for this element?
   b) Use a data book to find the properties of the element and check Mendeléev's predictions.
   c) How accurate were Mendeléev's predictions?

3 Look at Figure 10.2.
   a) Why did Newlands use the word 'octaves'?
   b) How does the order of elements in Newlands' first three octaves compare with the order of elements in Mendeléev's table?
   c) Suggest the name of an element discovered between 1864 and 1869.

4 Why was Mendeléev more successful than Newlands?

1.11 Modern Periodic Tables

Mendeléev's Periodic Table was a model to help explain the behaviour of the known elements. It has been modified over time, but still retains all the key features that Mendeléev stated. The discovery of helium in 1895 required the Periodic Table to add a whole new group we now call the noble gases, and to start a search for the rest of the group that had not been discovered. A good scientific model is one that allows new discoveries to be incorporated successfully into it. The Periodic Table is such a model.

Figure 11.1 This airship contains helium, an element discovered in 1895, and successfully added into the Periodic Table.

■ The modern Periodic Table

All modern Periodic Tables are based on the one proposed by Mendeléev in 1869. A modern Periodic Table is shown in Figure 11.2. The elements are numbered along each horizontal period, starting with Period 1, then Period 2, etc. The number given to each element is called its **atomic number** (Chapter 1.6). Hydrogen has an atomic number of 1, helium 2, lithium 3, and so on.

There are several points to note about the modern Periodic Table.

Table 1 The names of groups in the Periodic Table.

Group number	Group name
1	alkali metals
2	alkaline-earth metals
7	halogens
0	noble (inert) gases

1 The most obvious difference between modern Periodic Tables and Mendeléev's is the position of the **transition elements**. These have been taken out of the numbered groups and placed between Group 2 and Group 3. Period 4 is the first to contain a series of transition elements. These include chromium, iron, nickel and copper.
2 Some groups have names as well as numbers. These are summarised in Table 1.
3 Metals are clearly separated from non-metals. The 20 or so non-metals are packed into the top right-hand corner above the thick stepped line in Figure 11.2. Some elements close to the steps are metalloids. These elements have some properties like metals and some properties like non-metals.

Key

H	← symbol
hydrogen	← name
1	← atomic number

Group → / Period ↓	1 Alkali metals	2 Alkaline-earth metals	transition elements										3	4	5	6	7 Halogens	0 Noble gases
1										H hydrogen 1								He helium 2
2	Li lithium 3	Be beryllium 4											B boron 5	C carbon 6	N nitrogen 7	O oxygen 8	F fluorine 9	Ne neon 10
3	Na sodium 11	Mg magnesium 12											Al aluminium 13	Si silicon 14	P phosphorus 15	S sulfur 16	Cl chlorine 17	Ar argon 18
4	K potassium 19	Ca calcium 20	Sc 21	Ti 22	V 23	Cr chromium 24	Mn manganese 25	Fe iron 26	Co 27	Ni 28	Cu copper 29	Zn zinc 30	Ga 31	Ge 32	As 33	Se 34	Br bromine 35	Kr krypton 36
5	Rb 37	Sr 38	Y 39	Zr 40	Nb 41	Mo 42	Tc 43	Ru 44	Rh 45	Pd 46	Ag silver 47	Cd 48	In 49	Sn tin 50	Sb 51	Te 52	I iodine 53	Xe 54
6	Cs 55	Ba 56	La* lanthanum 57	Hf 72	Ta 73	W 74	Re 75	Os 76	Ir 77	Pt platinum 78	Au gold 79	Hg mercury 80	Tl 81	Pb lead 82	Bi 83	Po 84	At 85	Rn 86
7	Fr 87	Ra 88	Ac* actinium 89	Rf 104	Db 105	Sg 106	Bh 107	Hs 108	Mt 109	Ds 110	Rg 111							

Figure 11.2 The modern Periodic Table (*the lanthanides (atomic numbers 58–71) and the actinides (atomic numbers 90–103) have been omitted).

4 Apart from the noble gases, the most reactive elements are near the left- and right-hand edges of the Periodic Table. The least reactive elements are in the centre. Sodium and potassium, two very reactive metals, are on the left-hand edge. The next most reactive metals, such as calcium and magnesium, are in Group 2, whereas less reactive metals (such as iron and copper) are in the centre of the table. Carbon and silicon, unreactive non-metals, are also near the centre of the Periodic Table. Sulfur and oxygen, which are nearer the right-hand edge, are more reactive. Fluorine and chlorine, the most reactive non-metals, are very close to the right-hand edge.

Group	1	2											3	4	5	6	7	0
Period 1					H													He
Period 2	Li	Be											B	C	N	O	F	Ne
Period 3	Na	Mg											Al	Si	P	S	Cl	Ar
Period 4	K	Ca	Sc	Ti	V	Cr	Mn	Fe	Co	Ni	Cu	Zn	Ga	Ge	As	Se	Br	Kr
Period 5	Rb	Sr	Y	Zr	Nb	Mo	Tc	Ru	Rh	Pd	Ag	Cd	In	Sn	Sb	Te	I	Xe
Period 6	Cs	Ba	La	Hf	Ta	W	Re	Os	Ir	Pt	Au	Hg	Tl	Pb	Bi	Po	At	Rn
Period 7	Fr	Ra	Ac	Rf	Db													

Figure 11.3 Blocks of similar elements in the Periodic Table.

STUDY QUESTIONS

1 In modern Periodic Tables, you can pick out five blocks of elements with similar properties. These blocks are shown in different colours in Figure 11.3.

a) The five blocks of similar elements are called non-metals, noble gases, poor metals, reactive metals and transition metals. Which name belongs to which coloured block in Figure 11.3?

b) Which groups make up the reactive metals?

c) In the transition metals, the elements resemble each other across the series as well as down the groups. Pick out two sets of three elements to illustrate these similarities.

d) Some non-metals have properties like poor metals. Give two examples of this.

e) The noble gases are very unreactive. The first noble gas compound was not made until 1962. Today, several compounds of them are known.

i) The noble gases were once called 'inert gases'. Why was this?

ii) Why do you think their name was changed?

iii) Why are there no noble gases in Mendeléev's Periodic Table?

2 Draw an outline of the Periodic Table similar to Figure 11.3. On your outline, indicate where you would find:

A metals
B non-metals
C metalloids
D elements with atomic numbers 11 to 18 inclusive
E the alkaline-earth metals
F the most reactive metal
G the most reactive non-metal
H an element that is used as a disinfectant
I gases
J a magnetic element
K an element used in jewellery
L elements with the highest densities.

3 Suppose you are Mendeléev. The year is 1869. You are just about to announce the creation of your Periodic Table by writing a letter to the President of the Russian Academy of Sciences. Write down what you would say.

1.12 The noble gases

In 1868, a yellow line was noticed in the spectrum of light from the Sun. The wavelength of this light could not be identified, so scientists concluded that the Sun's atmosphere contained an element that had not been found on the Earth. The element was named helium, which comes from the Greek word *helios* meaning Sun. The first noble gas had been identified.

Helium

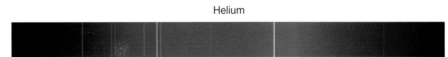

Figure 12.1 Emission spectrum of helium showing the yellow spectral line first observed in 1868 in the Sun's spectrum.

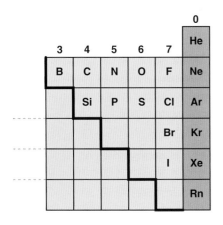

Figure 12.2 Group 0: the noble gases.

Figure 12.2 shows the position of the noble gases in Group 0 of the Periodic Table. After the discovery of helium, scientists realised that there must be other noble gases. They looked for them and gradually discovered each one. The discovery of the noble gases showed the value of the Periodic Table in encouraging research.

■ Finding helium on Earth

In 1890, two scientists tried to prepare pure nitrogen by removing oxygen, water vapour and carbon dioxide from air. But, the density of the gas they obtained was 0.5% greater than that of pure nitrogen. Further experiments on the impure nitrogen from the air showed that it contained another new element, argon, with a relative atomic mass of 40.

In 1894, traces of helium were found on Earth and the gas was shown to be very similar to argon. These two elements were very different from any other elements, which suggested that there was another group in the Periodic Table. The group was called Group 0 and the search began for the other elements in it.

The fractional distillation of liquid air in 1898 led to the discovery of neon, krypton and xenon. Radon, Rn, was discovered in 1900 as a product from the breakdown of the radioactive element radium.

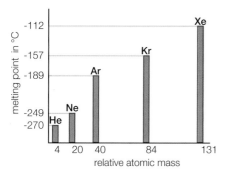

Figure 12.3 A graph showing the increase in the melting points of the noble gases as their relative atomic masses increase.

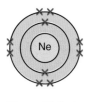 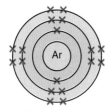

Figure 12.4 Electronic configurations of neon and argon.

Properties of the noble gases

Table 1 lists some properties of the noble gases. They are all colourless gases at room temperature with very low melting points and boiling points. Their melting points, boiling points and densities show a steady increase as their relative atomic mass increases. The graph in Figure 12.3 shows the steady increase in melting point with relative atomic mass.

Table 1 Properties of the noble gases.

Element	Relative atomic mass	Melting point in °C	Boiling point in °C	Density at 20 °C and atm. pressure in g / dm³
helium	4	−270	−269	0.17
neon	20	−249	−246	0.83
argon	40	−189	−186	1.7
krypton	84	−157	−152	3.5
xenon	131	−112	−108	5.5

The noble gases all exist as separate single atoms (i.e. monatomic molecules). Other gaseous elements at room temperature are diatomic, for example hydrogen (H_2), oxygen (O_2), nitrogen (N_2), fluorine (F_2) and chlorine (Cl_2).

Until 1962, no compounds of the noble gases were known. Chemists thought they were completely unreactive. Because of this, they were called the *inert* gases. Nowadays, several compounds of them are known and the name *inert* has been replaced by *noble*. The word *noble* was chosen because unreactive metals like gold and silver are called *noble metals*.

Figure 12.4 shows the electronic configuration of neon and argon. They do not easily lose, gain or share electrons.

Obtaining the noble gases

Neon, argon, krypton and xenon are obtained industrially by the fractional distillation of liquid air. There are only minute traces of helium in air. It is more economical to extract helium from the natural gas in oil wells.

Uses of the noble gases

Helium is used in meteorological balloons and airships because of its very low density and because it is non-flammable.

The noble gases produce coloured glows when their atoms are bombarded by a stream of electrons. The stream of electrons can be produced from a high voltage across terminals either in a discharge tube or in a laser. Neon and argon are used in discharge tubes to create fluorescent advertising signs (neon – red; argon – blue), whilst krypton and xenon are used in lasers.

Figure 12.5 A technician inflates a research balloon with helium. The balloon will carry instruments to measure the levels of ozone in the upper atmosphere over the Arctic.

Argon and krypton are also used in electric filament light bulbs. If there is a vacuum inside the bulbs, metal atoms evaporate from the very, very hot tungsten filament. To reduce this evaporation and prolong the life of the filament, the bulb is filled with an unreactive gas which cannot react with the hot tungsten filament.

Figure 12.6 The bright fluorescent lights of Las Vegas.

STUDY QUESTIONS

1 **a)** Which elements make up the noble gases?
   b) Why are they called *noble* gases?
   c) Why were they once called inert gases?
2 Use the values in Table 1 to plot a graph of the boiling points of the noble gases (vertically) against their relative atomic masses (horizontally).
   a) How do the boiling points vary with relative atomic mass?
   b) Explain the pattern shown by the graph.
   c) Use the graph to predict the boiling point of radon (A_r(Rn) = 222).

3 Suppose liquid air contains oxygen (boiling point = −183 °C), nitrogen (boiling point = −196 °C) water (boiling point = 100 °C), neon, argon, krypton and xenon. In fractional distillation, the liquid with the lowest boiling point distils off first. If liquid air is fractionally distilled, what is the order in which the constituents boil off?
4 Make a summary of the properties of the noble gases.

Summary

I am confident that:

✓ **I understand the arrangement of particles in solids, liquids and gases, and how these are interconverted**
- Solids melt to become liquids that boil to become gases.
- Gases condense to become liquids which freeze to become solids.

✓ **I understand methods of separating mixtures, including:**
- filtration and evaporation
- simple distillation and fractional distillation
- paper chromatography, and I can calculate R_f values from provided data.

✓ **I understand the differences between elements, mixtures and compounds in terms of atoms and their bonding**
- Atoms are the smallest particles of elements.
- Compounds are made from atoms of two or more different elements chemically combined.
- Mixtures are substances with more than one type of particle that are not chemically combined.
- Pure substances have fixed melting and boiling points. Mixtures melt and boil over a range of temperatures.

✓ **I am able to describe the structure of an atom in terms of:**
- protons, neutrons in the nucleus
- electrons orbiting the nucleus in shells.

✓ **I understand that the Periodic Table is an arrangement of elements in order of atomic number, and I can use the Periodic Table to find:**
- the number of protons of an atom
- the number of neutrons of an atom
- the relative atomic mass (A_r) of an atom.

✓ **I can work out the electronic configurations of the first 20 elements from their positions in the Periodic Table**
- Find the element's number of electrons.
- Then place them into shells, 2 in the first shell, 8 in the second shell, 8 in the third shell, and the rest in the fourth shell.

✓ **I can work out the number of outer electrons in a main group element from its position in the Periodic Table**
- The number of outer electrons an atom has is the same as the Group number of the element.

✓ **I can calculate the relative atomic mass of an element from the relative abundances of its isotopes**
- Multiply the atomic mass of each isotope by its abundance, either as a percentage or in terms of the ratio of atoms.
- Then add the values together and divide by 100 if percentages are used, or by the total number of atoms in the ratio.

Sample answers and expert's comments

1   The diagram represents an atom of an element.

    a) i)   State the atomic number and mass number of this element.   (2)

       ii) State the electronic configuration of this element.   (1)

       iii) Name this element.   (1)

    b) i)   Which group is this element in?   (1)

       ii) Name a different element in the same group.   (1)

       iii) Name a different element in the same period.   (1)

       iv) Explain how you chose your answer to part ii).   (2)

                                      (Total for question = 9 marks)

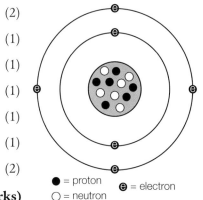

● = proton   ◉ = electron
○ = neutron

Student response Total 9/9	Expert comments and tips for success
a) i) Atomic number is 6, ✓ the mass number is 12 ✓	Knowing that the nucleus contains protons and neutrons, the mass number is found by counting all the dots in the nucleus. As there are six shaded and six unshaded dots, the atomic number must be six.
ii) 2, 4 ✓	The electronic configuration can be determined by counting the electrons in each shell.
iii) Carbon ✓	Carbon is the element in the Periodic Table with atomic number 6.
b) i) Group 4 ✓	The group numbers run across the top of the table.
ii) Silicon ✓	Correct choice from the vertical group.
iii) Oxygen ✓	Correct choice from the horizontal period.
iv) It is in the same group as carbon and elements in the same group ✓ have the same number of outer electrons. ✓	The answer clearly states the relationship between the number of outer electrons and the group number.

2 A student investigated what happened when some crushed ice was heated using a Bunsen burner. The diagrams show her investigation at the start and the end.

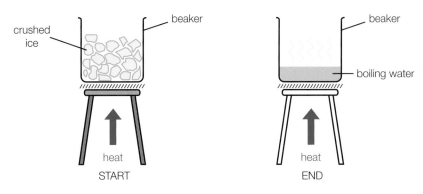

a) At first the solid ice turns to water. Give the name of the process and describe the changes in the arrangement, and movement of the particles as the ice becomes water. (3)

b) After further heating the water starts to boil. After 5 minutes the level of water in the beaker is half the original water level. Explain why the water level has dropped by describing the changes in the movement and energy of the particles as the water's temperature approaches boiling point. (4)

c) The water vapour turns back to liquid water on a nearby cold glass. Give the name of the process, and describe how the arrangement and energy of the particles changes as the gas becomes a liquid. (3)

(Total for question = 10 marks)

Student response Total 7/10	Expert comments and tips for success
a) The process is <u>melting</u>. ✓ In ice the particles are held together in a <u>regular arrangement</u> and are <u>not free to move.</u> <u>They vibrate</u>, getting faster as melting point is reached. ✓	The process is named correctly, and gains a mark. The answer is then split into two parts dealing with the arrangement and movement of particles in ice, and then in water.
As the ice melts the particles become <u>free to move around each other</u> having <u>no regular arrangement</u>; ✓ they are just random.	If you separate your answer into parts like this it is easier for the examiner to find the credit-worthy parts and give you the marks.
b) Some of the water has evaporated after five minutes at boiling point.	The question does not ask for the name of the change of state, so no marks.
This happens because the water particles gain enough energy to <u>separate from each other and go into the air</u>. ✓	The description of the particles' movement gains a mark. An explanation for the drop in water level is needed for a second mark.
As they gain energy they move quicker.	To gain a mark the answer needs to relate the particle energy and movement to temperature. You need to understand the practical described before making the answer.
c) The water appears by <u>condensation</u>. ✓ In the gas the particles are arranged randomly and are spread apart. As the water vapour cools the particles lose energy ✓ and get closer together and form a liquid on the cold surface. ✓	This is a good, well-structured answer. The process is correctly named, with good descriptions.

Exam-style questions

1 A few crystals of a green salt are placed in a beaker of cold water. The crystals start to dissolve.

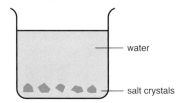

a) Describe how the appearance of the contents of the beaker change over a period of a few days. [2]

b) Name the process that occurs after the crystals dissolve. [1]

c) How will the results of the experiment differ if hot water is used in place of cold water? Explain your answer. [2]

2 a) The diagrams below show the particles present in four gases. Each circle represents an atom.

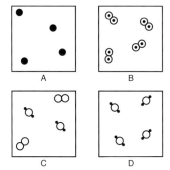

Which diagram represents:

i) nitrogen

ii) steam

iii) a mixture of gases

iv) a monatomic gas? [4]

b) Copy the next diagram and draw circles in the box to represent the arrangement of particles in a solid element. One particle has been drawn for you. [2]

c) Describe how the arrangement and movement of particles in a solid change when it is heated until it is liquid. [4]

3 Use words from the following list to complete the sentences. Each word may be used once, more than once or not at all.

allotropes   carbon   compounds   electrons
elements   hydrogen   neutrons   protons

a) Atoms of the same element always contain the same number of _____. [1]

b) Isotopes are atoms of the same element which contain different numbers of _____. [1]

c) Substances containing atoms all with the same number of protons are _____. [1]

d) Substances whose molecules contain more than one element are _____. [1]

e) The negatively charged particles in an atom are _____. [1]

f) In the definition of relative atomic mass, the mass of an atom is compared to the mass of an atom of _____. [1]

4 A sample of copper contains two isotopes.

a) What are isotopes? [2]

b) i) Copy and complete the following table for these isotopes of copper.

Atomic number	Mass number	Number of protons	Number of neutrons	Percentage of each isotope in sample
29	63			69
		29	36	31

[3]

ii) Use information from the table to calculate the relative atomic mass of this sample of copper. Give your answer to one decimal place. [2]

c) Identify the element, and its mass number, which is used in the definition of relative atomic mass. [2]

d) Why do the two isotopes of copper have the same chemical properties? [1]

5 a) Atoms contain smaller particles. Copy and complete the table to show the relative mass and relative charge of each particle.

Particle	Relative mass	Relative charge
electron		
neutron	1	
proton		+1

[4]

b) Use the Periodic Table on page 273 to name the element whose atoms have the electronic configuration 2, 8, 4. [1]

c) Scientists think they will soon make an element that will go directly below astatine in the Periodic Table. Suggest how many electrons an atom of this element would have in its outer electron shell. [1]

d) The diagrams show the electronic configurations of helium and neon.

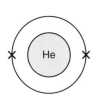 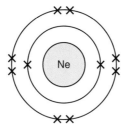

    i) What is the similarity in the outer electron shells of these two atoms? [1]

    ii) What effect does this similarity have on the chemical reactivity of helium and neon? [1]

6 Scientists have been able to make new elements in nuclear reactors. One of these new elements is fermium. An atom of fermium is represented by the symbol below.

$$^{257}_{100}\text{Fm}$$

a) How many protons does this atom contain? [1]

b) How many neutrons does this atom contain? [1]

7 Sodium chloride or cooking salt can be obtained by the purification of rock salt. Rock salt is a mixture of sand and sodium chloride. Sodium chloride dissolves in water.

A student wanted to obtain a pure sample of sodium chloride from some crushed rock salt.

a) The student dissolved the rock salt in hot water.

    i) Suggest why the student used hot water. [1]

    ii) How could the student separate the sand from the salt solution? [1]

b) The student then obtained the salt from the salt solution.

    i) Describe in detail how the student did this. [2]

    ii) The student then placed the damp salt crystals obtained in an oven. What did this do to the damp salt crystals? [1]

8 Two students were given some seawater. They placed the liquid in the apparatus shown below.

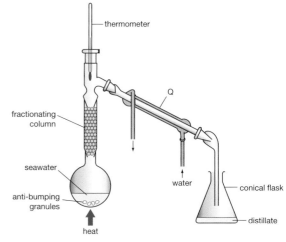

a) Name the process being used. [1]

b) Name the liquid in the conical flask. [1]

c) **i)** Name the part labelled Q. [1]

    ii) What happens in part Q? [1]

d) What is left in the flask at the end of the process? [1]

e) Explain how heating the seawater produces pure water. [3]

9 A, B,C, D, and E are five different inks. The dyes in the inks can be separated using chromatography. This chromatogram shows the results.

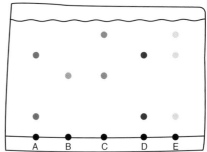

a) Which two inks have the same dyes in them? [1]

b) Which ink has only a single dye? [1]

The R_f value for a dye can be used to identify a dye. It is calculated using this formula:

$$R_f = \frac{\text{distance moved by dye}}{\text{distance moved by solvent front}}$$

c) In the ink chromatogram the solvent front is 8 cm above the position of the original ink spots. Calculate the R_f value of the dye in ink D that has moved 2.8 cm from its original position. [2]

10 Part of the modern Periodic Table is shown below.

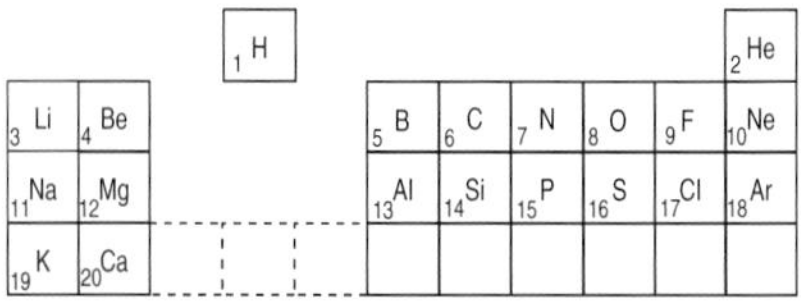

a) Copy and complete the sentence below by writing in the missing words.

Elements in the modern Periodic Table are arranged in order of increasing _____. [1]

b) i) Name a metal in the same group as beryllium. [1]

ii) Name a non-metal in the same period as sodium. [1]

c) The following table contains some information about two elements.

Element	Symbol	Number of		
		protons	neutrons	electrons
fluorine	F	9	10	9
chlorine	Cl	17	18	17
chlorine	Cl	17	20	17

i) In terms of atomic structure, state **one** feature that both these elements have in common. [1]

ii) There are two isotopes of chlorine shown in the table. How do these isotopes differ? [2]

EXTEND AND CHALLENGE

DNA testing: a tricky separation

Have you ever watched *CSI: Miami*? If your answer is 'yes', then you have watched one of the world's most popular television series. Many people, wherever they live, enjoy crime-based television dramas, which explains why these programmes are so popular.

Figure 1 A glamorous location, but full of crime according to *CSI: Miami*.

The *CSI* series of programmes are particularly popular and have led to a great increase in the number of people wanting to be forensic science investigators. There has been a downside to this, however, as fewer people come forward as witnesses to crimes. This is because *CSI*-style programmes lead them to think that crimes can always be solved by the evidence left behind as DNA, without the need for people to confirm this evidence.

A DNA sample is obtained, usually from saliva or blood. The DNA is separated from the nucleus of the cell and then mixed with enzymes. These break down the large DNA molecules into smaller sections and some of these, known as short tandem repeats (STRs), are analysed. These STRs are highly specific to individuals. In the USA 13 different types of STRs are used; in the UK only 11 types.

The actual DNA testing is an electrical current-assisted form of chromatography. There are two types, gel electrophoresis and capillary electrophoresis. The STR mixture is placed on a gel that behaves in a similar way to a piece of wet chromatography paper. An electric current is passed through the gel, and this separates out the different STR sections, producing an image like the one in Figure 2. False matches are extremely unlikely. When they do occur they are usually the result of contamination of a sample by the DNA of another person.

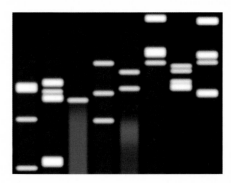

Figure 2 A gel electrophoresis DNA profile.

Sometimes at the scene of a crime there is insufficient DNA evidence. This has led to the development of 'low count' methods of analysis. The small amount of DNA collected is subjected to the same enzymes that make DNA replicate (reproduce). The small amount of DNA then makes more identical DNA until there is sufficient to test.

1 What is the difference between paper chromatography and gel electrophoresis?
2 What does STR stand for?
3 What are STRs?
4 Suggest two ways in which using an electric current may help the separation of different STRs.
5 A contaminated DNA sample explains most false DNA matches, but there is another cause of false matches. Suggest what it is, and explain why it occurs.
6 Describe the effect of carrying out a DNA test with insufficient amounts of DNA.
7 At first 'low count' DNA testing was not accepted as evidence in courts. Prepare a short summary to explain to a judge why 'low count' DNA testing techniques should be accepted.

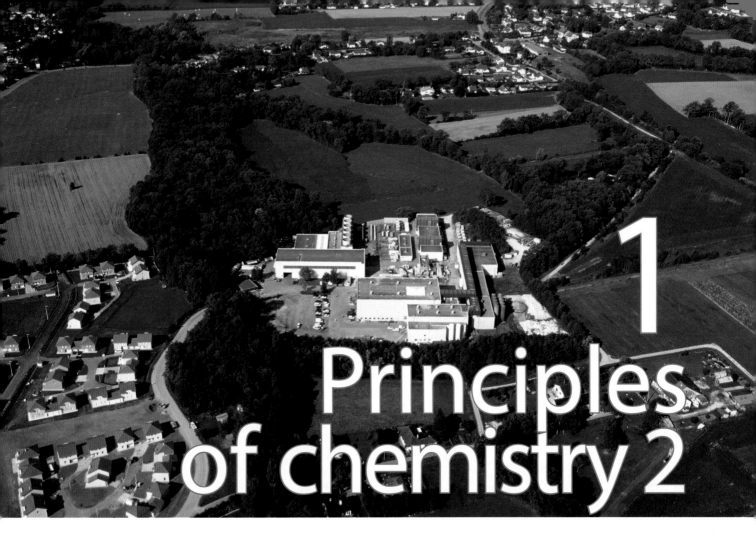

1 Principles of chemistry 2

DISCUSS • PRESENT

1 Over 20 different European countries are members of the European Organization for Nuclear Research. Suggest why so many countries are all working together to investigate the structure of matter.

2 The cost of building the Large Hadron Collider was approximately $10 billion. List two or three other things we might have spent the money on that would have helped people across the world. Do you think the cost of the Large Hadron Collider is justified? Explain your answer.

3 Find out the contribution of these scientists to the study of matter: John Dalton, Ernest Rutherford, Hans Geiger, J.J. Thomson, James Chadwick and Enrico Fermi.

In chemistry we study the interactions of atoms, because the atom model we use is still the best way to explain how substances are made and how they can be changed from one substance into other more useful materials. Research into the structure of matter at sub-atomic level continues.

Probably the most important research facility into the structure of matter today is at CERN, Geneva, shown in the aerial photo. This is the centre and research facility of the European Organization for Nuclear Research. Lying beneath the houses and fields is the Large Hadron Collider, a 27-kilometre circular tunnel used to investigate the fundamental particles of matter. In July 2012 CERN announced the discovery of a small particle known as the Higgs boson, believed to link energy and matter.

In the short term the discovery of the Higgs boson is unlikely to make a large impact on our lives, but it will contribute further to our understanding of how matter is joined together and how it behaves on a cosmological scale.

> **By the end of this section you should:**
> * be able to calculate empirical and molecular formulae
> * be able to describe a chemical reaction with a word equation and a balanced symbol equation
> * be able to calculate reacting masses and percentage yields
> * be able to describe the differences between ionic and covalent compounds in terms of their bonding and electronic configurations
> * know the structures of ionic crystals, giant covalent structures and metals
> * be able to describe the processes taking place during electrolysis.

1.13 Using relative atomic masses

How do you make sure you have the right number of very small atoms when doing a reaction? The atoms are too small to either weigh or handle individually. Instead, scientists use ideas that other people have used.

Look at Figure 13.1. You can weigh the brick to find out how much the pallet of bricks weighs. Alternatively, you could weigh the pallet of bricks to find the mass of one brick. For both methods you need to know the number of bricks. Scientists use these ideas to help them use the right number of reactants in chemical reactions.

Figure 13.1 Knowing the number of a bricks in the pallet and the mass of a brick allows builders to find the mass of the pallet of bricks.

■ The mole

> The relative atomic mass of an element in grams is sometimes called one **mole** (abbreviated as mol).

The word 'mole' comes from a Latin word meaning a heap or a pile.

So,   12 g of carbon = 1 mol of carbon, C

1 g of hydrogen = 1 mol of hydrogen, H

24 g of carbon = 2 mol of carbon, C

$$\text{Number of moles} = \frac{\text{mass}}{\text{relative atomic mass}}$$

So, for example, you can find the number of moles of aluminium in an aluminium colander by weighing it and dividing by its relative atomic mass (Figure 13.2).

Figure 13.2 The photo shows an aluminium colander (mass 108 g), a copper bracelet (mass 31.8 g), some iron nails (mass 5.6 g) and some barbecue charcoal (mass 150 g). How many moles of each element do the objects contain? (Relative atomic masses: Al = 27, Cu = 63.5, Fe = 56, C = 12).

■ The Avogadro number

Relative atomic masses show that one atom of carbon is 12 times as heavy as one atom of hydrogen. So, 12 g of carbon will contain the same number of atoms as 1 g of hydrogen. An atom of oxygen is 16 times as heavy as an atom of hydrogen, so 16 g of oxygen will also contain the same number of atoms as 1 g of hydrogen.

The relative atomic mass in grams (i.e. one mole) of every element (1 g of hydrogen, 12 g carbon, 16 g oxygen, etc.) will contain the same number of atoms. This number is called the **Avogadro number**. The term was chosen in honour of the Italian scientist Amedeo Avogadro.

Experiments show that the Avogadro number is 6×10^{23}. Written out in full this is 600 000 000 000 000 000 000 000. Thus:

> 1 mole of atoms of an element always contains 6×10^{23} atoms.

Using moles

Using the mole idea we can count (calculate) the number of atoms in a sample of an element. For example:

12 g (1 mol) of carbon contains 6×10^{23} atoms

so 1 g ($\frac{1}{12}$ mol) of carbon contains $\frac{1}{12} \times 6 \times 10^{23}$ atoms

$\Rightarrow$ 10 g ($\frac{10}{12}$ mol) of carbon contains $\frac{10}{12} \times 6 \times 10^{23} = 5 \times 10^{23}$ atoms

Chemists often need to count atoms. In industry, nitrogen is reacted with hydrogen to form ammonia, NH_3, which is then used to make fertilisers. In a molecule of ammonia, there is one nitrogen atom and three hydrogen atoms. In order to make ammonia, chemists must therefore react:

1 mol of nitrogen atoms + 3 mol of hydrogen atoms

(14 g of nitrogen)   (3 × 1 g = 3 g of hydrogen)

not 1 g of nitrogen and 3 g of hydrogen.

Because chemists often need to measure amounts that contain a known number of atoms, it is helpful to work in moles, as one mole (or 1 mol) of atoms of an element always contains 6×10^{23} atoms. So chemists use the mole (and not the kilogram) as their unit for the amount of an element. In effect, it is their counting unit.

■ Finding formulae

We have used some formulae already, but how do we know what the formula of a compound is? How do we know, for example, that the formula of water is H_2O? All formulae are obtained by doing experiments to find the masses of elements which react.

When water is decomposed into hydrogen and oxygen, results show that:

18 g of water gives 2 g of hydrogen + 16 g of oxygen

= 2 mol of hydrogen atoms, H + 1 mol of oxygen atoms, O

= $2 \times 6 \times 10^{23}$ atoms of hydrogen + $6 \times 10^{23} \times$ atoms of oxygen

12×10^{23} hydrogen atoms combine with 6×10^{23} atoms of oxygen, so 2 hydrogen atoms combine with 1 oxygen atom. Therefore, the formula of water is H_2O.

These results are set out in Table 1. By finding the masses of reacting elements, we can use relative atomic masses to calculate the number of moles of atoms that react. This gives the ratio of atoms that react and so gives the empirical formula of a compound. The empirical formula of a compound is the simplest ratio in which the atoms combine. It may not be the molecular formula of the compound; ethane has an empirical formula of CH_3, but the molecular formula is C_2H_6.

Table 1 Finding the formula of water.

	H	O
masses reacting	2 g	16 g
mass of 1 mole	1 g	16 g
∴ moles reacting	2	1
ratio of atoms	2	1
⇒ formula	H_2O	

Finding the formula of magnesium oxide

When magnesium ribbon is heated, it burns with a very bright flame to form white, powdery magnesium oxide.

magnesium + oxygen → magnesium oxide

If you try this experiment, wear eye protection.

Weigh accurately 2.4 g of clean magnesium ribbon. Heat this strongly in a crucible until all of it forms magnesium oxide (Figure 13.3). Have a lid on the crucible to stop magnesium oxide escaping, but keep a small gap so that air can enter. When the magnesium has finished reacting, reweigh the crucible + lid + magnesium oxide.

Calculate the mass of oxygen reacting from the mass of magnesium oxide minus the mass of magnesium.

Table 2 shows how to obtain the formula of magnesium oxide from the results.

crucible containing magnesium ribbon

pipe clay triangle

tripod

Bunsen burner with roaring flame

Figure 13.3 Heating magnesium to form magnesium oxide.

REQUIRED PRACTICAL

This experiment is a good way to work out a formula. It often appears in exams where the reacting masses are given and you have to work out the formula.

PRACTICAL

This suggested practical relates to specification point 1.31.

Table 2 Finding the formula of magnesium oxide.

Mass of magnesium reacting = 2.4 g
Mass of magnesium oxide produced = 4.0 g

	Mg	O
masses reacting	2.4 g	1.6 g
mass of 1 mole	24 g	16 g
∴ moles reacting	0.1	0.1
ratio of moles	1	1
∴ ratio of atoms	1	1
⇒ empirical formula	MgO	

Finding the formula of a hydrated salt

Some compounds such as copper(II) sulfate can form crystals that contain water of *crystallisation*. These salts are called hydrated salts. To determine the formula of a hydrated salt you need to know how much of the hydrated salt is water.

1. Find the mass of a clean dry evaporating basin.
2. Put about 5 g of your hydrated salt into the basin and re-weigh it.
3. Heat gently, stirring with a dry glass rod.
4. When the crystals appear to have changed to a powder allow the basin and contents to cool and re-weigh them.
5. Repeat steps 3 and 4 until the mass of the basin and salt remain constant.

Note: **Wear eye protection for this practical.** Do not heat too strongly as some hydrated salts may decompose producing toxic gases.

The mass of the water in the hydrated salt is the difference in the mass readings in steps 2 and 5. The mass of the anhydrous salt (without the water) is the difference between the mass readings in steps 1 and 5.

If you used $CuSO_4.xH_2O$ and found that 1.80 g of water had been lost and that 3.15 g of $CuSO_4$ remained then by knowing the relative formulae masses of water and $CuSO_4$ you can find the number of molecules of water in hydrated copper sulfate like this.

Relative formula mass of water $= 2 + 16 = 18$

Relative formula mass of $CuSO_4 = 63.5 + 32 + 16 + 16 + 16 + 16 = 159.5$

$$H_2O : CuSO_4$$

Ratio of grams $1.80 : 3.15$

Ratio of moles $\dfrac{1.80}{18} : \dfrac{3.15}{159.5}$

$$= 0.10 : 0.019\ 749$$

reacting ratio $= 0.1 : 0.02$ or $5 : 1$

5 moles of water are in 1 mole of hydrated copper(II) sulfate, and so the empirical formula is $CuSO_4.5H_2O$.

MATHS TIP

In calculations using experimental data you should round ratios. Notice that the number of moles of 0.019 749 for $CuSO_4$ has been rounded to 0.02. There are two reasons to do this. The first is that some random errors in the measuring of the masses will be present, and the second is that by rounding to two significant figures it makes the calculation of the reacting ratios much easier. Using the full 0.019 749 would give a ratio of 1 : 5.063 492, and since you can only have complete molecules of water 1 : 5 would still be the answer.

STUDY QUESTIONS

1. How many moles are there in:
   a) 52 g chromium (Cr = 52)
   b) 2.8 g nitrogen (N = 14)
   c) 0.36 g carbon (C = 12)
   d) 20 g bromine (Br = 80)?
2. What is the mass of:
   a) 3 mol of bromine atoms (Br = 80)
   b) ¼ mol of calcium atoms (Ca = 40)
   c) 0.1 mol of sodium atoms (Na = 23)?
3. Methane in natural gas is found to contain 75% carbon and 25% hydrogen by mass. Calculate the empirical formula of methane using a method like that in Tables 1 and 2.
4. What are the empirical formulae of the following compounds?
   a) A compound in which 10.4 g chromium (Cr = 52) combines with 48 g bromine (Br = 80).
   b) A nitride of chromium in which 0.26 g chromium forms 0.33 g of chromium nitride (N = 14).

5. a) What masses of calcium, carbon and oxygen react to form one mole of calcium carbonate ($CaCO_3$)? (Ca = 40, C = 12, O = 16)
   b) What are the percentages by mass of calcium, carbon and oxygen in calcium carbonate?
6. A student heated 12.7 g of copper in oxygen to make some copper oxide. After five minutes the student weighed the sample, then heated the sample for another minute and re-weighed it. The student repeated the heating and weighing until the mass was 15.9 g on two consecutive weighings.
   a) Why did the student keep heating and weighing until the mass was constant?
   b) Use the masses given to calculate:
      i) the mass of oxygen that reacted with the copper
      ii) the formula of the copper oxide made.
   c) Calculate the number of moles of copper oxide made.

1.14 Writing formulae

The formula of any compound is very useful. It tells you the elements in the compound, how many atoms of each element are present, and is a quick way of writing the compound without using the words. If you look at the bottles of chlorides in Figure 14.1 you will see that they each have different numbers of chlorine atoms. Knowing the formula of a compound can give you more information about the elements in the compound. Although the only sure way of knowing the formula of a compound is by experiment, the formulae of most compounds can be predicted from a few simple rules.

Figure 14.1 Bottles of chlorides, showing their different formulae.

■ Compounds of non-metals with non-metals

Water, carbon dioxide and hydrogen chloride are examples of compounds containing non-metals combined or bonded with other non-metals.

In these compounds, the atoms combine in small groups to form **molecules**. For example, water contains one oxygen atom bonded to two hydrogen atoms and the formula of the molecule is H_2O. Hydrogen chloride contains one hydrogen atom bonded to one chlorine atom and the formula of the molecule is HCl.

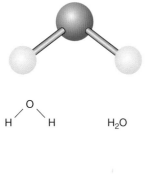

H_2O

Figure 14.2 shows three ways of representing molecules of water and hydrogen chloride. Models like those in the first structure in each case represent the atoms as little spheres.

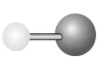

H—Cl   HCl

Figure 14.2 Ways of representing molecules of water and hydrogen chloride.

These compounds of non-metals which are composed of small molecules are usually called **molecular compounds**. It is possible to work out the formulae of most non-metal compounds if you know how many bonds the atoms usually form (Table 1).

Sometimes there are double bonds and even triple bonds between the atoms in non-metal compounds.

O=C=O

Figure 14.3 Bonding in carbon dioxide showing the double bonds between atoms.

Figure 14.3 shows the bonds in carbon dioxide and its formula. Carbon atoms form four bonds and oxygen atoms form two bonds.

To satisfy and link all the bonds, two oxygen atoms combine with one carbon atom by double bonds, so the formula of carbon dioxide is CO_2.

Notice that there is a strict colour code for the atoms of different elements in molecular models. These colours are shown in Table 1.

Table 1 The symbols, number of bonds and colour codes of some non-metals.

Element	Symbol	Number of bonds formed	Colour in molecular models
carbon	C	4	black
nitrogen	N	3	blue
oxygen	O	2	red
sulfur	S	2	yellow
hydrogen	H	1	white
chlorine	Cl	1	green

In practice, it is not possible to predict the formulae of all non-metal compounds. The bonding rules in Table 1, for example, cannot account for the formulae of carbon monoxide, CO, or sulfur dioxide, SO_2.

■ Compounds of metals with non-metals

Common salt (sodium chloride), iron ore (brown iron oxide) and copper sulfate are compounds of metals with non-metals. These metal/non-metal compounds are usually called **ionic compounds** because they are composed of ions and *not* molecules like compounds of non-metals.

Ions are charged particles formed from atoms by the loss or gain of electrons. Tables 2 and 3 show the positive and negative charges on important ions. For example, sodium chloride consists of sodium ions, Na^+, and chloride ions, Cl^-. Its formula is NaCl because the single positive charge on one Na^+ ion is balanced by the single negative charge on one Cl^- ion.

Brown iron oxide is composed of iron ions, Fe^{3+}, and oxide ions, O^{2-}. Its formula is Fe_2O_3 because the six positive charges on two Fe^{3+} ions are balanced by the six negative charges on three O^{2-} ions.

The correct chemical name for brown iron oxide is iron(III) oxide. It is called iron(III) oxide and not simply iron oxide because iron can form two ions, Fe^{3+} and Fe^{2+}. So there is a second iron oxide, correctly called iron(II) oxide, with the formula FeO.

The only other common metal that can form two different ions is copper, which forms Cu^+ and Cu^{2+}. Copper(I) compounds are very rare.

In metal/non-metal compounds, the metal ions are always positive and the non-metal ions are negative.

Figure 14.4 The gas in the cylinder is butane. This contains carbon atoms with four bonds and hydrogen atoms with one bond. Its formula is C_4H_{10}.

Table 2 The charges on some common positive ions.

Positive ion	Formula of ion
lithium	Li^+
sodium	Na^+
potassium	K^+
magnesium	Mg^{2+}
calcium	Ca^{2+}
aluminium	Al^{3+}
silver	Ag^+
copper	Cu^{2+}
iron (II)	Fe^{2+}
iron(III)	Fe^{3+}
lead	Pb^{2+}
zinc	Zn^{2+}
ammonium	NH_4^+

Rules for the ions in metal/non-metal compounds

Positive metal ions

There is one simple rule that you must learn for the charges on metal ions.

> All common metal ions have a charge of 2+ except:
>
> - Ag^+, Na^+ and K^+ (remember this as 'agnak') with a charge of 1+
> - Cr^{3+}, Al^{3+} and Fe^{3+} (remember this as 'cralfe') with a charge of 3+.

EXAM TIP

You must learn the formulae and the charges of the ions in Tables 2 and 3.

Negative non-metal ions

The charges on common ions of non-metals are shown in Table 3. Notice that some of the negative ions contain two non-metals.

Table 3 The charges on some common negative ions.

Negative ion	Formula	Negative ion	Formula	Negative ion	Formula
fluoride	F^-	oxide	O^{2-}	hydroxide	OH^-
chloride	Cl^-	sulfide	S^{2-}	nitrate	NO_3^-
bromide	Br^-	nitride	N^{3-}	carbonate	CO_3^{2-}
iodide	I^-	phosphide	P^{3-}	sulfate	SO_4^{2-}

When you write the formulae of metal/non-metal compounds, be careful not to confuse nitride, N^{3-}, and nitrate, NO_3^- also sulfide, S^{2-} and sulfate SO_4^{2-} .

Using the rules

Let's practise these rules for positive and negative ions by working out the formula for aluminium sulfate.

From the rules for positive ions, you should know that the formula of an aluminium ion is Al^{3+}. From Table 3, you will see that the formula of a sulfate ion is SO_4^{2-}. When ionic compounds form, the positive and negative charges must balance. So in this case, the six positive charges on two Al^{3+} ions will balance the six negative charges on three SO_4^{2-} ions, and the formula of aluminium sulfate is $Al_2(SO_4)_3$ or $(Al^{3+})_2(SO_4^{2-})_3$.

Notice that brackets are needed around the sulfate ions in $Al_2(SO_4)_3$ because the SO_4^{2-} ion is a single unit containing one sulfur and four oxygen atoms bonded together with a charge of 2–.

Other ions containing two or more atoms, such as OH^-, NO_3^- and CO_3^{2-}, must also be treated as single units and put in brackets when there is more than one of them in a formula.

Figure 14.5 The Taj Mahal is composed largely of marble, which is mainly calcium carbonate. What ions does calcium carbonate contain and what is its formula?

STUDY QUESTIONS

1 Write symbols for these pairs of elements:
   a) potassium and phosphorus
   b) cobalt and copper
   c) nitrogen and nickel
   d) silver and silicon.

2 Use the different ways shown in Figure 14.2 to represent the following compounds:
   a) methane
   b) carbon disulfide.

3 Work out the formulae of:
   a) hydrogen sulfide
   b) dichlorine oxide
   c) hydrogen nitride (ammonia).

4 The formula of calcium hydroxide must be written as $Ca(OH)_2$. Explain why $CaOH_2$ is wrong?

5 Write the formulae of the following:
   a) copper(II) chloride
   b) lead nitrate
   c) sodium sulfide
   d) iron(II) sulfate
   e) zinc carbonate
   f) iron(III) hydroxide
   g) silver oxide.

6 Give the name and number of each type of atom in the following formulae:
   a) NaCl
   b) $MgBr_2$
   c) $AgNO_3$
   d) K_2SO_4
   e) $CaCO_3$
   f) $Cu(NO_3)_2$
   g) $Fe_2(SO_4)_3$
   h) H_2SO_4
   i) $Ca(OH)_2$
   j) C_2H_5OH.

1.15 Particles in reactions – equations

Figure 15.1 Sparklers produce white sparks using the reaction of magnesium powder with oxygen in the air.

The sparks from these sparklers in Figure 15.1 are bits of burning magnesium. Sparklers are made by gluing gunpowder and metal filings such as magnesium to a steel wire. The burning gunpowder ignites the metal filings, letting them burn with oxygen from the air.

Chemists describe reactions such as magnesium burning with oxygen with equations. Word equations describe the reactants (the starting substances) and the products (the final substances). Chemical or symbol equations describe what happens to the atoms, and how many of each there are in the reaction.

■ Burning magnesium

When magnesium burns in air, it reacts with oxygen to form magnesium oxide. The word equation for this is:

$$\text{magnesium} + \text{oxygen} \rightarrow \text{magnesium oxide}$$

Chemists usually write symbols and formulae rather than names in equations. So, in this word equation, we should write Mg for the element magnesium, O_2 for oxygen and MgO for magnesium oxide, which is composed of Mg^{2+} and O^{2-} ions.

$$Mg + O_2 \rightarrow MgO$$

But, notice that this doesn't balance. There are two oxygen atoms in O_2 on the left and only one oxygen atom in MgO on the right. So, MgO must be doubled to give:

$$Mg + O_2 \rightarrow 2MgO$$

Unfortunately, the equation still doesn't balance. There are now two Mg atoms on the right in 2MgO, but only one on the left in Mg. This is easily corrected by writing 2Mg on the left to give:

$$2Mg + O_2 \rightarrow 2MgO$$

The numbers of different atoms are now the same on both sides of the arrow. This is a **balanced chemical equation**.

■ Writing a balanced equation

A balanced chemical equation is a summary of the starting substances (reactants) and the products in a chemical reaction, in which the numbers of atoms of each element are the same on both sides of the arrow.

The example above shows the three key steps in writing an equation. These can be summarised as follows.

Remember that fluorine, oxygen, nitrogen, hydrogen and chlorine are diatomic so they are written as F_2, O_2, N_2, H_2 and Cl_2. All other elements are shown as single atoms, i.e. Zn for zinc, C for carbon, etc.

Step 1   Write a word equation for the reaction:
for example hydrogen + oxygen → water

Step 2   Write symbols for the elements and formulae for the compounds in the word equation:
for example $H_2 + O_2 \rightarrow H_2O$

Step 3   Balance the equation by making the number of atoms of each element the same on both sides:
for example $2H_2 + O_2 \rightarrow 2H_2O$

Remember that *you must never change a formula* to make an equation balance. The formula for water is always H_2O and never HO or HO_2. Similarly, the formula of magnesium oxide is always MgO.

You can only balance an equation by putting numbers in front of symbols or in front of formulae, i.e. 2Mg and $2H_2O$.

Why balanced equations are so useful

Balanced chemical equations are more useful than word equations because they show:

■ the symbols and formulae of the reactants and products
■ the relative numbers of atoms and molecules of the reactants and products.

Balanced equations also help us to understand how the atoms are rearranged in a reaction. You can see this even better using models as in Figure 15.2.

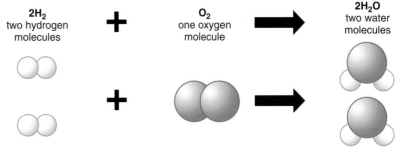

Figure 15.2 Using models to represent the reaction between hydrogen and oxygen to form water.

State symbols

State symbols are used in equations to show the state of a substance. (s) after a formula indicates the substance is a solid. (l) is used for liquid; (g) for gas; and (aq) for an aqueous solution (i.e. a substance dissolved in water). For example,

zinc + sulfuric acid → zinc sulfate + hydrogen

$$Zn(s) + H_2SO_4(aq) \rightarrow ZnSO_4(aq) + H_2(g)$$

Figure 15.3 When natural gas burns, methane (CH_4) reacts with oxygen in the air to form carbon dioxide and water. Write a word equation and then a balanced chemical equation for this reaction.

Figure 15.4 The copper dome on Brighton Pavilion is green because the copper has reacted with oxygen in the air to form copper(II) oxide (CuO). This has then reacted very slowly with water and carbon dioxide to form basic copper(II) carbonate, a compound containing both copper(II) hydroxide ($Cu(OH)_2$) and copper(II) carbonate ($CuCO_3$). Write word equations and then balanced chemical equations for these two reactions.

STUDY QUESTIONS

1 Write balanced chemical equations for the following word equations.
   a) sodium + oxygen $\rightarrow$ sodium oxide (Na_2O)
   b) sodium oxide + water $\rightarrow$ sodium hydroxide (NaOH)
   c) hydrogen + chlorine $\rightarrow$ hydrogen chloride
   d) zinc + hydrochloric acid (HCl) $\rightarrow$ zinc chloride ($ZnCl_2$) + hydrogen

2 Look at the photos on this page and answer the questions in the captions.

3 Write word equations and then balanced chemical equations for the following reactions:
   a) aluminium with oxygen to give aluminium oxide
   b) copper oxide with sulfuric acid to give copper(II) sulfate and water
   c) nitrogen with hydrogen to give ammonia
   d) charcoal (carbon) burning in oxygen to give carbon dioxide
   e) iron with chlorine to give iron(III) chloride.

1.16 Formulae and equations

After a plane is manufactured it is easy to weigh it. The problem aircraft designers have is to make sure before they build a new aircraft that the mass of the components used will be equally distributed over the entire frame, so the aircraft doesn't fly with one wing lower than the other, or nose down. The designers estimate the mass of every component and place them so that the mass of each wing is identical. They know if they add up the mass of each component, then the total mass of each wing should equal the sum of the components. Chemists use the same idea to work out the relative formula mass of compounds.

Figure 16.1 How do you design a jumbo jet so the mass is evenly distributed, so it will fly level?

■ Relative formula masses

We have learnt that relative atomic masses can be used to compare the masses of different atoms. Relative atomic masses can also be used to compare the masses of molecules in different compounds. The relative mass of a compound is called the **relative formula mass** (symbol M_r).

Calculating relative formula masses

The relative formula mass of a compound is obtained by adding up the relative atomic masses of all the atoms in its formula.

For example:

The relative formula mass of water, H_2O, is:

$$M_r(H_2O) = 2 \times \frac{\text{relative atomic}}{\text{mass of hydrogen}} + \frac{\text{relative atomic}}{\text{mass of oxygen}}$$

$$= (2 \times 1) + 16 = 18$$

The relative formula mass of sulfuric acid, H_2SO_4, is:

$$M_r(H_2SO_4) = 2 \times A_r(H) + A_r(S) + 4 \times A_r(O)$$

$$= (2 \times 1) + 32 + (4 \times 16) = 98$$

The relative formula mass of aluminium sulfate $Al_2(SO_4)_3$ is:

$$Al_2(SO_4)_3 = 2 \times A_r(Al) + (3 \times (A_r(S) + (4x\ A_r(O)))$$

$$= (2 \times 27) + (3 \times (32 + (4 \times 16))) = (2 \times 27) + (3 \times 96)$$
$$= 342$$

Relative formula masses and moles

The relative formula mass of a compound in grams is sometimes called one **mole** in the same way that the relative atomic mass of an element in grams is also called one mole. So:

1 mole of water is 18 g
0.1 mole of water is $0.1 \times 18 = 1.8$ g
1 mole of aluminium oxide is 102 g
3 moles of aluminium oxide is $3 \times 102 = 306$ g

Calculating the percentage of an element in a compound

Relative atomic masses can also be used to calculate the percentage of different elements in a compound. For example:

carbon dioxide (CO_2) contains 12 g of carbon and 2×16 g of oxygen in 44 g of carbon dioxide.

So, in terms of mass, it contains $\dfrac{12}{44}$ parts carbon and $\dfrac{32}{44}$ parts oxygen

$= \dfrac{12}{44} \times 100 = 27\%$ carbon and $\dfrac{32}{44} \times 100 = 73\%$ oxygen

■ Using equations to calculate the amounts of reactants and products

In industry, and wherever chemists convert reactants to products, it is important to know the amounts of reactants that are needed for a chemical process and the amount of product that can be obtained. Chemists can calculate these amounts using equations with relative atomic and formula masses.

There are four important steps in solving problems using equations.

Step 1   Write a balanced equation for the reaction.
Step 2   Write down the amounts in moles of the relevant reactants and products.
Step 3   Calculate masses from the amounts in moles.
Step 4   Scale the masses to the quantities required.

Figure 16.2 The saucer contains 58.5 g (one mole) of common salt, sodium chloride (NaCl).
M_r (NaCl) = A_r (Na) + A_r (Cl)
$= 23 + 35.5 = 58.5$

As an example, let's calculate the mass of tin, Sn, we could obtain by heating 1 kg of pure tin(IV) oxide (SnO_2) with coke (carbon). (Sn = 119, O = 16)

Step 1   tin(IV) oxide + carbon → tin + carbon monoxide
$SnO_2 + 2C \rightarrow Sn + 2CO$

Step 2   1 mol $SnO_2 \rightarrow$ 1 mol Sn

Step 3 M_r $(SnO_2) = 119 + (2 \times 16) = 151$

A_r (Sn) = 119

so, 151 g $SnO_2 \rightarrow$ 119 g Sn

Step 4   151 g $SnO_2 \rightarrow$ 119 g Sn

$\therefore$ 1 g $SnO_2 \rightarrow \dfrac{119}{151}$ g Sn = 0.79 g Sn

$\therefore$ 1 kg of pure SnO_2 produces 790 g of tin

Now try to answer Study Questions 1–3.

■ Volumes of gases in reactions

The volume of a gas depends on three things:

- the amount of gas in moles
- the temperature
- the pressure.

At a fixed temperature and fixed pressure, the volume of a gas depends only on the amount of gas in moles. The kind of gas and its formula don't matter.

After hundreds of measurements, chemists have found that the volume of 1 mole of every gas is 24 dm^3 (24 000 cm^3) at room temperature and pressure (r.t.p.), which is 25 °C and 1 atm.

> The volume of 1 mole of gas at r.t.p. is called the **molar volume**.

So, 1 mole of oxygen (O_2), 1 mole of nitrogen (N_2) and 1 mole of carbon dioxide (CO_2) each occupies 24 dm^3 at room temperature and pressure. Therefore, at r.t.p.:

2 moles of O_2 will occupy 48 dm^3
0.5 moles of N_2 will occupy 12 dm^3
10 moles of CO_2 will occupy 240 dm^3.

Notice from these simple calculations that:

> **volume of gas** in cm^3 at r.t.p. =
>
> **amount of gas** in moles × 24 000 cm^3 / mol

graduated 100 cm^3 gas syringe

dilute hydrochloric acid

small piece of magnesium

Figure 16.3 Measuring the volume of hydrogen produced when magnesium reacts with dilute hydrochloric acid.

Measuring the volumes of gases in reactions

The apparatus in Figure 16.3 can be used to measure the volume of hydrogen produced and from this work out the equation for the reaction when magnesium reacts with hydrochloric acid.

A small piece of magnesium (mass 0.061 g) was added to excess dilute hydrochloric acid (HCl)(aq). A vigorous reaction occurred and 60 cm^3 of hydrogen gas (H_2) was produced at r.t.p.

Eventually, all the magnesium had reacted and the reaction stopped.

Changing gas volumes to moles

During the experiment reacting magnesium with hydrochloric acid:

0.061 g magnesium (Mg) produces 60 cm³ of hydrogen (H_2) at r.t.p.

$\therefore \dfrac{0.061}{24}$ mol Mg produce $\dfrac{60}{24\,000}$ mol of H_2

$\Rightarrow$ 0.0025 mol Mg produce 0.0025 mol of H_2

$\therefore$ 1 mol Mg produces 1 mol of H_2

Assuming that magnesium chloride, $MgCl_2$, is also a product, we can write a balanced equation for the reaction, with state symbols, as:

$$Mg(s) + 2HCl(aq) \rightarrow MgCl_2(aq) + H_2(g)$$

PRACTICAL

This suggested practical relates to specification point 1.35C.

Calculating the molar volume of a gas

The apparatus in Figure 16.3 can also be used to calculate the molar volume of a gas.

If 0.060 g of magnesium (= 0.0025 mol Mg) produces 60 cm³ of hydrogen gas we can find the molar volume of a gas. We know that 1 mole of magnesium produces 1 mole of hydrogen (H_2) gas, so 60 cm³ of gas is the volume of 0.0025 moles of gas. So 60 / 0.0025 = 24 000 is the volume of 1 mole of gas in cm³, which is 24 dm³.

Gas volume calculations

When all the relevant substances in a reaction are gases, gas volume calculations are fairly straightforward. In these cases, the ratio of the number of moles in the equation is the same as the ratio of gas volumes in the reaction.

MATHS TIP

In this answer the line
$N_2(g) + 3H_2(g) \rightarrow 2NH_3(g)$
shows the reacting ratio, 1:3 and the ratio of products to reactants, 2:4 or 1:2

Example

What volume of hydrogen will react with 50 cm³ of nitrogen and what volume of ammonia is produced if all volumes are measured at room temperature and pressure?

Answer

The equation for the reaction is:

	nitrogen	+	hydrogen	$\rightarrow$	ammonia
	$N_2(g)$	+	$3H_2(g)$	$\rightarrow$	$2NH_3(g)$
So	1 mol N_2	+	3 mol H_2	$\rightarrow$	2 mol NH_3
	$\therefore 24\,000$ cm³		$3 \times 24\,000$ cm³		$2 \times 24\,000$ cm³
	$\Rightarrow 1$ cm³		3 cm³		2 cm³
	$\therefore 50$ cm³		150 cm³		100 cm³

So, 50 cm³ nitrogen will react with 150 cm³ of hydrogen to produce 100 cm³ of ammonia.

■ Percentage yields

If a chemical reaction is totally efficient, all the starting reactant is converted to the product according to the balanced equation for the reaction. This gives a 100% yield. It is the maximum possible yield if the reaction goes exactly as shown in the balanced equation. This maximum possible yield is usually called the **theoretical yield**. In practice, very few reactions give 100%

yields and many reactions give low yields. There are various reasons why the **actual yields** in reactions are not 100%.

- The reactants may not be pure.
- Some of the product may be lost during transfer from one container to another when it is separated from the reaction mixture.
- There may be side reactions in which the reactants form different products.
- Some of the reactants may not react because the reaction is too slow (Chapter 3.4) or because it comes to equilibrium (Chapter 3.8).

In order to assess the efficiency of reactions, we can calculate the **percentage yield**. This is the actual yield as a percentage of the theoretical yield.

$$\text{percentage yield} = \frac{\text{actual yield}}{\text{theoretical yield}} \times 100\%$$

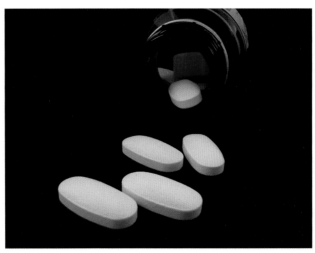

Figure 16.4 The production of ibuprofen is an excellent example of improving percentage yields. Ibuprofen is an important medicine which reduces pain and swelling in joints. In the 1960s, ibuprofen was made in five steps with a very poor percentage yield. Now, it can be produced in just two steps with a much higher percentage yield.

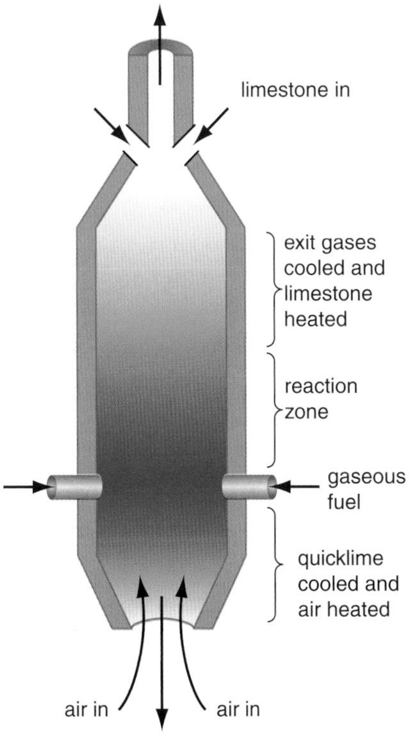

Calculating percentage yields

Example

Figure 16.5 shows a modern gas-fuelled lime kiln. Kilns like this produce about 500 kg of calcium oxide, CaO (quicklime), from 1000 kg of crushed calcium carbonate, $CaCO_3$ (limestone). What is the percentage yield of calcium oxide?

Answer

We know the actual yield of calcium oxide is 500 kg. So, we must use the equation for the decomposition of calcium carbonate to calculate the theoretical yield of calcium oxide from 1000 kg of $CaCO_3$.
(Ca = 40, C = 12, O = 16)

CO₂ and other gases out

limestone in

exit gases cooled and limestone heated

reaction zone

gaseous fuel

quicklime cooled and air heated

air in   air in

quicklime out

Figure 16.5 A modern gas-fuelled lime kiln.

The equation for the reaction is:

calcium carbonate $\rightarrow$ calcium oxide + carbon dioxide

$$CaCO_3 \quad \rightarrow \quad CaO \quad + \quad CO_2$$

So,   1 mol of $CaCO_3$ $\rightarrow$ 1 mol of CaO

$$M_r\,(CaCO_3) = 40 + 12 + (3 \times 16) = 100$$

$$M_r\,(CaO) = 40 + 16 = 56$$

$\therefore$ 100 g $CaCO_3 \rightarrow$ 56 g CaO

and   1 g $CaCO_3 \rightarrow$ 0.56 g CaO

$\Rightarrow$ 1000 kg $CaCO_3 \rightarrow$ 560 kg CaO

So, the theoretical yield of CaO = 560 kg

and the actual yield of CaO = 500 kg

$\therefore$ percentage yield of CaO $= \dfrac{500}{560} \times 100 = 89\%$

STUDY QUESTIONS

1 60 g of a metal M (M = 60) combine with 24 g of oxygen (O = 16).
   a) How many moles of O react with one mole of M?
   b) What is the empirical formula of the oxide of M?

2 The fertiliser 'Nitram' (ammonium nitrate) has the formula NH_4NO_3.
   a) What are the masses of nitrogen, hydrogen and oxygen in 1 mole of Nitram? (N = 14, H = 1, O = 16)
   b) What are the percentages of nitrogen, hydrogen and oxygen in Nitram?

3 Iron is manufactured by reducing iron ore (Fe_2O_3) with carbon monoxide (CO).
   $Fe_2O_3 + 3CO \rightarrow 2Fe + 3CO_2$
   a) What does this equation tell you?
   b) What mass of iron is obtained from 1 mole of Fe_2O_3? (Fe = 56, O = 16)
   c) What mass of iron is obtained from one tonne of Fe_2O_3?

4 How many moles of gas at r.t.p. are there in:
   a) 240 000 cm^3 of hydrogen
   b) 480 cm^3 of oxygen
   c) 6 dm^3 of nitrogen?

5 What is the volume at r.t.p. of:
   a) 5 mol of ammonia
   b) 0.02 mol of argon?

6 a) Copy and balance the following equation:
       $CH_4(g) + \_O_2(g) \rightarrow CO_2(g) + \_H_2O(g)$
   b) What volume of oxygen reacts with 600 cm^3 of methane (CH_4) and what volume of carbon dioxide is produced? (All volumes are measured at r.t.p.)
   c) What is the mass of carbon dioxide produced?

7 Aluminium is manufactured by electrolysis of molten aluminium oxide. The products are aluminium and oxygen. (Al = 27, O = 16)
   a) Write a balanced equation for the decomposition of aluminium oxide forming aluminium and oxygen.
   b) What is the theoretical yield of aluminium from 1 tonne (1000 kg) of aluminium oxide?
   c) The actual yield of aluminium from 1 tonne of aluminium oxide is 440 kg. Calculate the percentage yield of aluminium.

8 When ethanol, C_2H_5OH, is manufactured by hydration of ethene, C_2H_4, the percentage yield is 50%.
   a) Write an equation for the reaction involved.
   b) What mass of ethene is required to produce 10 tonnes of ethanol?

1.17 Chemical bonding

Whenever you want to stick things together at home you get out the glue. Bricklayers stick bricks together with a special glue called mortar made from sand, cement and water. For scientists, the glue that holds atoms together are the outer electrons of the atoms. How they interact is the key to making molecules and compounds.

Figure 17.1 Mortar is used to stick bricks together to make a wall. What sticks atoms together to make compounds?

■ Types of bonding

When atoms react together to form compounds their outer electrons interact to form chemical bonds. Depending on the types of atoms reacting together, either ionic bonds or covalent bonds are formed.

- Metal atoms often lose electrons and become charged particles called positive ions.
- Non-metal atoms can either gain electrons and become negatively charged ions, or they can share some of their electrons with other non-metal atoms.

These ideas form the basis of the **electronic theory of chemical bonding**. This theory says that when some atoms react, they lose, gain or share electrons.

Two kinds of bond are formed when atoms react with each other – ionic bonds and covalent bonds.

Ionic bonds are formed when metals react with non-metals. Metals form positive ions and non-metals form negative ions. The attraction between ions of opposite charge forms the ionic bond. Ionic bonds are sometimes called electrovalent bonds.

Covalent bonds are formed when non-metals react with each other. Covalent bonds involve a sharing of electrons. The positive nucleus of each non-metal attracts the shared negative electrons and this forms the covalent bond.

A covalent bond is the electrostatic attraction between the shared pair of electrons and the nuclei of the two atoms bonded together.

■ Ionic bonding: transfer of electrons

Figure 17.2 shows what happens when sodium chloride (Na^+Cl^-) is formed. Electronic configurations are shown for the sodium and chlorine atoms and for their respective ions.

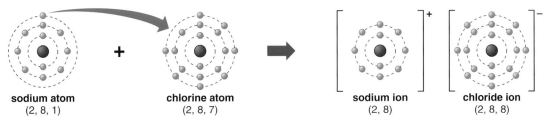

sodium atom   chlorine atom   sodium ion   chloride ion
(2, 8, 1)   (2, 8, 7)   (2, 8)   (2, 8, 8)

Figure 17.2 Electron transfer during the formation of sodium chloride.

The sodium atom has one electron in its outer shell and chlorine has seven. During the reaction, the sodium transfers its one outer electron into the outer shell of the chlorine atom. This produces:

■ a sodium ion (Na^+) with the same electronic configuration as the noble gas neon, and

■ a chloride ion (Cl^-) with the same electronic configuration as the noble gas argon.

So, the formation of sodium chloride involves the *complete transfer* of an electron from a sodium atom to a chlorine atom, forming Na^+ and Cl^- ions.

> Ionic (electrovalent) bonds result from the electrostatic attraction between oppositely charged ions.

Using dot and cross diagrams for ionic bonding

The formation of sodium chloride in Figure 17.2 can be summarised by showing only the outer shell electrons.

(2, 8, 1)   (2, 8, 7)   (2, 8)   (2, 8, 8)

Figure 17.3 'Dot and cross' diagram for the formation of sodium chloride.

This is called a 'dot and cross' diagram because the electrons of the different atoms are shown as either dots or crosses. Remember though that all electrons are identical.

Compounds containing ions with ionic bonds are called **ionic compounds**. The structure, bonding and properties of ionic compounds are discussed in Chapter 1.20.

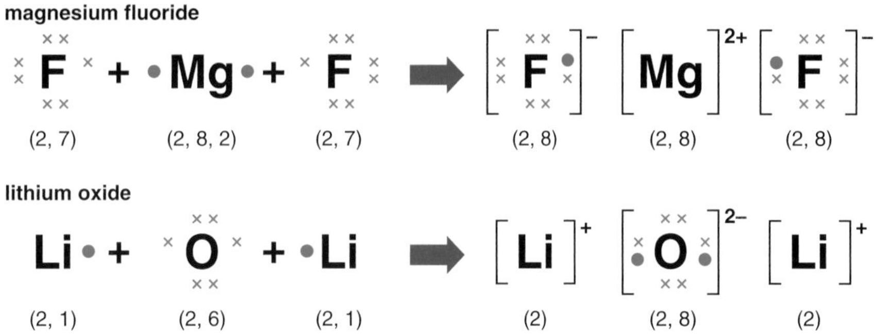

magnesium fluoride

$$\text{F} + \bullet\text{Mg}\bullet + \text{F} \implies \left[\text{F}\right]^{-} \left[\text{Mg}\right]^{2+} \left[\text{F}\right]^{-}$$

(2, 7) (2, 8, 2) (2, 7)   (2, 8) (2, 8) (2, 8)

lithium oxide

$$\text{Li}\bullet + \text{O} + \bullet\text{Li} \implies \left[\text{Li}\right]^{+} \left[\text{O}\right]^{2-} \left[\text{Li}\right]^{+}$$

(2, 1) (2, 6) (2, 1)   (2) (2, 8) (2)

Figure 17.4 Electron transfers in the formation of magnesium fluoride and lithium oxide.

Figure 17.4 shows two more dot and cross diagrams of electron transfer and ionic bonding. Notice the following points in these dot and cross diagrams.

- Transfer of electrons to form ionic bonds is typical of the reactions between metals and non-metals.
- Atoms sometimes form ions with electronic configuration like noble gases, for example helium (2), neon (2, 8) and argon (2, 8, 8).
- One magnesium atom has two electrons in its outer shell (Figure 17.4). It reacts with two fluorine atoms, each of which takes one electron. The Mg^{2+} ion and the two F^- ions all finish with an electronic configuration like neon.
- Two Li atoms react with one O atom to form lithium oxide (Figure 17.4). In this case, the two Li^+ ions have an electronic configuration like helium and the O^{2-} ion has an electronic configuration like neon.

■ Covalent bonds: sharing electrons

Bonding in chlorine (Cl_2)

A chlorine atom is very unstable. Its outer shell contains seven electrons. At normal temperatures, chlorine atoms join up in pairs to form Cl_2 molecules. Why is this? If two chlorine atoms come close together, the electrons in their outer shells can overlap. Each chlorine atom can share one of its electrons with the other atom (Figure 17.5). The two atoms share a pair of electrons and each atom obtains the electronic configuration of argon.

The shared electrons attract the positive nuclei of both atoms and this holds the atoms together. This attraction is known as a covalent bond. Notice in the dot and cross diagram in Figure 17.5 that:

- the shared pair of electrons contribute to the outer shell of both chlorine atoms
- circles are used to enclose the outer shell electrons of each chlorine atom
- the chlorine atoms have bonded together forming an uncharged molecule.

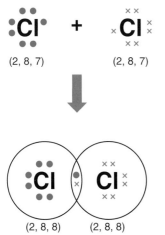

(2, 8, 7)   (2, 8, 7)

(2, 8, 8) (2, 8, 8)

Figure 17.5 Electron sharing in the covalent bond of a chlorine molecule.

A covalent bond is formed by the sharing of a pair of electrons between two atoms. Each atom contributes one electron to the bond.
A covalent bond is the electrostatic attraction between a shared pair of electrons and the nuclei of the two atoms bonded together.

Other non-metal covalent molecules

Other non-metal atoms are unstable by themselves. Like chlorine they share electrons to make covalent bonds. Figure 17.6 shows how two hydrogen atoms share their electrons to make a single covalent bond. Each of the hydrogen atoms achieves the electronic structure of the noble gas helium.

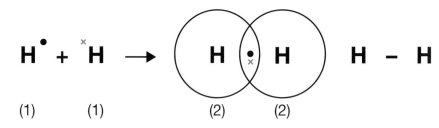

Figure 17.6 Electron sharing in the covalent bond of a hydrogen molecule (H_2).

In both chlorine and hydrogen each individual atom contributes a single electron to make a single covalent bond. Oxygen is different. Oxygen shares two electrons from each atom to achieve the electronic structure of the noble gas neon. Figure 17.7 shows how the electrons are shared in an oxygen molecule. Oxygen shares two pairs of electrons so there are two covalent bonds. This is referred to as a double (covalent) bond. Only the outer electrons are shown to make the diagram easier to understand.

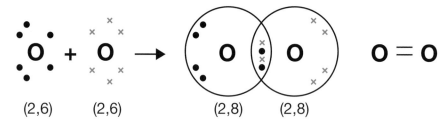

Figure 17.7 Electron sharing in the covalent double bonds of an oxygen molecule (O_2).

Nitrogen has five outer electrons and so each atom shares three electrons to obtain the electronic structure of neon. Fig 17.8 shows how nitrogen atoms share three electrons to make three covalent bonds. These three covalent bonds are known as a triple (covalent) bond. When drawing displayed formula of covalent compounds each bond is represented by a single line as shown in Figures 17.6, 17.7 and 17.8.

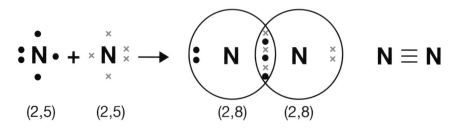

Figure 17.8 Electron sharing in the covalent triple bonds of a nitrogen molecule (N_2).

When non-metal atoms react, they form **molecules**. In these molecules, the atoms are joined by covalent bonds. The covalent bonding and electron structures of some common molecules are shown in Figure 17.9.

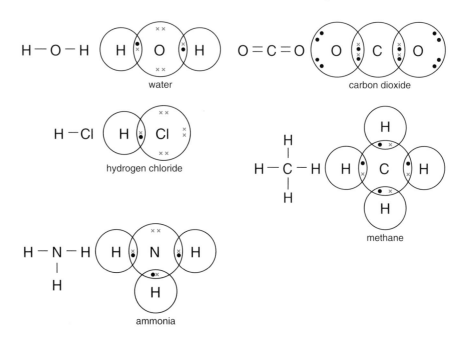

Figure 17.9 The covalent bonding and electron structures of some common molecules.

Check the following points in Figure 17.9.

- The electronic configurations of these molecular compounds can be related to the displayed formulae shown on the left-hand side of each dot and cross diagram. In the displayed formulae, each covalent bond is shown as a line between atoms (for example H—O—H for water).
- H atoms always have one bond. Cl atoms always have one bond. Oxygen atoms have two bonds, nitrogen atoms have three bonds and carbon atoms have four bonds.
- **Double covalent bonds** result from the sharing of two pairs of electrons, as in oxygen and carbon dioxide.

STUDY QUESTIONS

1 Look at Figure 17.4.
  a) How many electrons do lithium and oxygen atoms lose or gain in forming lithium oxide, Li_2O?
  b) Which noble gases have electronic configurations like the ions in lithium oxide?
  c) Why do two lithium atoms react with one oxygen atom in forming lithium oxide?
2 Draw a diagram similar to those in Figure 17.4 to show what happens when potassium reacts with fluorine to form potassium fluoride, KF. Show the dot and cross structures and electronic configurations.
3 Draw dot and cross diagrams to show the bonding in:
  a) hydrogen, H_2
  b) nitrogen, N_2
  c) ethane, CH_3—CH_3
  d) ethene, CH_2=CH_2.

1.18 Electricity in everyday life

It's hard to imagine life without electricity. Every day we depend on electricity for cooking, for lighting and for heating. At the flick of a switch, we use electric heaters, electric kettles and dozens of other electrical gadgets. All these electrical appliances use mains electricity. The electricity is generated in power stations from coal, oil, natural gas or nuclear fuel. Heat from the fuel is used to boil water. The steam produced drives turbines and generates electricity. In this way, chemical energy in the fuel is converted into electrical energy.

In addition to the many appliances which use mains electricity, there are others, like torches, mobile phones and calculators, that use electrical energy from cells and batteries.

Figure 18.1 A city at night. How could we survive without electricity?

■ Electricity and chemistry

The many everyday uses of electricity show why it is so important in our lives.

- ■ It can be used to transfer energy easily from one place to another.
- ■ It can be converted into other forms of energy and used to warm a room, light a torch or cook a meal.

Electricity can also be used to manufacture some important chemicals. For example, salt (sodium chloride) cannot be decomposed using heat, but it can be decomposed using electricity. Sodium hydroxide, chlorine and hydrogen are manufactured by passing electricity through concentrated sodium chloride solution (brine).

$$\text{sodium chloride solution} \xrightarrow{\text{electricity}} \text{sodium hydroxide} + \text{chlorine} + \text{hydrogen}$$

Figure 18.2 Plastic and glass insulators are used to hold the cables carrying electricity to pylons.

■ Electrical conductors and insulators

Some materials, like wood, rubber and plastics, will not allow electricity to pass through them. These materials are called **insulators**. Plastics like polythene and PVC are used to insulate electrical wires and cables.

Materials, like metals, that do allow electricity to pass through them are called **conductors**. See Table 1.

Table 1 Some conductors and insulators.

Conductors			Insulators
Good	Moderate	Poor	
metals, e.g.	carbon (graphite)	water	plastics, e.g.
copper	silicon		polythene
aluminium			PVC
iron			rubber
			wood
			glass
			ceramics

Figure 18.3 The cut-away end of an electrical cable carrying copper wires used in the electricity circuits in our homes. Copper is used because it is such a good conductor. Plastic covering around the copper provides insulation and protection.

■ What is an electric current?

Copper, iron and aluminium, which are easily made into wire, are used for fuses, wires and cables in electrical machinery. Copper is used more than any other metal in electrical circuits because electricity moves through it easily. It is a very good conductor of electric charge.

> An electric current is a flow of charge.

When a copper wire is attached to both terminals of a battery (Figure 18.4), negative electrons in the outer parts of the copper atoms are attracted towards the positive terminal of the battery. At the same time, extra electrons are repelled into the copper wire from the negative terminal of the battery.

Electrons flow through the copper rather like water flows through a pipe or traffic moves along a road.

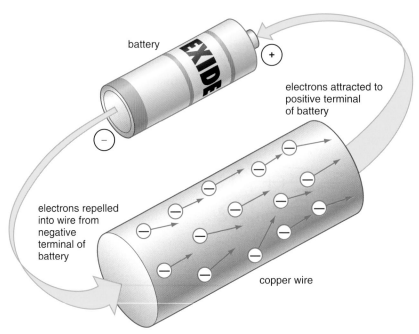

battery

electrons attracted to positive terminal of battery

electrons repelled into wire from negative terminal of battery

copper wire

Figure 18.4 An electric current in a metal wire is a flow of electrons.

STUDY QUESTIONS

1 Electricity is used more widely than gas for our energy supplies. Why is this?

2 **a)** List four important uses of electricity in your home.
   b) How might the jobs in **(a)** be done without electricity?

3 What is:
   a) an electric current
   b) a conductor
   c) an insulator?

4 **a)** Name four elements which conduct electricity when solid.
   b) Name four elements which conduct electricity when liquid.
   c) Name four elements which do **not** conduct electricity when solid.

5 Design an experiment to compare the conduction of electricity by thin copper wire and thick copper wire.
   a) Draw a diagram of the apparatus you would use.
   b) Say what you would do.
   c) Say what measurements you would make.
   d) Say how you would compare the two wires.

1.19 Which substances conduct electricity?

The type of bonding present in a molecule or compound is reflected in its properties. Some substances do not conduct electricity at all; others conduct electricity in some circumstances, but not in others. Some substances have low melting points and others have high melting points. All these properties give us clues as to how the atoms in the substances are chemically combined or bonded to each other.

Figure 19.1 Water and solid sodium chloride do not conduct electricity. Dissolve the salt in the water and the solution conducts electricity. How can this knowledge help us to understand the bonding in substances?

■ Which solids conduct electricity?

The apparatus in Figure 19.2 can be used to test whether a solid conducts electricity. If the solid conducts, what happens when the switch is closed? Experiments like this show that:

> The only common solids which conduct electricity are metals and graphite.

When metals and graphite conduct electricity, electrons flow through the material, but there is *no chemical reaction*.

No solid compounds conduct electricity.

■ Which liquids conduct electricity?

Pure water does not readily conduct electricity. But, water containing a little sulfuric acid will readily conduct electricity. Unlike metals, the dilute sulfuric acid changes when it conducts electricity. It is decomposed, forming hydrogen and oxygen. Electricity is a form of energy like heat. We can use it to boil water, to cook food and to cause chemical reactions.

> The decomposition of a substance, such as dilute sulfuric acid, by electricity is called **electrolysis**.
>
> The compound which is decomposed is called an **electrolyte** and we say that it has been **electrolysed**. Compounds which don't conduct electricity and don't get decomposed are called **non-electrolytes**.

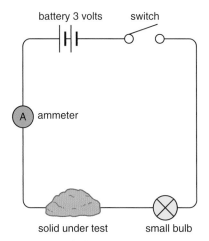

battery 3 volts   switch

A ammeter

solid under test   small bulb

Figure 19.2 Which solids conduct?

PRACTICAL

It is important to know how to test both solids and liquids, including solutions, for conductivity.

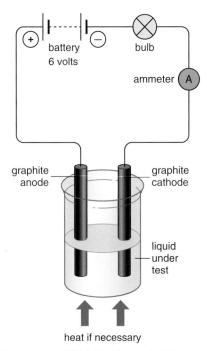

Figure 19.3 Which liquids conduct?

Conductivity of liquids and aqueous solutions

Figure 19.3 shows how we can test the conductivity of liquids. The terminals through which the current enters and leaves the electrolyte are called **electrodes**. They are made from unreactive or inert materials such as platinum. In the diagram graphite is used as it is only slightly reactive, but is much cheaper than a metal such as platinum.

> The electrode connected to the positive terminal of the battery is positively charged and is called the **anode**.

> The electrode connected to the negative terminal of the battery is negatively charged and is called the **cathode**.

Table 1 Testing to see which liquids and aqueous solutions conduct electricity.

Pure liquids	Does the liquid conduct?	Aqueous solutions	Does the solution conduct?
bromine*	no	sugar ($C_{12}H_{22}O_{11}$)	no
mercury*	yes	ethanoic acid (CH_3COOH)	yes
molten sulfur*	no	1M solution sulfuric acid (H_2SO_4)	yes
molten zinc*	yes	copper(II) sulfate ($CuSO_4$)	yes
water (H_2O)	no	potassium iodide (KI)	yes
ethanol (alcohol) (C_2H_5OH)	no	sodium chloride (NaCl)	yes
molten sodium chloride (NaCl)	yes		
molten lead bromide ($PbBr_2$)*	yes		

*These liquids should only be tested carefully in a fume cupboard, as a demonstration by the teacher.

Analysing the results

Look at the results in Table 1.
The two liquid metals (mercury and zinc) conduct electricity, but neither of the liquid non-metal elements (bromine and sulfur) conduct electricity.

Look at the compounds that contain only non-metal elements and which are liquids (water and ethanol). These compounds are covalently bonded (see Chapter 1.17). They do not conduct electricity.

Molten sodium chloride and molten lead bromide conduct electricity.

Look at the aqueous solutions of compounds that contain only non-metal elements. An aqueous solution of sugar does not conduct electricity as all the bonds in a sugar molecule are covalent. Aqueous solutions of sulfuric acid and ethanoic acid do conduct electricity as they can produce charged ions in water.

The compounds that contain both metal ions and non-metal ions have ionic bonds. All of them conduct electricity when dissolved in water. The examples in Table 1 are copper(II) sulfate, potassium iodide and sodium chloride.

Table 2 The conduction of electricity by elements and compounds.

Does the substance conduct as a ...	Elements		Compounds	
	Metals and graphite (e.g. Fe, Zn)	Non-metals except graphite (e.g. Br_2, S)	Metal/non-metal, ionic (e.g. NaCl, $CuSO_4$)	Non-metal, covalent (e.g. C_2H_5OH, CCl_4)
solid	yes	no	no	no
liquid	yes	no	yes	no
aqueous solution			yes (and acids)	no (except acids)

The results can be summarised (see Table 2):

- Metals conduct electricity when solid or liquid.
- Non-metals do not conduct electricity, except for graphite (see Chapter 1.23).
- Ionic compounds (metal atoms bonded with non-metal atoms) conduct electricity when molten or in an aqueous solution, but not when they are solid.
- Non-metal compounds that only have covalent bonds do not conduct electricity. If they conduct in aqueous solutions then the molecule has been separated into ions.

Conductivity tests are a very useful tool. Finding out if a substance conducts electricity when solid, molten or in aqueous solution allows chemists to deduce the type of bonding in the substance.

Figure 19.4 Aluminium is manufactured by electrolysis from aluminium oxide. At this factory, molten aluminium is removed from the electrolysis tanks using the suspended and moveable vat shown in the photo.

STUDY QUESTIONS

1 Explain the following words: *electrolysis, electrolyte, electrode, anode, cathode.*
2 From the following list name:
   a) two metals
   b) two non-metals
   c) two electrolytes
   d) two pure liquids at 20 °C
   e) two elements which conduct
   f) two compounds that are gases at 110 °C
   g) three compounds that are non-electrolytes.

calcium, carbon disulfide, copper sulfate solution, lead, carbon, water, methane (natural gas), phosphorus, dilute sulfuric acid

3 a) Write down the rule about the conduction of electricity by compounds containing only non-metal elements.
   b) Write down the rule about the conduction of electricity by compounds containing metal and non-metal elements.

1.20 Giant ionic structures

Whenever you grow crystals of sodium chloride or copper sulfate they always have the same shapes. An early space experiment was to see if the shape of crystals could be changed by growing them without gravity. It made no difference. Crystal shapes reveal something about the arrangement of the particles in the crystal, which is always the same.

Figure 20.1 Sodium chloride and copper sulfate crystals always have the same shapes. Why is this?

■ Forming ionic compounds by electron transfer

We saw in Chapter 1.17 that ionic compounds form when metals react with non-metals. For example, when sodium burns in chlorine, sodium chloride is formed. This contains sodium ions (Na^+) and chloride ions (Cl^-).

$$Na + Cl \rightarrow Na^+ \quad Cl^-$$

sodium atom   chlorine atom   sodium ion chloride ion

These ions form by transfer of electrons. During the reaction, each sodium atom gives up one electron and forms a sodium ion.

$$Na \rightarrow Na^+ + e^-$$

The electron is taken by a chlorine atom to form a chloride ion.

$$Cl + e^- \rightarrow Cl^-$$

When ionic compounds form, metal atoms lose electrons and form positive ions, while non-metal atoms gain electrons and form negative ions. This transfer of electrons from metals to non-metals explains the formation of ionic compounds.

Figure 20.3 shows what happens when calcium reacts with oxygen to form calcium oxide. In this case, two electrons are transferred from each calcium atom to each oxygen atom.

Figure 20.2 Chalk cliffs are composed of an ionic compound, calcium carbonate, containing calcium ions (Ca^{2+}) and carbonate ions (CO_3^{2-}).

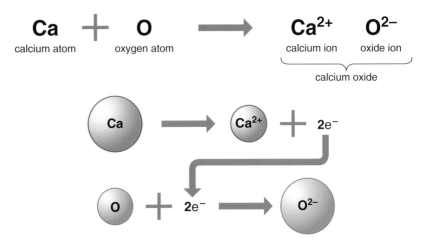

Figure 20.3 The formation of calcium oxide.

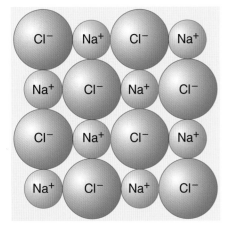

Figure 20.4 The arrangement of ions in one layer of a sodium chloride crystal.

■ Bonding and structure

In solid ionic compounds, the ions are held together by the electrostatic attraction between positive ions and negative ions. This force of attraction between oppositely charged ions is called an **ionic** or **electrovalent bond**.

Figure 20.4 shows how the ions are arranged in one layer of sodium chloride and Figure 20.5 is a 3-D model of its structure. Notice that Na^+ ions are surrounded by Cl^- ions and that Cl^- ions are surrounded by Na^+ ions.

Each Na^+ ion is surrounded by six Cl^- ions which are strongly attracted to it. Each Cl^- ion is surrounded by six Na^+ ions which are strongly attracted to it.

This kind of arrangement in which large numbers of ions are packed together in a regular pattern as a giant three-dimensional lattice is an example of a **giant structure**.

Giant ionic structures are held together very firmly by ionic bonds – strong electrostatic attractions between oppositely charged ions. This explains the properties of ionic compounds.

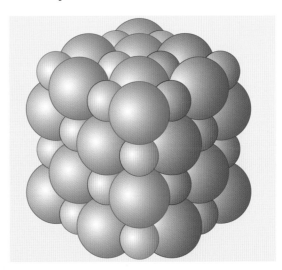

Figure 20.5 A 3-D model of the structure of sodium chloride. The larger green balls represent Cl^- ions ($A_r = 35.5$). The smaller red balls represent Na^+ ions ($A_r = 23$).

■ Properties of ionic compounds

- **Ionic compounds have high melting points and high boiling points**. In general, the melting points and boiling points of ionic compounds increase as the charges on the ions increase, because larger charges result in stronger ionic bonds. For example, the melting point of sodium fluoride, Na^+F^-, is 993 °C, whereas that of sodium oxide, $(Na^+)_2O^{2-}$, is 1275 °C and that of magnesium fluoride, $Mg^{2+}(F^-)_2$, is 1261 °C.
- **Ionic compounds do not conduct electricity when solid**, because the ions can only vibrate about fixed positions in the solid lattice. They cannot move freely towards the electrodes.
- **Ionic compounds conduct electricity when molten or in aqueous solution** as the charged ions can move freely in the liquid towards the electrode of opposite charge (see Chapters 1.19 and 1.25).

■ The formulae of ionic compounds

The formulae of ionic compounds, like sodium chloride (NaCl) and calcium oxide (CaO), can be obtained by balancing the charges on their positive and negative ions (Chapter 1.14). For example, the formula of calcium chloride is $CaCl_2$. Here, two Cl^- ions balance the charge on one Ca^{2+} ion.

Can you see that the number of charges on an ion is a measure of its 'combining power'? Na^+ has a combining power of 1, whereas Ca^{2+} has a combining power of 2. This means that Na^+ can combine with only one Cl^- to form NaCl, whereas Ca^{2+} can combine with two Cl^- ions to form $CaCl_2$.

Table 1 shows the names and formulae of some ionic compounds. Notice that the formula of calcium nitrate is $Ca(NO_3)_2$. The brackets around NO_3^- show that it is a single unit with one negative charge. Thus, two NO_3^- ions balance one Ca^{2+} ion. Other ions such as SO_4^{2-}, CO_3^{2-} and OH^- must also be put in brackets when there are two or three of them in a formula.

Table 1 The names and formulae of some ionic compounds.

Name of ionic compounds	Formula
calcium nitrate	$Ca^{2+}(NO_3^-)_2$ or $Ca(NO_3)_2$
zinc sulfate	$Zn^{2+}SO_4^{2-}$ or $ZnSO_4$
sodium carbonate	$(Na^+)_2CO_3^{2-}$ or Na_2CO_3
potassium iodide	K^+I^- or KI

STUDY QUESTIONS

1 Which of the following substances conduct electricity
   a) when liquid
   b) when solid?
   diamond, potassium chloride, copper, carbon disulfide, sulfur

2 Look at Figures 20.4 and 20.5.
   a) How many Cl^- ions surround one Na^+ ion in the 3-D crystal?
   b) How many Na^+ ions surround one Cl^- ion in the 3-D crystal?

3 Write the symbols for the ions and the formulae of the following compounds:
   potassium hydroxide, iron(III) nitrate, barium chloride, calcium carbonate, silver sulfate, sodium sulfate, aluminium oxide, zinc bromide, copper(II) nitrate, magnesium sulfide.

4 Sodium fluoride and magnesium oxide have the same crystal structure and similar distances between ions. The melting point of NaF is 993 °C, but that of MgO is 2640 °C. Why is there such a big difference in their melting points?

1.21 The structure of substances

The uses of materials depend on their properties. For example, copper is used for electrical wires and cables because it can be drawn into wires and it's a good conductor of electricity. Clay is used for pots and crockery because it's soft and easily moulded when wet, but becomes hard and rigid when heated (fired) in a furnace.

Figure 21.1 Metal was used to make suits of armour in the Middle Ages. Why do you think metal was used?

■ The importance of particles

All substances are made up of particles. If we know how these particles are arranged (the **structure**) and how the particles are held together (the **bonding**), we can explain the **properties** of substances. For example, copper is a good conductor because its metallic bonding allows electrons to move through the structure when it is connected to a battery. And copper can be drawn into wires because its layers of atoms can slide over each other in their close-packed structure.

Figure 21.2 Soft wet clay is easily moulded to make objects that, when fired, are hard and rigid. What do you think happens to the structure of the damp clay when fired?

Wet clay is soft and easily moulded because water molecules can get between its flat two-dimensional structure. When clay is fired, all the water molecules are driven out. Atoms in one layer bond to those in the layers above and below. This gives the clay a three-dimensional structure, making it hard, rigid and useful for pots and crockery.

Notice how:

- the structure and bonding of a substance determine its properties
- the properties of a substance determine its uses.

■ Linking structure, bonding and properties

The links from structure and bonding to properties help us to explain the uses of materials. They explain why metals are used as conductors, why graphite is used in pencils and why clay is used to make pots.

Using X-ray analysis, we can find out how the particles are arranged in a substance (its structure), but it is more difficult to study the forces between these particles (its bonding).

You know that all substances are made up from only three kinds of particle – atoms, ions and molecules. These three particles give rise to four different types of solid structures:

- giant ionic structures
- simple molecular structures
- giant covalent structures
- giant metallic structures.

Table 1 shows the particles in these four structures, the types of substances they form and examples of these substances.

Table 1 The four types of solid structure and the particles they contain.

Type of structure	Particles in the structure	Types of substance	Examples
giant ionic	ions	compounds of metals with non-metals	Na^+Cl^- (salt) $Ca^{2+}O^{2-}$ (quicklime) $Cu^{2+}SO_4^{2-}$ (copper(II) sulfate)
simple molecular	molecules	non-metals, or non-metal compounds	I_2 (iodine) O_2 (oxygen) H_2O (water) CO_2 (carbon dioxide)
giant covalent	atoms	non-metals, or non-metal compounds	diamond, graphite, sand (silicon dioxide, SiO_2)
giant metallic	atoms	metals and alloys (mixtures of metals)	Na, Fe, Cu, steel, brass

Giant ionic structures and the properties they lead to have been considered in Chapter 1.20. Simple molecular, giant covalent and metallic structures will be considered in the next three chapters.

Figure 21.3 A large natural diamond embedded in volcanic igneous rock. How do the structure and properties of diamond lead to its use in jewellery?

Figure 21.4 A sample of lead sulfide (galena) crystals. What particles will lead sulfide contain? How do you think the particles are arranged?

STUDY QUESTIONS

1 Get into a small group with two or three others. Look at the photos in this chapter and discuss the questions in the captions.

2 Look at Table 1. Suggest two differences in the properties of simple molecules with covalent bonding and giant covalent structures.

3 What type of structure will the following substances have:

chlorine, limestone (calcium carbonate), silver, air, rubber, bronze, wood?

4 Conductivity tests can give evidence for the particles in a substance and its type of structure. Describe:
   a) the tests you would carry out
   b) the results you would expect
   c) the conclusions you would make from your results for each structure type.

1.22 Simple molecular substances

Water is an extraordinary compound. As well as being a liquid between 0 °C and 100 °C, it is one of the few substances that expands on cooling. So ice is less dense than water, and floats on the surface of lakes and the seas. Life can exist in the liquid water beneath the polar ice, insulated from the extreme cold (Figure 22.1). Without these properties life on Earth could never have evolved.

Figure 22.1 Under the polar ice there is liquid water and life.

What is a simple molecular substance?

Oxygen (O_2) and water (H_2O) are good examples of **simple molecular** substances. They have simple molecules containing a few atoms. Most non-metals and non-metal compounds are also made of simple molecules. For example, hydrogen is H_2, chlorine is Cl_2, carbon dioxide is CO_2 and methane in natural gas is CH_4. Sugar ($C_{12}H_{22}O_{11}$) has much larger molecules than these substances, but it still counts as a simple molecule.

Forces of attraction between molecules

In simple molecular substances, the atoms are held together in each molecule by strong covalent bonds, but there are only weak forces between the separate molecules (Figure 22.2). The weak forces between separate molecules are called **intermolecular forces.**

The properties of simple molecular substances

The properties of simple molecular substances can be explained in terms of their structure and the weak forces between their molecules. In simple molecular substances, there are no ions (as in ionic compounds) or freely moving electrons (as in metals). So there are no forces between oppositely charged ions, or between electrons and positive ions, holding them together.

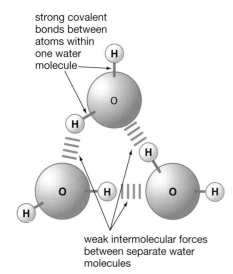

strong covalent bonds between atoms within one water molecule

weak intermolecular forces between separate water molecules

Figure 22.2 Covalent bonds and intermolecular forces in water. Water is a simple molecular substance. In each water molecule, there are strong covalent bonds between the two hydrogen atoms and the oxygen atom. But the separate water molecules are held together by only relatively weak intermolecular forces.

Some simple molecular substances, like water and sugar, exist as liquids and solids, so there must be some forces holding their molecules together.

- **Simple molecular substances have low melting points and boiling points**. Because of their weak intermolecular forces, it takes much less energy to separate the molecules in simple molecular substances than to separate ions in ionic compounds, or atoms in metals. So, simple molecular compounds have much lower melting points and boiling points than ionic compounds and metals.
- **Simple molecular substances do not conduct electricity**. Simple molecular substances have no delocalised electrons like metals. They have no ions either. This means that they cannot conduct electricity as solids, as liquids or in aqueous solution, unless the substance reacts when added to water to form a solution containing ions.
- **Simple molecular substances and relative molecular mass.** As the relative molecular mass of simple molecular substances increases the melting points and boiling points also increase. The intermolecular forces of attraction increase as molecules have a greater mass. This means more energy is needed to overcome the intermolecular force of attraction. The need for more energy to break the attraction means that the temperatures at which the forces are overcome become higher. Table 1 shows some examples of the trend.

EXAM TIP

Watch out for negative numbers in questions. −114 is lower than −51. Hydrogen iodide has a higher melting point than hydrogen chloride. Don't be caught out!

Table 1 Melting points and boiling points of some simple molecular substances.

Simple molecular substance	Formula	Relative molecular mass	Melting in °C	Boiling point in °C
carbon monoxide	CO	28	-205	-191
hydrogen chloride	HCl	36.5	-114	-85
carbon disulfide	CS_2	76	-112	46
hydrogen bromide	HBr	81	-87	-67
hydrogen iodide	HI	128	-51	-35

■ Molecular compounds

Metals can be mixed to form alloys, but they *never* react with each other to form compounds. For example, zinc and copper will form the alloy brass, but the two metals cannot react chemically because they both want to lose electrons and form positive ions.

Unlike metals, non-metals can react with each other and form a compound. These non-metal compounds consist of both simple molecular compounds and giant covalent compounds, like silica (silicon dioxide, SiO_2) and polymers.

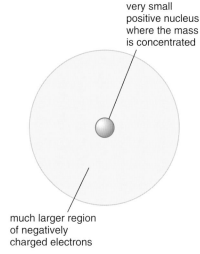

much larger region
of negatively
charged electrons

Figure 22.3 A simple picture of atomic structure.

Forming molecular compounds – electron sharing

All atoms have a small positive nucleus, surrounded by a very large region in which negatively charged electrons move (Chapter 1.5). The negative charge on the electrons is balanced by positive charge in the nucleus, so that the whole atom is neutral. Almost all the mass of the atom is concentrated in the nucleus (Figure 22.3). Different atoms have different numbers of electrons. Hydrogen atoms are the smallest with only one electron, helium atoms have two electrons and oxygen atoms have eight electrons.

When two non-metals react to form a molecule, the regions of electrons in their atoms overlap so that each atom gains negative charge. The positive nuclei of both atoms attract the electrons in the region of overlap and this holds the atoms together (Figure 22.4). This type of bond formed by electron sharing between non-metals is a **covalent bond** (Chapter 1.17). Notice that covalent bonding, like ionic bonding, involves attraction between opposite charges.

Covalent bonds hold atoms together *within* a molecule but there are also intermolecular forces holding the separate molecules together in simple molecular liquids like water and simple molecular solids like sugar.

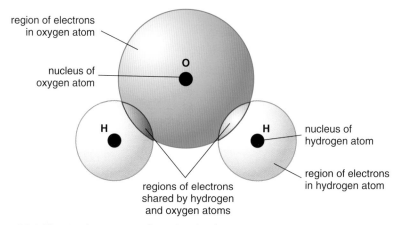

region of electrons
in oxygen atom

nucleus of
oxygen atom

O

H

H

nucleus of
hydrogen atom

region of electrons
in hydrogen atom

regions of electrons
shared by hydrogen
and oxygen atoms

Figure 22.4 The simple structure of a molecule of water.

Formulae of molecular compounds

Table 2 includes the formulae and structures of some well-known simple molecular compounds. In some simple molecular substances, such as oxygen (O_2), two atoms share two pairs of electrons and so have two covalent bonds (a double bond) holding them together.

Formulae that show all the bonds between atoms in a molecule, such as H—H for hydrogen and O=C=O for carbon dioxide, are called **displayed formulae**. These show the number of covalent bonds to each atom. Notice that hydrogen can form one bond with other atoms (H—), so its combining power (Chapter 1.20) is 1.
The combining powers of chlorine and bromine are also 1. Oxygen forms two bonds with other atoms (—O— or O=). Its combining power is therefore 2. Nitrogen atoms form three bonds and carbon atoms form four bonds, so their combining powers are 3 and 4 respectively.

Table 2 Formulae and structures of some simple molecular substances.

Name and formula	Displayed formula	Model of structure
hydrogen, H_2	H — H	
oxygen, O_2	O = O	
water, H_2O	H—O—H (bent)	
methane, CH_4	H—C—H with H above and below	
hydrogen chloride, HCl	H — Cl	
chlorine, Cl_2	Cl — Cl	
carbon dioxide, CO_2	O = C = O	

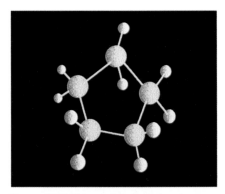

Figure 22.5 This model of a molecule was drawn using a computer to analyse the results obtained during the investigation of various organic substances.

You could use a molecular model kit to make models in 3D of these substances.

Although we can predict the formulae of molecular compounds from the number of bonds which the atoms form, the only sure way of knowing a formula is by chemical analysis. For example, carbon forms four bonds and oxygen forms two bonds, so we would predict that carbon and oxygen will form a compound O=C=O. This compound, carbon dioxide, does exist, but so does carbon monoxide, CO, which we could not predict.

STUDY QUESTIONS

1 Explain the meaning of the following:
covalent bond, intermolecular force, simple molecule, displayed formula, nucleus.

2 Simple molecular substances often have a smell, but metals do not. Why is this?

3 What properties does butter have to show that it contains simple molecular substances?

4 Assuming the usual combining powers of the elements, draw the structures of the following compounds (show each bond as a line —).
Dichlorine oxide (Cl_2O), tetrabromomethane (carbon tetrabromide, CBr_4), nitrogen trichloride (NCl_3), hydrogen peroxide (H_2O_2), ethane (C_2H_6), ethene (C_2H_4)

1.23 Diamond, graphite and fullerenes

Diamond and graphite are both made of pure carbon but these two solids have very different properties and uses. Diamond is hard and clear, whereas graphite is soft and black. Diamonds are used to cut stone and engrave glass (Figure 23.1), but graphite in pencils is used by artists to achieve a soft, shaded effect.

Figure 23.1 Diamonds that are not good enough for jewellery are used in glass cutters and in diamond-studded saws. This photo shows an engraver using a diamond-studded wheel to make patterns in a glass vase.

■ Allotropes of carbon

The different forms of solid carbon are called **allotropes**. A few other elements also have allotropes. Oxygen has two allotropes – oxygen (O_2) and ozone (O_3).

> Allotropes are different forms of the same element in the same state.

Diamond and graphite have different properties and different uses because *they have different structures*. They both contain carbon, but the carbon atoms are packed in different ways. The arrangement of carbon atoms in diamond and graphite has been studied by X-ray analysis.

■ Diamond

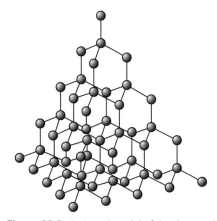

Figure 23.2 An 'open' model of the diamond structure. Each black ball represents a carbon atom and each line is a covalent bond.

In diamond, carbon atoms are joined to each other by strong covalent bonds. Inside the diamond structure (Figure 23.2), each carbon atom forms covalent bonds with four other carbon atoms. Check this for yourself in Figure 23.2. These strong covalent bonds extend through the whole diamond, forming a three-dimensional giant structure.

The structure of diamond is described as a **giant covalent structure**. Only a small number of atoms are shown in the model in Figure 23.2. In a real diamond, this arrangement of carbon atoms is extended millions and millions of times. Every perfect diamond is a giant structure with covalent bonds linking one carbon atom to the next.

The properties and uses of diamond

- **Diamonds are very hard** because the carbon atoms are linked by very strong covalent bonds. Another reason for its hardness is that the atoms are not arranged in layers so they cannot slide over one another like the atoms in metals. Most industrial uses of diamond depend on its hardness. Diamonds that are not good enough for gems are used in glass cutters and in diamond-studded saws. Powdered diamonds are used as abrasives for smoothing very hard materials.
- **Diamond has a very high melting point**. Carbon atoms in diamond are held in the giant structure by very strong covalent bonds and there are many of them. This means that the atoms cannot vibrate fast enough to break away from their neighbours until very high temperatures are reached. So, the melting point of diamond is very high.
- **Diamond does not conduct electricity**. Unlike metals, diamond has no delocalised electrons. All the electrons in the outer shell of each carbon atom are held firmly in covalent bonds. So there are no delocalised electrons in diamond to form an electric current.

■ Graphite

Figure 23.3 shows a model of part of the structure of graphite. Notice that the carbon atoms are arranged in parallel layers. Each layer contains millions and millions of carbon atoms arranged in hexagons. Each carbon atom is held strongly in its layer by strong covalent bonds to three other carbon atoms. So graphite is a **giant covalent structure**, like diamond. The distance between neighbouring carbon atoms in the same layer is only 0.14 nm, but the distance between the layers is 0.34 nm.

Figure 23.4 A can of lubricating oil containing graphite. Graphite has a layered structure. The layers slip and slide over one another very easily. This makes graphite an excellent material to improve the lubricating action of oils.

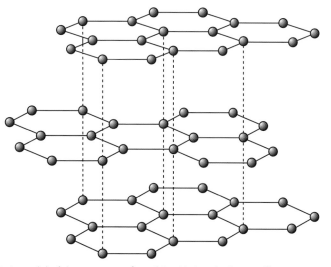

Figure 23.3 A model of the structure of graphite. Notice the layers of hexagons, one on top of the other.

The properties and uses of graphite

- **Graphite is soft and can act as a solid lubricant**. In graphite, each carbon atom is linked by strong covalent bonds to three other atoms in its layer. But, the layers are 2½ times further apart than carbon atoms in the same layer. This means that the forces between the layers are weak. If you rub graphite, the layers slide over each other and onto your fingers. This property has led to the use of graphite as the 'lead' in pencils and as a lubricant. The layers of graphite slide over each other like a pile of wet microscope slides (Figure 23.5).

- **Graphite has a high melting point**. Although the layers of graphite move over each other easily, it is difficult to break the strong covalent bonds between carbon atoms within one layer. The covalent bonds are strong and there are so many of them. Because of this, graphite does not melt until 3730°C and it does not boil until 4830°C. So, it is used to make crucibles for molten metals. The bonds between carbon atoms in the layers of graphite are so strong that graphite fibres with the layers arranged along the fibre are stronger than steel. These fibres are used to reinforce metals and broken bones.

- **Graphite conducts electricity**. The electrons can move along the layers from one atom to the next when graphite is connected to a battery. So graphite will conduct electricity, unlike diamond and other non-metals. Because of this unusual property, graphite is used for electrodes in industry and as the positive terminals in dry cells (batteries).

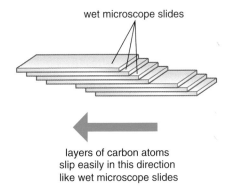

Figure 23.5 The layers in graphite slide over each other like wet microscope slides. The wet slides stick together and it is difficult to pull them apart. But, a force parallel to the slides pushes them over each other easily and smoothly.

Figure 23.6 Graphite fibres have been used to reinforce the shaft of this badminton racket.

■ Fullerenes

Expo67 in Montreal, Canada had as its centre piece an architectural structure called a geodesic dome designed by Buckminster Fuller (Figure 23.7).

In 1985 a fresh form of carbon was discovered. It was very similar in shape to the dome at Expo67. The scientists named it Buckminsterfullerene. It was the first of a series of new structures of carbon atoms very similar to graphite and graphene. Figure 23.8 shows the structure of Buckminsterfullerene, C_{60}.

Figure 23.7 Geodesic dome at Expo67, Montreal.

The properties and uses of fullerenes

- The carbon atoms are covalently bonded to each other into a strong structure. C_{60} sublimes rather than melts as the intermolecular forces holding the C_{60} molecules together are overcome. The C_{60} molecules separate and become a gas.
- **Fullerenes have many properties**. The discovery of buckminsterfullerene led to the discovery of a large number of other similar carbon-based structures, such as **nanotubes**, and **graphene**. Owing to nanotubes massive surface areas they are useful to coat with catalysts to speed up chemical reactions. Nanotubes also have pharmaceutical uses based on their ability to enclose a toxic chemical and transport it to a specific site in the body where the fullerene can then be broken down releasing the toxic compound. Trials are underway to use this as a form of chemotherapy treatment for cancer patients. Hi-tech companies are trialing roll-up TV and monitor screens using Graphene, and are developing clothing that contains flexible solar cells that can recharge your mobile phone from your t-shirt!

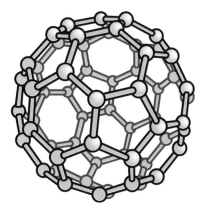

Figure 23.8 The structure of the fullerene C_{60}.

STUDY QUESTIONS

1 Why is diamond called a 'giant structure'?
2 **a)** Give two uses of diamond.
 b) Explain how these uses depend on the properties and structure of diamond.
3 The largest natural diamond is the Cullinan diamond. This weighs about 600 g.
 a) How many moles of carbon does it contain? (C = 12)
 b) How many atoms of carbon does it contain?
4 'Diamonds are a girl's best friend'. Is this true? What do you think?
5 **a)** Describe the structure of graphite.
 b) Explain why the melting point of graphite is very high.
6 Make a table to show the similarities and differences between diamond, graphite and fullerene C_{60}.

7 **a)** Why is a zip-fastener rubbed with a soft pencil to make it move more freely?
 b) Why is pencil used rather than oil?
 c) Why is graphite better than oil for lubricating the moving parts of hot machinery?
8 Graphite powder is mixed with clay to make pencil 'lead'. How does the hardness of a pencil depend on the amounts of graphite and clay in it?
9 Explain why fullerenes such as C_{60} may revolutionise:
 a) the treatment of diseases such as cancer
 b) the production of mobile phones and portable computers.

(You may find the Extend and challenge text at the end of this section helpful.)

1.24 The properties of metals

For thousands of years people have known that you can bend metals to make the shape you want. This is different from non-metals, where attempting to bend and shape them in this way usually means they break. There is something different about the arrangement of atoms in metals compared with that of non-metals that allows metals to change their shape without breaking.

Figure 24.1 This metal press is cold-pressing parts for the body work of a motor car. Why does the metal bend into shape rather than shatter?

■ Classifying elements

For centuries chemists have classified elements as metals and non-metals.

- Metals are elements that conduct electricity (Chapter 1.19) and have basic oxides (Chapter 2.6).
- Non-metals are elements that don't conduct electricity and have acidic oxides.

Classifying elements in this way is not always clear cut, but it has proved very useful.

■ Properties of metals

Metals are important and useful materials. Just look around and notice the uses of different metals – cutlery, cars, ornaments, jewellery, pipes, radiators, girders and bridges. The properties of metals lead to these and many other important uses.

In general, metals:

Figure 24.2 Blacksmiths rely on the malleability of metals to hammer and bend them into useful shapes.

- have high densities
- have high melting points and high boiling points
- are good conductors of heat and electricity
- are malleable (can be hammered into different shapes).

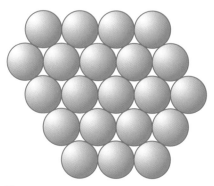

Figure 24.3 Close packing of atoms in a metal.

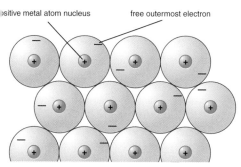

positive metal atom nucleus   free outermost electron

Figure 24.4 The outermost electrons of each atom move around freely in the metal structure.

Density

X-ray analysis shows that the atoms in most metals are packed as close together as possible. This arrangement is called **close packing**. Figure 24.3 shows a few atoms in one layer of a metal.

In metals the outer electrons of the atoms are delocalised. The metal atoms pack together through an electrostatic attraction between the positively charged nuclei of the metal atoms and the negatively charged delocalised outer electrons.

Notice that each atom in the middle of the crystal touches six other atoms in the same layer. When a second layer is placed on top of the first, atoms in the second layer sink into the dips between atoms in the first layer. This allows atoms in one layer to get as close as possible to those in the next layer. This close packing of atoms in metals helps to explain their high densities.

Melting and boiling points

High melting points and high boiling points suggest that there are strong forces holding the atoms together in metal crystals. The electrostatic forces of attraction between the nuclei of the atoms and delocalised electrons are strong and hence a lot of energy is required to overcome them.

Conductivity

When a metal is heated, energy is transferred to the electrons. The electrons move around even faster and conduct the heat (energy) to other parts of the metal.

When a metal is connected to a battery in a circuit, delocalised electrons in the metal move towards the positive terminal. At the same time, electrons can be fed into the other end of the metal from the negative terminal (Figure 24.5). This flow of electrons through the metal forms the electric current.

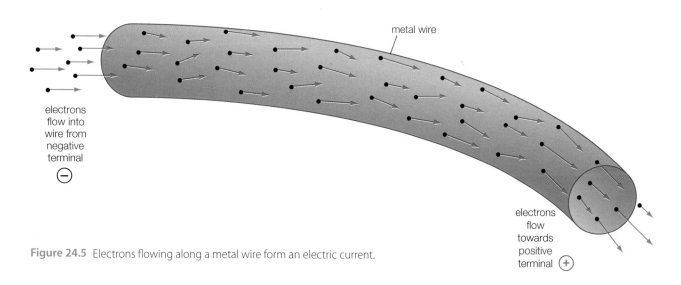

electrons flow into wire from negative terminal

metal wire

electrons flow towards positive terminal

Figure 24.5 Electrons flowing along a metal wire form an electric current.

Malleability

The forces of attraction between nuclei of the atoms and delocalised electrons in a metal are strong, but they are *not* rigid. When a force is applied to a metal, the layers of atoms can 'slide' over each other. This is known as **slip**. After slipping, the ions settle into position again and the close-packed structure is restored. Figure 24.6 shows the positions of ions before and after slip.

This is what happens when a metal is hammered into different shapes.

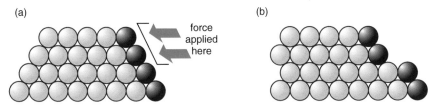

Figure 24.6 The positions of ions in a metal crystal, (a) before and (b) after 'slip' has taken place.

Alloys

Many common metals are a mixture of two metals. Examples are brass (copper and zinc), pewter (lead and tin) and bronze (copper and tin). These mixtures are called **alloys**. The addition of small quantities of the second metal, which has different sized atoms, significantly changes the physical properties of the main metal by making it harder for the ions to slide over each other. This results in the alloy being harder than either of the original metals, reducing the malleability, and often causing it to be more brittle. Alloys are often far more useful than the pure metals from which they are made.

STUDY QUESTIONS

1 Explain the following terms: *close packing, slip, malleable.*
2 Explain why metals:
   a) have a high density
   b) have a high melting point
   c) are good conductors of heat
   d) are malleable.
3 A substance is a non-conductor of electricity in the solid state. It melts at 217 °C and boils at 685 °C. Could this substance be:
   a) a metal:
   b) a non-metal:
   c) a giant covalent substance:
   d) an ionic solid:
   e) a simple molecular solid?

4 Answer *true* or *false* to parts a) to f). Some reasons for classifying magnesium as a metal are:
   a) it burns to form an oxide
   b) it reacts with non-metals
   c) it reacts only with non-metals
   d) it is magnetic
   e) it conducts electricity
   f) it has a high density.
5 a) Why do you think blacksmiths dip red-hot steel objects into cold water?
   b) Why do you think sodium has a much lower density and melting point than most metals?

1.25 Investigating electrolysis

This drawing in Figure 25.1 of an old chemical works producing sodium hydroxide by electrolysis from sodium chloride looks a lot cleaner than the works probably did in operation. Using electrolysis to break down compounds into their elements or to make more useful chemicals can be very hazardous, as often lots of toxic gases are produced that need to be dealt with safely.

Figure 25.1 An early chemical works using electrolyis to produce sodium hydroxide and chlorine.

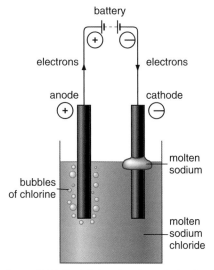

Figure 25.2 Explaining the electrolysis of molten sodium chloride.

■ What are the products of electrolysis?

When compounds are electrolysed, new substances are produced at the electrodes. For example, when electricity is passed through molten sodium chloride, pale green chlorine gas comes off at the anode and shiny molten sodium forms at the cathode. This electrolysis can be written as a chemical equation because a chemical change has taken place.

$$\text{sodium chloride} \rightarrow \text{sodium} + \text{chlorine}$$

$$2\text{NaCl(l)} \rightarrow 2\text{Na(l)} + \text{Cl}_2\text{(g)}$$

Figure 25.2 shows the electrolysis of molten sodium chloride. In the laboratory you would use graphite to make the electrodes as the graphite would be inert. This is important as you do not want the electrodes to react with the products of the electrolysis.

The positive sodium ions are attracted to the negative cathode. Positive ions that are attracted to the cathode are called **cations**. Figure 25.3 shows that at the cathode each sodium ion takes an electron and changes to a sodium atom. This change can be written as a **half equation** which explains half of the full equation for the reaction.

$$\text{Na}^+ + \text{e}^- \rightarrow \text{Na}$$

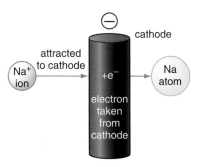

Figure 25.3

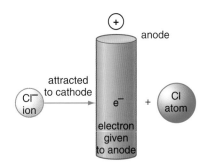

Figure 25.4

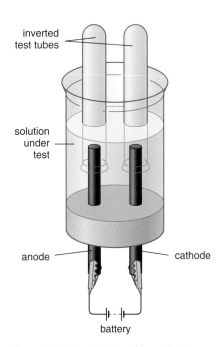

Figure 25.5 Investigating the products when solutions are electrolysed.

The negative chloride ions are attracted to the positive anode. Negative ions that are attracted to the anode are called **anions**. Figure 25.4 shows that at the anode each chloride ion donates an electron to become a chlorine atom.

$$Cl^- \rightarrow Cl + e^-$$

The Cl atoms then pair up to form Cl_2 molecules

$$Cl + Cl \rightarrow Cl_2$$

The reaction at the anode can be summarised as a half equation:

$$2Cl^- \rightarrow Cl_2 + 2e^-$$

The equation summarising the reaction at one electrode is called a half-equation because it summarises only half of the overall reaction. It shows the changes in the electrons that would not otherwise be shown in the equation for the overall reaction.

■ Electrolysis of molten lead bromide

If molten lead bromide is electrolysed using the same apparatus as in Figure 25.2 then the lead bromide is split by the electrolysis into molten lead and bromine gas.

$$\text{lead bromide} \rightarrow \text{lead} + \text{bromine}$$

$$PbBr_2(l) \rightarrow Pb(l) + Br_2(g)$$

As with sodium chloride, we can write half-equations to show how the electrons from the battery cause the chemical change. For the lead, which needs two electrons:

$$Pb^{2+} + 2e^- \rightarrow Pb$$

and for the bromide:

$$Br^- \rightarrow Br + e^-$$

Again, because bromine forms a diatomic molecule, two bromine atoms combine to make a bromine molecule:

$$Br + Br \rightarrow Br_2$$

■ Electrolysis of aqueous solutions

To investigate the electrolysis of aqueous solutions in the laboratory the apparatus shown in Figure 25.5 is used. By collecting the gases produced and identifying them the electrolysis can be explained.

Electrolysis of sodium chloride solution

When a solution of sodium chloride is electrolysed the electrodes are made of platinum. Hydrogen gas is produced at the test tube over the cathode. Chlorine gas is produced at the test tube over the anode. Figure 25.6 shows the results of the electrolysis if a small amount of red litmus solution is added to the solution before starting.

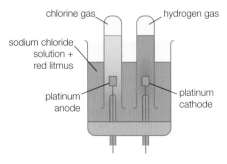

chlorine gas   hydrogen gas

sodium chloride
solution +
red litmus

platinum
anode

platinum
cathode

Figure 25.6 Electrolysis of sodium chloride solution using litmus indicator to identify the products.

As in the electrolysis of molten sodium chloride, the chloride anions (Cl^-) are attracted to the anode where each chloride ion gives up an electron:

$$Cl^- \rightarrow e^- + Cl$$

and they then pair up to make chlorine molecules:

$$Cl + Cl \rightarrow Cl_2$$

As chlorine gas is produced the investigation should be done in a fume cupboard. In Figure 25.6, this process can be seen in the test tube over the anode where the solution is bleached by the chlorine gas.

At the cathode the solution is turning blue. Water molecules gain electrons at the cathode.

$$2H_2O + 2e^- \rightarrow H_2 + 2OH^-$$

The hydroxide ions formed make the solution alkaline.

Eye protection should be worn for this practical.

Electrolysis of copper(II) sulfate solution

The same apparatus can be used to investigate what happens when copper(II) sulfate ($CuSO_4(aq)$) is electrolysed. When a current is passed through a solution of copper(II) sulfate then the copper(II) sulfate separates into $Cu^{2+}(aq)$ cations and $SO_4^{2-}(aq)$ anions, along with $H^+(aq)$ ions and $OH^-(aq)$ ions from the water. The positive cations of copper are attracted to the cathode where they become copper atoms and coat the cathode with an orange red deposit of copper:

$$Cu^{2+} + 2e^- \rightarrow Cu$$

At the anode water molecules lose electrons.

$$2H_2O \rightarrow 4H^+ + O_2 + 4e^-$$

Eye protection should be worn for this practical.

Electrolysis of dilute sulfuric acid

Dilute sulfuric acid ($H_2SO_4(aq)$) contains only three different ions: $H^+(aq)$ cations and $SO_4^{2-}(aq)$ anions from the sulfuric acid and more $H^+(aq)$ cations and $OH^-(aq)$ anions from the water. When electrolysed with inert platinum electrodes the hydrogen cations are attracted to the cathode where they gain electrons and become hydrogen gas:

$$H^+ + e^- \rightarrow H$$

The H atoms then pair up to make hydrogen molecules:

$$H + H \rightarrow H_2$$

The formation of hydrogen can also be explained via the equation:

$$2H_2O + 2e^- \rightarrow H_2 + 2OH^-$$

In this case, the solution around the cathode does not become alkaline, as in the electrolysis of sodium chloride solution, because the hydroxide ions formed react with the hydrogen ions present in the acidic solution.

At the anode water molecules lose electrons.

$$2H_2O \rightarrow 4H^+ + O_2 + 4e^-$$

If the hydrogen and oxygen gases are collected using the apparatus shown in Figure 25.6 then twice the volume of hydrogen gas is collected to that of oxygen. This is explained as each hydrogen ion needs to gain one electron to become a hydrogen atom, but each oxygen ion needs to lose two electrons to become an oxygen atom.

■ Understanding electrolysis

Electrolysis only happens when an electric current is passed through an ionic compound where the ions are free to move. This can only happen when the compound is either molten or is in solution. The compound is then broken down by the transfer of electrons from the source of electricity. The electrons that are accepted by the cation come from the source of the electricity, not from the anion. Similarly, the anion's electrons are given to the source not to the cation. It is the transfer of the electrons that cause the chemical changes.

The migration of ions

1 Cut a piece of filter paper so that it fits a microscope slide. Draw a pencil line across the middle of the filter paper.
2 Wet the filter paper with tap water. (Tap water is used as it is a solution that can conduct electricity.)
3 With forceps place a single crystal of potassium manganate(VII) on the pencil line.
4 Connect the filter paper to a battery, as shown in Figure 25.7, and allow a current to flow for 10 minutes.

You should see a smear of purple colour from the pencil line towards the anode as the purple manganate(VII) ions are attracted to the positive charge. You should be able to explain why the potassium ions are not visible as they migrate to the cathode.

Electrolysis as oxidation–reduction reactions

When an ion or molecule accepts electrons we say the ion is being **reduced**. So when copper ions accept two electrons to become copper atoms we say that the copper ions are reduced.

When an ion or molecule loses electrons we say the ion is being **oxidised**. When chloride ions lose electrons to become chlorine atoms we say that the chloride ions are oxidised.

Reduction and oxidation always happen together. If one substance is reduced, then another substance in the reaction is being oxidised. Chemists refer to these reactions as oxidation–reduction reactions or **REDOX** reactions.

PRACTICAL

This suggested practical relates to specification point 1.60C.

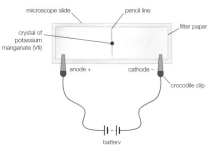

Figure 25.7 Migration of ions. **Wear eye protection.**

A **reduction** reaction is a chemical reaction where a particle **gains** electrons.

An **oxidation** reaction is a chemical reaction where a particle **loses** electrons.

■ Uses of electrolysis

PRACTICAL

This suggested practical relates to specification point 1.58C.
Wear eye protection for this practical.

Investigating the mass changes at the electrodes when copper(II) sulfate solution is electrolysed using copper electrodes

- Place 50 cm³ of copper(II) sulfate solution into a beaker.
- Make two electrodes out of pieces of copper foil.
- Weigh and record the mass of one of these electrodes and attach it via a wire to the positive terminal of your battery. This is your anode.
- Weigh and record the mass of the remaining electrode and attach it via a wire to the negative terminal of your battery. This is your cathode.
- Pass a current through the solution for about 5 minutes. Observe what happens at the anode and the cathode.
- At the end of the time carefully remove each electrode, dry them very carefully, and re-weigh them.

The cathode will weigh more than at the start as it has been coated with more copper metal. The anode weighs less as it has dissolved into the solution to provide the copper ions to be plated onto the cathode.

If you change the copper cathode for a metal object, such as a teaspoon, you can electroplate the spoon with a thin layer of copper. This is how many items are plated with another metal.

STUDY QUESTIONS

1 When molten lead bromide, $PbBr_2$, is electrolysed lead forms at the cathode and orange-brown bromine gas forms at the anode.
   a) What ions are present in $PbBr_2$?
   b) Write half-equations for the reactions at the anode and cathode during electrolysis.
2 Which of the following substances are electrolytes? copper, molten wax, hydrochloric acid, alcohol, aqueous magnesium chloride

3 What are the products at the electrodes when the following compounds are electrolysed:
   a) molten calcium chloride
   b) hydrobromic acid
   c) aqueous zinc sulfate?
4 Copy and balance the following half-equations for reactions at electrodes.
   a) $H^+ + e^- \rightarrow H_2$
   b) $O^{2-} \rightarrow e^- + O_2$
   c) $Al^{3+} + e^- \rightarrow Al$

Summary
I am confident that:

✓ **I understand the terms atomic number, mass number, isotope and relative atomic mass (A_r)**

✓ **I can calculate relative formula masses (M_r) from relative atomic masses (A_r)**
- Add together the relative atomic mass of each atom in the formula.

✓ **I can carry out calculations using the mole and molar volumes**
- 1 mole of an element is the relative atomic mass in grams.
- 1 mole of a compound is the relative formula mass in grams.
- 1 mole of a compound or element always contains Avogadro's number of particles.
- 1 mole of gas always has a volume of $24\,dm^3$ at room temperature and pressure (r.t.p.).

✓ **I can work out the formula of a compound from the charges on its ions**

✓ **I can work out the formula of a compound from experimental data that gives the reacting masses of the elements that make up the compound**
- Work out the ratio of atoms of each element by dividing the mass or percentage by the relative atomic mass of the element.
- Then divide each element's ratio by the lowest ratio to find the numbers of each atom in the compound, and so its formula.

✓ **I can write word and balanced chemical equations**
- Use the correct formulae of each reactant and product.
- Balance the equation, remembering to leave the balancing of oxygen and hydrogen to the end.
- Use state symbols (s), (l), (g) and (aq) to describe each substance in the equation.

✓ **I can calculate the masses of reactants and products and the percentage yield**
- Find the reacting ratio of the reactant to the product.
- Calculate the number of moles used by dividing the mass of reactant by its relative formula mass.
- Calculate the amount of product formed, multiplying the reacting ratio and the number of moles used to find the number of moles made.
- Then multiply the number of moles made by the relative atomic or formula mass of the product.
- Percentage yield = actual yield ÷ theoretical yield × 100%

✓ **I can describe how ions are made by the gain or loss of electrons**
- Positive ions have lost electrons.
- Negative ions have gained electrons.
- The number of electrons lost or gained is given by the number of the charge.

✓ **I can use electronic configurations of atoms to work out the charge on an element's ion**
- Ions have the electronic configuration of the nearest noble gas.
- For metal elements the outer electrons are lost.
- For non-metal elements electrons are gained.

✓ **I can use dot and cross diagrams to explain the formation of ionic compounds**

✓ **I know that ionic compounds form enormous three-dimensional crystals**
- The oppositely charged ions are electrostatically attracted to one another.
- The crystals have very strong structures.
- They have high melting and boiling points.
- The melting and boiling points increase as the number of charges on the ions increase.
- The crystals do not conduct electricity.

✓ **I know that a covalent bond is the electrostatic attraction between a shared pair of electrons and the nuclei of the two atoms bonded together.**
- More than one shared pair of electrons can hold atoms together.

✓ **I can use dot and cross diagrams to explain the bonding of:**
- the elements hydrogen, chlorine, oxygen and nitrogen.
- the compounds hydrogen chloride, water, methane, ammonia and carbon dioxide.

✓ **I understand why compounds with simple molecular structures have low melting and boiling points**
- The intermolecular forces are weak.

✓ **I know that some covalent substances such as diamond and graphite form giant covalent structures**
- The structures of diamond and graphite are very different and this explains their different properties and uses.
- They both have high melting points.
- Graphite conducts electricity but diamond does not.

✓ **I can explain the electrical conductivity and malleability of metals**
- The atoms are arranged in a lattice as positive nuclei with delocalised electrons that are free to flow through the metal.
- The flow of electrons is an electric current.
- The atoms in the lattice can slide past each other when a force is applied.
- In an alloy different sizes of atoms make it harder for the atoms to slide past each other.

✓ **I can explain the differences in conductivity between covalent compounds and ionic compounds and use this to identify the bonding in a compound**
- When molten or in solution, ions are free to move, carrying electric charge and so conducting electricity.
- Covalently bonded compounds have no ions or delocalised electrons so they cannot conduct electricity.

✓ **I understand that electrolysis involves the formation of new substances**
- An electric current can flow through the molten or dissolved substance.
- The electric current flow transfers electrons from negative ions to positive ions, turning the ions back to atoms.
- The positive ions are attracted to the negative electrode, and the negative ions are attracted to the positive electrode.

✓ **I can write ionic half-equations for the reactions at the anode and the cathode during the electrolysis of:**
- sodium chloride
- lead bromide
- copper sulfate
- dilute sulfuric acid.

Sample answers and expert's comments

1   A student wanted to find the formula of magnesium oxide.
    The student used this apparatus for the investigation.

Mass of crucible and lid   = 16.81 g

Mass of crucible, lid and magnesium   = 18.24 g

Mass of crucible, lid and magnesium oxide made = 19.16 g

a) Calculate the mass, in grams, of magnesium that was used.   (1)

b) Calculate the amount, in moles, of magnesium that was used.   (2)

c) Calculate the mass, in grams, of oxygen that was used.   (1)

d) Calculate the amount, in moles, of atoms of oxygen that
   combined with the magnesium.   (2)

e) Calculate the empirical formula of magnesium oxide.   (2)

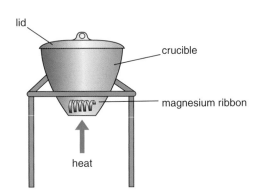

(Total for question = 8)

Student response Total 8/8	Expert comments and tips for success
a) $18.24 - 16.81$; $1.43 g$ ✓	Clearly shown calculation with units.
b) $\frac{1.43}{24}$ ✓ ; $0.060 \ mol$ ✓	The calculation is correct and the answer is rounded up to only two significant figures to make later calculations easier.
c) $19.16 - 18.24 = 0.92 g$ ✓	Correct subtraction gains the mark.
d) $\frac{0.92}{16}$ ✓ $= 0.058 \ mol$ ✓	The calculation is correct. For the unit you can use either mol (the symbol) or moles.
e) $0.060 : 0.058 = 1 : 1$ ✓ so MgO is the formula ✓	Remember that answers from practical work will not always give exact answers. Realising that 0.060 is virtually the same as 0.058 allows the correct formula to be given.

2 The table shows the properties of five different substances.

Substance	Melting point in °C	Boiling point in °C	Conducts electricity as a	
			Solid	Liquid
P	−114	−85	no	no
Q	714	1418	no	yes
R	3550	4827	no	no
S	−39	357	yes	yes
T	6	15	no	no

Use the information in the table to answer the following questions.

a) Which substance has the lowest melting point? (1)

b) Which substance is a liquid at room temperature (20 °C)? (1)

c) Which substance is a metal? Explain your answer. (2)

d) Which substance has a giant covalent structure? Explain your answer. (2)

(Total for question = 6 marks)

Student response Total 6/6	Expert comments and tips for success
a) P ✓	Correctly identifies −114 °C as the lowest melting point.
b) S ✓	Correct choice.
c) S ✓, as metals conduct electricity as both solids and liquid. ✓	You do not have to memorise data, but you must know the key features of each type of substance and be able to find it in the table, e.g. metals conduct electricity as both solids and liquids, and are usually solids at room temperature.
d) R, ✓ as it has high melting and boiling points, and doesn't conduct electricity, ✓ so it must be covalent with a crystal lattice.	A clear answer which uses information from more than one column of the table to choose the substance and explains the choice using known properties of covalent substances.

Exam-style questions

1 Look at the Periodic Table on page 273.

a) Give the symbol of the element that has the atomic number of 12. [1]

b) Give the symbol of the element that has a relative atomic mass of 12. [1]

c) Give the number of the group that contains the noble gases. [1]

d) Which group contains elements whose atoms form ions with a 2+ charge? [1]

e) Which group contains elements whose atoms form ions with a 1– charge? [1]

2 Epsom salts are hydrated magnesium sulfate. Their formula is sometimes written as $MgSO_4.xH_2O$. Knowing that Epsom salts decompose on strong heating to form anhydrous magnesium sulfate, a student obtained the following results.

Mass of dry test tube = 5.30 g

Mass of dry test tube + Epsom salts = 6.30 g

Mass of dry test tube + anhydrous salt = 5.79 g

a) The student heated the anhydrous salt left in the test tube a second time and found that the mass of the dry test tube + anhydrous salt was still 5.79 g. Why did he do this? [1]

b) From the results above calculate:

   i) the mass of hydrated magnesium sulfate taken [1]

   ii) the mass of water in this hydrated salt [1]

   iii) the mass of $MgSO_4$ in this hydrated salt. [1]

c) Calculate the relative formula mass of:

   i) water, H_2O [1]

   ii) magnesium sulfate, $MgSO_4$. [1]

d) Determine the number of water molecules in Epsom salts. [4]

3 Lithium and fluorine react together to form the ionic compound lithium fluoride.

a) i) What is the formula of each of the elements before the reaction occurs? [2]

   ii) What is the symbol of each of the ions formed in the reaction? [2]

b) The diagrams show the electronic configurations of lithium and fluorine atoms.

Draw diagrams to show the arrangement of the electrons in the ions formed in lithium fluoride. [2]

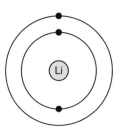 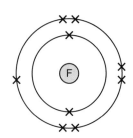

4 The table shows some properties of diamond and graphite.

Diamond	Graphite
colourless, transparent, crystalline solid	black, shiny solid
very hard but brittle	flakes easily
non-conductor of electricity	conductor of electricity

a) Why might you expect diamond and graphite to have the same properties? [1]

b) Explain why diamond and graphite have different properties. Your answer should refer to their different structures. [4]

c) Explain why graphite conducts electricity but diamond does not. [2]

5 Potassium chloride, KCl, is an ionic compound.

a) Explain why KCl has a high melting point and a high boiling point. [2]

b) Explain why molten KCl conducts electricity, but solid KCl does not. [1]

c) Chlorine gas, Cl_2, consists of molecules. Name the type of bonding between:

   i) Cl atoms in Cl_2 [1]

   ii) Cl_2 molecules in Cl_2. [1]

6 a) Magnesium, atomic number 12, reacts with sulfur, atomic number 16, to form magnesium sulfide.

   i) Give the electronic configuration of the two elements magnesium and sulfur. [2]

   ii) Explain, by means of a diagram or otherwise, the changes in electronic configurations that take place during the formation of magnesium sulfide. Include the charges on the ions. [2]

   iii) Explain why the bonding in magnesium sulfide produces a solid with a high melting point. [1]

b) Hydrogen, atomic number 1, forms hydrogen molecules, H_2.

Draw a dot-and-cross diagram to show the arrangement of the outer electrons in a molecule of hydrogen. [2]

7 Use the Periodic Table of elements on page 273 to help you answer this question.

Sodium chloride (NaCl) can be made by burning sodium metal in chlorine gas.

a) Copy and balance this equation for the reaction:

$Na(s) + Cl_2(g) \rightarrow NaCl(s)$ [1]

b) Use dot and cross diagrams to show the arrangement of the electrons in:

   i) an atom of sodium [1]

   ii) an ion of sodium [1]

   iii) an atom of chlorine [1]

   iv) a chloride ion. [1]

c) Chlorine gas has covalent bonds.

   i) What is a covalent bond? [1]

   ii) Draw a dot-and-cross diagram to show the arrangement of the outer electrons in a molecule of chlorine. [2]

d) Sodium chloride is an ionic compound.

   i) How are the ions attracted to one another in sodium chloride? [1]

   ii) Draw a dot-and-cross diagram to show the arrangement of the outer electrons in the ions present in sodium chloride. [3]

8 A student investigated the electrolysis of copper(II) sulfate solution using the apparatus shown. The two

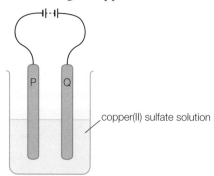

copper(II) sulfate solution

electrodes **P** and **Q** were made of two carbon rods. The student passed a current through the copper sulfate solution for 5 minutes.

a) Which of the two electrodes **P** or **Q** is the anode? [1]

b) i) What would you expect to see at electrode P? [1]

   ii) Write a half equation for the reaction occurring at electrode **P**. [1]

c) i) What would you expect to see at electrode Q? [1]

   ii) Write a half equation for the reaction occurring at electrode **Q**? [2]

9 The table shows the properties of four substances, **A–D**.

Sub-stance	Does it dis-solve in water?	Melting point in °C	Boiling point in °C	Does it conduct electricity when …	
				solid?	dis-solved in water?
A	yes	808	1465	no	yes
B	yes	1610	2230	no	no
C	no	-114	78	no	no
D	yes	-114	-85	no	yes

Choose your answers from the four substances, A–D.

a) a gas at room temperature? [1]

b) liquid at room temperature? [1]

c) an ionic compound? [1]

d) has a giant structure? [1]

EXTEND AND CHALLENGE

Graphene, a breakthrough for display screens

Graphene is a new 'wonder' material. It is made of a sheet of graphite that is only one layer of hexagons thick. It is claimed to be a better electrical conductor than any metal and threatens to replace silicon chips completely. A million sheets of graphene have a thickness of 1 mm.

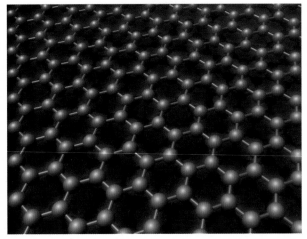

Figure 1 Artist's impression of a sheet of graphene.

James Hone of Columbia University said, 'Our research establishes graphene as the strongest material ever measured, some 200 times stronger than structural steel.'

1   Use your knowledge of the structure of graphite and how metals conduct electricity to suggest how graphene is able to conduct electricity. A diagram may help your explanation.

Samsung industries are already using graphene to make flexible display screens, like the one in Figure 2, for mobile phones.

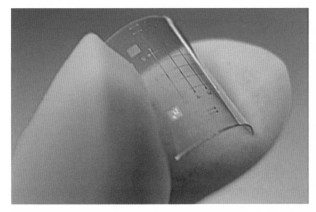

Figure 2 Flexible display screen.

Advertisers and packaging companies are also investigating possible applications for graphene. Computer companies are predicting the roll-up portable computer.

2   You have been asked to market the idea of a roll-up computer screen to a computer manufacturer. Suggest five points, with reasons, that you could make to persuade them that flexible computers are the next great innovation. You should also consider some good answers to any possible objections they may have.

The researchers who discovered graphene also discovered that a good way of obtaining a layer of graphene was to get a piece of graphite, cover it with a strip of self-adhesive tape, and then rip the tape off.

3   Explain how this produced a piece of graphene from the graphite and suggest how you could separate the graphene from the self-adhesive strip.

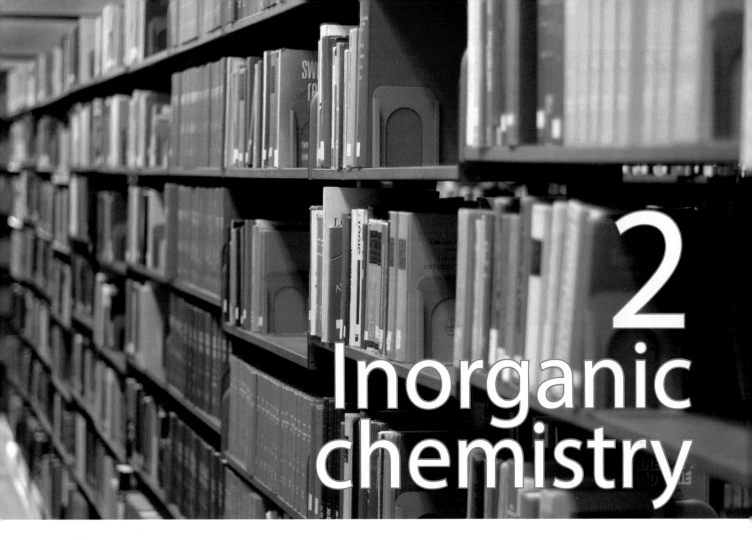

2
Inorganic chemistry

A library uses a pattern to help you find books easily. Fiction books are usually arranged by author's name, non-fiction books by a number system that groups books on the same topic on the same shelves.

Chemists use patterns to help explain chemical reactions and to predict possible useful substances. In developing pharmaceutical drugs, chemists look for chemicals that are effective, then look for other chemicals with similar structures that might be even better. They are following patterns.

DISCUSS • CONSIDER

1 There are many different possible patterns in which you could arrange the files on your computer, each with its own benefits. Think of four ways of arranging your files. Suggest the benefits of each way of organising your files. Which method do you prefer?

2 The pattern of chemical elements we use today was developed over a period of 75 years. Think of the possible ways you could organise the chemical elements based on the information you know. How could you decide if the pattern you chose was useful?

3 There were only 64 known elements when the Periodic Table was developed. There are now 118 known elements. What features did the Periodic Table need to be able to cope with the large number of elements discovered after it was developed?

By the end of this section you should:

- know some of the reactions of Group 1 and Group 7 elements
- know the gases in the air and the proportions of those gases
- be able to describe the reactions of some metals with dilute acids, and other metal salt solutions, and use this information to construct a reactivity series of metals
- be able to describe a reaction as a thermal decomposition, oxidation, reduction or redox reaction
- be able to describe and explain how a metal can be extracted from its ore
- be able to describe the reactions of acids and bases and how to make salts
- be able to test unknown compounds and gases to identify the substances present.

2.1 Group 1 elements

Figure 1.1 Potassium ignites when it comes into contact with water.

The Group 1 metals are all highly reactive. Unlike other metals, they react very easily with water. The world would be very different if many metals were this reactive. Their ease of reactivity has enabled scientists to understand how ions form, and the reactivity of the metals.

■ Properties of Group 1 metals

The elements in Group 1 are sometimes called **alkali metals** because they react with water to form alkaline solutions. Lithium, sodium and potassium are the best known alkali metals. The other elements in Group 1 are rubidium, caesium and francium (Figure 1.2). Some properties of lithium, sodium and potassium are summarised in Table 1.

Group 1

| Li |
| Na |
| K |
| Rb |
| Cs |
| Fr |

Alkali metals

Figure 1.2 Group 1 alkali metals.

Table 1 Some properties of lithium, sodium and potassium.

Property	Lithium (Li)	Sodium (Na)	Potassium (K)
Reaction with air	Burns with red flame, forming white oxide $4Li + O_2 \rightarrow 2Li_2O$	Burns with yellow flame , forming white oxide $4Na + O_2 \rightarrow 2Na_2O$	Burns with lilac/purple flame, forming white oxide $4K + O_2 \rightarrow 2K_2O$
Reaction with water	Reacts steadily, floating on the surface, heating up and produces hydrogen gas. Alkaline solution made. $2Li + 2H_2O \rightarrow 2LiOH + H_2$	Reacts vigorously, floating on the surface, heating up, melting into a small ball and produces hydrogen gas. Alkaline solution made. $2Na + 2H_2O \rightarrow 2NaOH + H_2$	Reacts vigorously, floating on the surface, heating up, melting into a small ball and produces hydrogen gas. Alkaline solution made. $2K + 2H_2O \rightarrow 2KOH + H_2$
Type of compound and ion formed on reaction	Makes ionic compounds Li^+	Makes ionic compounds Na^+	Makes ionic compounds K^+
Colour of compounds	Lithium compounds are mostly white	Sodium compounds are mostly white	Potassium compounds are mostly white

PRACTICAL

You should be able to describe the reactions of lithium, sodium and potassium with water.
These reactions will be performed as teacher demonstrations only. Eye protection must be worn. Apparatus should be surrounded by safety screens.

The three metals, lithium, sodium and potassium, all react in the same way with water and oxygen. In each reaction the only difference in the products is the metal. Reaction with water always makes the hydroxide of the alkali metal used and hydrogen. The lower the metal is in the group the more violently it reacts. It is this similarity in the reactions and other properties that provides evidence that they are in the same chemical group.

Lithium, sodium and potassium have some unusual properties for metals.

■ They are soft enough to be cut with a knife.
■ Their melting points and boiling points are unusually low (Figure 1.4).
■ Their densities are so low that they float on water.

Notice how the elements react more vigorously with water moving down the group from lithium to potassium.

The alkali metals become more reactive as their relative atomic mass increases.

This trend in reactivity is largely due to the increasing size of their atoms. As their atoms get larger, the outer electrons are further from the nucleus (see Figure 1.3) and are not attracted to it so strongly. This allows the outer electrons to be lost more easily, forming compounds containing ions with a charge of 1+.

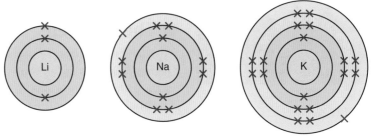

Figure 1.3 The electronic configurations of lithium, sodium and potassium.

Look at the physical properties of lithium, sodium and potassium shown in Table 2. These properties and the reactions of alkali metals illustrate another important feature of the Periodic Table.

Although the elements in a group have similar properties, there is a steady change in physical properties from one element to the next.

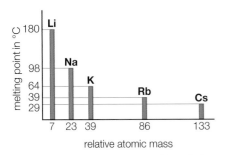

Figure 1.4 The melting points of the alkali metals.

Table 2 The physical properties of lithium, sodium and potassium.

Element	Relative atomic mass	Melting point in °C	Boiling point in °C	Density in g/cm³
lithium	7	180	1330	0.53
sodium	23	98	892	0.97
potassium	39	64	760	0.86

Figure 1.4 shows the steady change in the melting points of the alkali metals.

Once we know the general properties of the elements in a group, and how these properties vary from one element to the next, we can predict the properties of other elements in the group.

STUDY QUESTIONS

1 Write a word equation and then balance the equation with symbols for the reaction of chlorine with lithium.
2 Use the internet to find and watch videos of the following reactions:
  a) rubidium and water
  b) sodium and chlorine.
3 The metals in Group 2 are similar to those in Group 1, but not so reactive. Magnesium and calcium are the commonest metals in Group 2.
  a) What products will form when: **i)** magnesium reacts with oxygen; **ii)** calcium reacts with water?

  b) Which do you think is the more reactive, magnesium or calcium?
4 a) Use a data source to find the boiling points and relative atomic masses of rubidium and caesium.
  b) Use your values from part (a) and those in Table 2 to plot a graph of boiling point (vertically) against relative atomic mass for the elements in Group 1.
  c) How do the boiling points of the alkali metals change as their relative atomic masses increase?

2.2 Group 7 elements

In the First World War (1914–1918) the gas chlorine was used to kill soldiers on both sides. Chlorine is an element in Group 7 of the Periodic Table. It is vital for life in the compound sodium chloride, but deadly as the pure element.

Figure 2.1 Chlorine was used as a weapon during the First World War.

■ The halogens

The elements in Group 7 of the Periodic Table are called **halogens** (Figure 2.2). They are a group of reactive non-metals. The common elements in the group are fluorine (F), chlorine (Cl), bromine (Br) and iodine (I). The final element, astatine (At), does not occur naturally. It is an unstable radioactive element which was first synthesised in 1940.

■ Sources of the halogens

The halogens are so reactive that they very rarely occur naturally as elements. They are usually found combined with metals in salts such as sodium chloride (NaCl) and magnesium bromide ($MgBr_2$). This gives rise to the name 'halogens', which means 'salt formers'.

The most widespread compound containing fluorine is fluorspar or fluorite (CaF_2) which occurs in some rocks. The commonest chlorine compound is sodium chloride (NaCl) which occurs in seawater and in rock salt. Each kilogram of seawater contains about 30 g of sodium chloride. Seawater also contains small amounts of bromides and traces of iodides. Certain seaweeds also contain iodine.

	6	7	0
			He
	O	**F**	Ne
	S	**Cl**	Ar
		Br	Kr
		I	Xe
		At	Rn

Figure 2.2 The halogens in Group 7 of the Periodic Table.

Figure 2.3 *Laminaria* is a type of seaweed which contains iodine. You can often find *Laminaria* at low tide on rocky beaches.

■ Patterns in the physical properties of halogens

The halogens are typical of non-metals – soft when solid, like iodine, poor conductors of heat and electricity with low melting points and boiling points. Table 1 lists some physical properties of chlorine, bromine and iodine. Look at the table and note how their properties change as relative atomic mass increases.

Table 1 Physical properties of chlorine, bromine and iodine.

Element	Relative atomic mass	Colour and state at room temperature	Colour of vapour	Structure	Melting point in °C	Boiling point in °C
chlorine	35.5	pale green gas	pale green	Cl_2 molecules	−101	−35
bromine	80	red brown liquid	orange	Br_2 molecules	−7	58
iodine	127	dark grey solid	purple	I_2 molecules	114	183

As the relative atomic mass of the halogen increases:

■ the state at room temperature changes from gas to liquid to solid
■ the colour of vapour becomes darker
■ the melting point increases (Figure 2.4)
■ the boiling point increases (Figure 2.4).

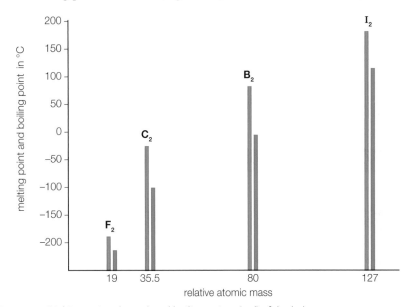

Figure 2.4 Melting points (green) and boiling points (red) of the halogens.

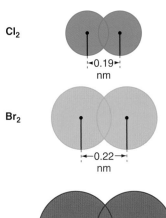

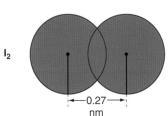

Figure 2.5 Sizes of halogen molecules (1 nm = 10^{-9} m).

The halogens have diatomic molecules

All the halogens exist as simple molecules containing two atoms – F_2, Cl_2, Br_2 and I_2. These are called **diatomic molecules**. Strong bonds hold the two atoms together as a molecule, but the forces of attraction between separate molecules are weak. This means that the molecules are easily separated, so they have low melting points and low boiling points. The relative sizes of these molecules (Figure 2.5) explain the changes in melting point and boiling point with increasing relative atomic mass.

The trend in melting and boiling points

Moving down the group, the halogen molecules get larger and heavier. The larger the molecule, the harder it is to break up the orderly arrangement within the solid and form a liquid. It is also more difficult to separate larger molecules and form gas. This is because there are stronger intermolecular forces between the larger molecules than the smaller ones.

Thus, more energy is needed to melt and to boil the elements with the larger molecules. So the melting points and boiling points increase with relative molecular mass. F_2 and Cl_2, the smallest halogen molecules, are gases at room temperature. Br_2 is a liquid and I_2 is a solid.

Figure 2.6 Chlorine gas, bromine liquid and solid iodine.

STUDY QUESTIONS

1 What are the halogens?
2 State a source of:
   a) chlorine
   b) bromine
   c) iodine.
3 List the characteristic physical properties of the halogens.
4 Use the information in this chapter to predict the following properties of:
   a) fluorine
   b) astatine.

i) colour
ii) state at room temperature
iii) structure
iv) melting point
v) boiling point

5 Explain the meaning of the following terms which are used in this chapter:
   a) unstable radioactive element
   b) synthesised
   c) diatomic molecule
   d) intermolecular forces.

2.3 Reactions of the halogens

The halogens are very useful elements. Their high reactivity means they readily form compounds that are very useful to us. Figure 3.1 shows just a few of the uses of chlorine in our everyday lives. A glance at the ingredients on many household products reveals the presence of fluorine, chlorine, iodine and bromine. You can spot chlorine as either chlorides or 'chloro' in the chemical names. Think how you could spot the presence of bromine or iodine in a product.

Properties of
CHLORINE

- pale green gas
- choking smell
- poisonous (toxic)
- denser than air
- dissolves in and reacts with water
- bleaches dyes and indicators
- reacts vigorously with most metals

Figure 3.1 Just a few of the many uses of chlorine.

Figure 3.2 The properties of chlorine.

■ Uses of halogens

Chlorine is the most important element in Group 7. Its properties are listed in Figure 3.2. Figure 3.1 shows some of its more familiar uses, but it has other uses. Most swimming pools use chlorine compounds to kill bacteria in the pool, making it safe for us all to swim together. When you have your clothes dry cleaned, then the 'dry' solvent they use is a compound called tetrachloroethene. Each solvent molecule has four chlorine atoms in it.

The other halogens also have familiar uses. Fluorine is used to make Teflon, the non-stick covering on cooking pans and baking trays. It is also used in PTFE tape to make watertight plumbing joints. Fluorides are added to toothpaste to harden the tooth enamel, and in some areas they are added to the water supply for the same reason. Bromine is used to make medicines, as is iodine. If you've had a minor operation the doctor may cover your skin with a brown liquid containing iodine to kill bacteria. Before the discovery of antibiotics iodine was widely used as an antiseptic.

■ Reactions with metals

The halogens react with a number of metals to form ionic compounds. These ionic compounds are salts, for example sodium chloride (NaCl, common salt) and calcium fluoride (CaF_2). The halogens occur as negative ions in salts – fluoride (F^-), chloride (Cl^-), bromide (Br^-) and iodide (I^-). Because of this, the salts are sometimes called **halides**.

■ Displacement reactions of halogens

Table 1 The colours of the halogens in water.

Name of halogen solution	Colour
chlorine water	very pale green
bromine water	orange
iodine solution	brown

Halogens dissolve easily in water and these solutions can be used to investigate the relative reactivity of each halogen. Bromine dissolves in water to form a solution called bromine water, which is coloured orange. The colours of the halogens in water are shown in Table 1.

If some bromine water is added to a solution of sodium iodide, the mixture changes colour to become brown as the bromine reacts with the sodium iodide to produce iodine.

bromine water + sodium iodide → iodine water + sodium bromide
$$Br_2(aq) + 2NaI(aq) → I_2(aq) + 2NaBr(aq)$$

The iodine has been displaced by the bromine from the sodium iodide. The reaction occurs because bromine is more reactive than iodine and can take electrons from the iodide ions, forming iodine molecules.

$$Br_2(aq) + 2I^-(aq) → 2Br^-(aq) + I_2(aq)$$

This is called a **displacement reaction**.

Adding chlorine water to salts containing either bromide or iodide ions results in displacement reactions. This shows that chlorine is more reactive than either bromine or iodine (see Figure 3.3).

The halogens get less reactive as their relative atomic mass increases.

Figure 3.3 Adding chlorine water to solutions of sodium chloride, sodium bromide and sodium iodide. Which is which?

Explaining the trend in reactivity of the halogens

With Group 1 metals the reactivity increases as the relative atomic mass increases (see Chapter 2.1 and Figure 1.3). With Group 7 non-metals the reverse occurs. Group 7 elements gain electrons to become negatively charged ions. As the atomic mass gets larger, so too does the size of the atom. This means that the outer electron orbit is further from the nucleus (see Table 2) and the force available to attract electrons to the atom is less.

Table 2 Atomic radii of some Group 7 atoms.

Group 7 atom	Relative atomic mass	Atomic radii in nm
F	19	0.135
Cl	35.5	0.180
Br	80	0.195
I	127	0.215

The same reason explains the trend in reactivity for both Group 1 and Group 7 elements. In Group 7 it has the opposite effect on the trend of reactivity. This is because metals lose electrons, but non-metals attract electrons; two opposite processes.

Displacement reactions are examples of oxidation and reduction

When chlorine water reacts with lithium bromide the following reaction takes place.

chlorine water + lithium bromide → bromine water + lithium chloride

The chlorine molecules gain electrons and are said to be **reduced**, while the bromide ions lose electrons and are said to be **oxidised**.

$$Cl_2(aq) + 2LiBr(aq) \rightarrow Br_2(aq) + 2LiCl(aq)$$

As one reactant is reduced in the reaction and another reactant is oxidised in the reaction, chemists refer to these reactions as **redox reactions**.

Redox reactions are discussed further in the next chapter.

REQUIRED PRACTICAL

You should be able to describe how to carry out a displacement reaction between a halogen dissolved in water and a halide salt. You should be able to describe the colour changes that occur in these displacement reactions and explain the changes in terms of atoms becoming ions and ions becoming atoms, using ionic equations.
Eye protection must be worn when carrying out these reactions. Avoid inhaling any gases produced by them.

EXAM TIP

Note that the trend in reactivity of the halogens is opposite to the trend in Group 1 where the alkali metals get more reactive with increasing relative atomic mass.

STUDY QUESTIONS

1 Describe experiments which show the relative reactivity of bromine, chlorine and iodine. Write equations for the reactions you describe.
2 Arrange the following pairs of elements in order of decreasing vigour of reaction:
   a) lithium and iodine
   b) potassium and chlorine
   c) potassium and fluorine
   d) sodium and chlorine
   e) sodium and iodine.
3 Fluorine ($A_r = 19$) is a member of Group 7. It is a toxic gas.
   a) Predict the reaction of fluorine gas with solid sodium bromide. Write a balanced chemical equation for the reaction.
   b) Explain what safety precautions you would take when doing this reaction.

2.4 Oxidation and reduction

The burning of a match (Figure 4.1) is a redox reaction. Match heads contain phosphorus or antimony compounds and substances containing oxygen. The head of the match or the strip on the box also contains finely powdered glass. When the match is struck, friction caused by the powdered glass creates heat to start a reaction in which phosphorus or antimony is oxidised to its oxide.

■ Combustion, respiration and rusting

Many reactions in everyday life involve substances reacting with oxygen to form oxides. Combustion, respiration and rusting are three important examples.

During **combustion**, fuels containing carbon and hydrogen react with oxygen to form carbon dioxide and water.

$$\text{fuel} + \text{oxygen} \rightarrow \text{carbon dioxide} + \text{water}$$

During **respiration**, foods containing carbon and hydrogen react with oxygen to form carbon dioxide and water.

$$\text{food} + \text{oxygen} \rightarrow \text{carbon dioxide} + \text{water}$$

During **rusting**, iron reacts with oxygen and water to form hydrated iron(III) oxide.

$$\text{iron} + \text{oxygen} + \text{water} \rightarrow \text{hydrated iron(III) oxide}$$

Chemists use a special word for a reaction in which a substance combines with oxygen. They call the reaction **oxidation** and the substance is said to be **oxidised**.

But if one substance combines with and gains oxygen, another substance (possibly oxygen itself) must be reduced.

Substances which lose oxygen in chemical reactions are said to be **reduced** and we call the process **reduction**.

Oxidation and reduction always happen together. If one substance combines with oxygen and is oxidised, another substance must lose oxygen and be reduced. We call the combined process **redox** (**RED**uction + **OX**idation).

Notice that some redox reactions, like burning and respiration, are very useful, but other redox reactions like rusting and the spoiling of food (Figure 4.2), are a problem.

Figure 4.1 What happens when you strike a match?

Figure 4.2 When food goes bad, substances in the food combine with oxygen in the air. The process involves oxidation. Carbon dioxide and water are produced.

■ Redox in industrial processes

Welding steel

A redox reaction is sometimes used in welding steel. A mixture of powdered aluminium and iron(III) oxide (known as 'thermit') is used. Aluminium is more reactive than iron, so it removes oxygen from the iron oxide to form aluminium oxide and iron (Figure 4.3).

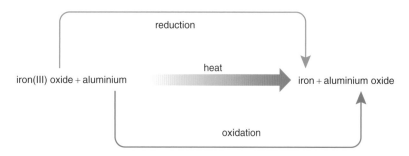

Figure 4.3 In a redox reaction oxidation is always accompanied by reduction.

Aluminium gains oxygen and is oxidised. The iron in iron(III) oxide loses oxygen and is reduced. The whole process involves both oxidation and reduction. It is an example of redox.

This reaction between aluminium and iron(III) oxide releases a lot of energy. The iron is produced in a molten state. As the iron solidifies, it will weld together two pieces of steel. Welding together railway lines using this method has increased the average 'life' of track from 23 to 30 years. Figure 4.4 shows the process in action.

Figure 4.4 The redox reaction between aluminium and iron(III) oxide can be used to weld railway lines together. Molten iron from the reaction runs into a mould around the rails to be joined. When the iron has cooled, the mould is removed and excess metal is trimmed off.

Extracting iron

Redox reactions also occur in the manufacture of metals. In a blast furnace, iron is extracted from iron ore (iron(III) oxide) by reaction with carbon monoxide.

iron(III) oxide + carbon monoxide → iron + carbon dioxide
(iron ore)

In this process, the iron in iron(III) oxide is reduced to iron, while the carbon in carbon monoxide is oxidised to carbon dioxide.

Extracting zinc

Zinc is extracted from zinc oxide by reaction with coke (carbon).

zinc oxide + carbon → zinc + carbon monoxide
(coke)

Which element is oxidised and which substance is reduced in this process?

Redox is studied further in Chapter 2.6.

STUDY QUESTIONS

1 Look at the photo of grapes going bad (Figure 4.2).
   a) What chemical processes occur when food decays?
   b) What methods and precautions do we use at home to stop food going off?
   c) How do these methods work?
2 Which element is oxidised and which is reduced in each of the following redox reactions?
   a) aluminium + water → aluminium oxide + hydrogen
   b) hydrogen + oxygen → water
   c) copper oxide + hydrogen → copper + water

3 a) Will copper oxide and magnesium react on heating? Explain your answer.
   b) Will magnesium oxide and copper react on heating? Explain your answer.
   c) Element W reacts with the oxide of element X but not with the oxide of element Y. Write W, X, and Y in order of reactivity (most reactive first).

2.5 The air

Figure 5.1 River water and seawater contain dissolved oxygen. Fish take in water through their mouths. This flows over their gills, which extract oxygen from the water.

Air is all around us. We need it to live. We need it to burn fuels to keep warm. We also obtain useful products from the air. These products include oxygen and nitrogen. Air is a mixture, but the substance in it that we need for both breathing and burning is oxygen.

■ What percentage of the air is oxygen?

Figure 5.2 shows an experiment to find the percentage of oxygen in air. Air is passed over heated copper. The hot copper reacts with oxygen in the air to form copper(II) oxide.

$$\text{copper} + \text{oxygen} \rightarrow \text{copper(II) oxide}$$

This removes oxygen from the air and its volume decreases.

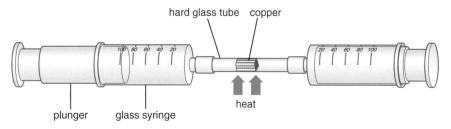

Figure 5.2 Finding the percentage of oxygen in the air. **Wear eye protection if you try this experiment.**

REQUIRED PRACTICAL

You need to be able to explain how to find the percentage of oxygen in air experimentally using all three methods shown in this chapter. You should also be able to explain how to show that air contains both water vapour and carbon dioxide.

At the beginning of the experiment, one syringe is empty and the other is filled with 100 cm³ of air. The hard glass tube is then heated strongly. When the copper is red hot, the syringes are used to push the air forwards and backwards over the heated copper, so that all the oxygen in the air reacts with the copper. The tube is now allowed to cool and the volume of gas in the syringes measured. Finally, the heating and cooling are repeated until the volume of gas that remains in the syringe is constant. Table 1 shows the results from one experiment.

Table 1 The results of an experiment to find the percentage of oxygen in air.

volume of air in syringe before heating	100 cm³
volume of gas after first heating and cooling	82 cm³
volume of gas after second heating and cooling	79 cm³
volume of gas after third heating and cooling	79 cm³

1 Has all the oxygen been used up after the first heating?
2 Has all the oxygen been used up after the second heating?
3 Why is the heating and cooling repeated three times?
4 How much oxygen did the copper remove?
5 What is the percentage of oxygen in the air?

Gases in the air

Table 2 gives some information about the main gases in clean, dry air.

Table 2 The main gases in the air.

Gas	% of air by volume	Boiling point in °C	Important uses
nitrogen	78.1	−196	making ammonia for nitric acid and fertilisers
oxygen	20.9	−182	steel making and welding
argon	0.9	−186	filling electric light bulbs (argon is very unreactive)
carbon dioxide	0.04	−78.5	fire extinguishers, oil recovery, refrigerants

Clean, dry air also contains small percentages of carbon dioxide, neon, krypton and xenon. Together, these gases make up about 0.1% of clean, dry air. Although clean, dry air contains nitrogen, oxygen, argon and small percentages of the four gases just mentioned, ordinary air also contains some water vapour and waste gases from industry (Chapter 4.2).

Other methods for determining the percentage of oxygen in air

Using iron

Some iron wool is placed in a measuring cylinder full of air and inverted over a trough of water as shown in Figure 5.3. The apparatus is left for a week. The iron reacts with the oxygen in the air to form rust, and the water level inside the measuring cylinder rises to replace the oxygen used up.

The percentage of oxygen in the air can be calculated by measuring the change in volume of the water in the measuring cylinder and dividing it by original volume of the air in the cylinder, then multiplying by 100.

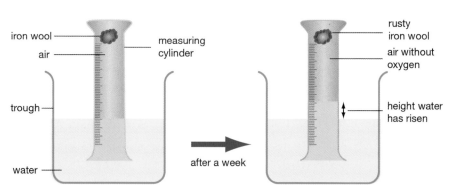

Figure 5.3 Another method for finding the percentage of oxygen in air.

Using phosphorus

White phosphorus is a non-metal element which must be stored under water. If it is allowed to dry out it will burst into flame in the air. If a small dry piece of white phosphorus is left inside a very large beaker of air it will ignite and burn with the oxygen in the air to form phosphorus oxide, which dissolves in water. Figure 5.4 shows how the experiment could be done. However, the experiment should not be done in school as white phosphorus catches fire spontaneously and is highly toxic.

In this experiment, to make the arithmetic easier, the height is used instead of the volume. This works because the volume equals the height × the area, and you assume the area remains constant inside the beaker. You calculate the change in height of the water and divide it by the original height of air, then multiply by 100.

PRACTICAL

This suggested practical relates to specification point 4.12.

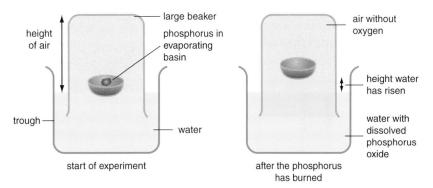

Figure 5.4 A third way of finding the percentage of oxygen in air.

Using a candle

You could also investigate exactly what is made when the candle burns in air. Candles are made from paraffin wax, a mixture of compounds that contain only hydrogen and carbon. If you use the apparatus in Figure 5.5 you can investigate the products of combustion.

Eye protection must be worn for this experiment.

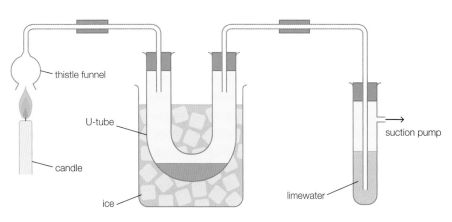

Figure 5.5 Investigating the products made when a candle burns.

Black soot forms from unburnt carbon on the thistle funnel, condensation of water appears in the cold U-tube, and the limewater turns milky white as it reacts with the carbon dioxide produced when the candle burns in oxygen. To prove the condensation is water you would find the boiling point of a small sample or test it (see Chapter 2.19). If the paraffin wax is given the formula of $C_{21}H_{44}$, the reaction can be summarised as

$$\text{paraffin wax} + \text{oxygen} \quad \rightarrow \quad \text{carbon dioxide} \quad + \quad \text{water}$$

$$C_{21}H_{44} \quad + \quad 32O_2(g) \quad \rightarrow \quad 21CO_2(g) \quad + \quad 22H_2O(l)$$

You can see from the equation that burning the paraffin wax uses an enormous quantity of oxygen for each mole of wax burnt.

STUDY QUESTIONS

1 Iron reacts slowly with oxygen and water to form hydrated iron(III) oxide. A student placed wet iron filings in the end of a graduated tube and set it up as in Figure 5.6.

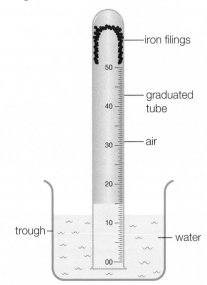

Figure 5.6 Wet iron filings in the end of a graduated tube.

Over several days the water rose up the graduated tube and eventually reached a constant level. The starting level of water in the graduated tube was at $15.00 \, cm^3$ and the final level was at $24.50 \, cm^3$.

a) Why does the water rise up the graduated tube?

b) Why is it not possible to calculate the initial volume of air in the graduated tube?

c) i) What other volume do you need to know in order to calculate the initial volume of air in the graduated tube?

   ii) If this other volume is $10.00 \, cm^3$, calculate the initial volume of air in the graduated tube.

d) Now calculate:

   i) the final volume of gas in the graduated tube

   ii) the volume of oxygen that reacts with the iron filings

   iii) the percentage by volume of oxygen in the air.

2.6 Oxygen

Iron from the blast furnace contains carbon and sulfur impurities. Before it can be called steel most of these impurities have to be removed. Oxygen is blown through the molten iron to react with the carbon to make carbon dioxide, and the sulfur reacts to become sulfur dioxide. These two gases then bubble out of the molten iron, leaving behind steel. For every 10 tonnes of steel made, 1 tonne of oxygen gas is needed.

Figure 6.1 Using oxygen to remove impurities from molten iron to make steel.

■ Preparing oxygen

It is not usually necessary to prepare oxygen in the laboratory because cylinders of oxygen are normally available. However, oxygen can be prepared if it is needed by decomposing compounds that contain high proportions of oxygen. The most convenient compound of this kind is hydrogen peroxide.

Hydrogen peroxide solution decomposes very slowly at room temperature to form water and oxygen.

$$\text{hydrogen peroxide} \rightarrow \quad \text{water} \quad + \text{ oxygen}$$
$$\text{(hydrogen oxide)}$$

If the hydrogen peroxide is mixed with manganese(IV) oxide, it decomposes much more quickly. The manganese(IV) oxide helps the hydrogen peroxide to decompose more easily, but it is not used up during the reaction. The manganese(IV) oxide acts as a catalyst (Chapter 3.7).

A suitable arrangement of apparatus for preparing and collecting oxygen in the laboratory is shown in Figure 6.2.

Eye protection must be worn for this procedure.

The aqueous solution of hydrogen peroxide should be added slowly to the solid manganese(IV) oxide. As soon as the hydrogen peroxide touches the manganese(IV) oxide, there is a vigorous reaction and oxygen is produced. The first gas jar to be filled with gas should be discarded as it will contain mainly air displaced from the flask and delivery tube. The oxygen can be collected over water even though it is slightly soluble.

PRACTICAL

Make sure you know how oxygen is produced using manganese(IV) oxide and hydrogen peroxide.

123

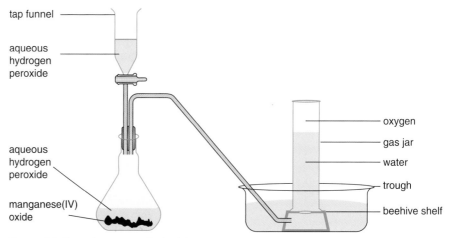

Figure 6.2 Preparing oxygen in the laboratory.

■ How does oxygen react with elements?

Some of the properties of oxygen are shown in Figure 6.3. One of its most important properties is the way it helps things to burn. If a substance burns in air, it will burn much more easily in oxygen.

The test for oxygen

The simple test for oxygen is that it will cause a glowing splint to relight (Figure 6.4).

Reaction with oxygen on heating

Most elements will react with oxygen on heating. Some elements react slowly at room temperature. Iron slowly develops a layer of rust (hydrated iron(III) oxide) on exposure to the air. Similarly, shiny aluminium surfaces become dull with a layer of white aluminium oxide. The iron and aluminium have reacted with oxygen in the air. Table 1 shows the results obtained when various elements are heated strongly in air.

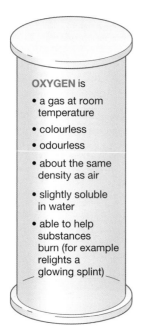

OXYGEN is

- a gas at room temperature
- colourless
- odourless
- about the same density as air
- slightly soluble in water
- able to help substances burn (for example relights a glowing splint)

Figure 6.3 Properties of oxygen.

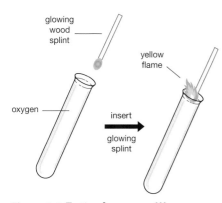

Figure 6.4 Testing for oxygen. **Wear eye protection.**

Table 1 Comparing the reactions of some elements with oxygen in air.

Element	Reaction with oxygen in air	Product	Shake product with water, then add universal indicator
sodium	bright yellow flame – white smoke and powder	white solid (sodium oxide)	dissolves pH = 11 alkaline
magnesium	dazzling white flame – white clouds and powder	white solid (magnesium oxide)	dissolves slightly pH = 8 alkaline
iron	glows red hot and burns with sparks	black-brown solid (iron oxide)	insoluble
copper	does not burn, but the surface turns black	black solid (copper(II) oxide)	insoluble
carbon	glows red hot, reacts slowly	colourless gas (carbon dioxide)	dissolves pH = 5 acidic
sulfur	burns readily with a blue flame	colourless gas (sulfur dioxide)	dissolves pH = 3 acidic
hydrogen	burns readily with a pale blue flame	colourless liquid (water)	pH = 7

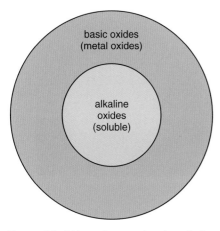

Figure 6.5 A Venn diagram showing alkaline oxides as a sub-set of basic oxides.

All the elements burn better in oxygen than in air. The substances produced are called oxides.

magnesium	+	oxygen	→	magnesium oxide
$2Mg(s)$	+	$O_2(g)$	→	$2MgO(s)$
hydrogen	+	oxygen	→	water
$2H_2(g)$	+	$O_2(g)$	→	$2H_2O(l)$
sulfur	+	oxygen	→	sulfur(IV)oxide
$S(s)$	+	$O_2(g)$	→	$SO_2(g)$

Notice in Table 1 that:

- The metal oxides (for example sodium oxide, magnesium oxide, iron(II) oxide and copper(II) oxide) are all solids. So are other metal oxides.
- The non-metal oxides (carbon dioxide and sulfur dioxide) are both gases.

■ How do oxides react with water?

Look at Table 1 again. Each of the oxides was shaken with water and the solution produced was then tested with universal indicator.

Sodium oxide and magnesium oxide both react with water to form alkaline solutions with a pH greater than 7 (pH > 7).

sodium oxide + water → sodium hydroxide
magnesium oxide + water → magnesium hydroxide

- The oxides of metals are called **basic oxides**. Basic oxides are bases – they react with acids to form salts (Chapter 2.16). Most metal oxides are insoluble in water but a few, like sodium oxide and magnesium oxide, react with it to form alkaline solutions. These oxides are called **alkaline oxides**. Figure 6.5 shows the relationship between basic oxides and alkaline oxides in a Venn diagram.
- The non-metal oxides react with water to form acidic solutions with a pH less than 7 (pH < 7). These oxides of non-metals which give acids in water are called **acidic oxides**.

carbon dioxide + water → carbonic acid
sulfur dioxide + water → sulfurous acid

As the chemical opposites of basic oxides, acidic oxides react with solutions of bases (alkalis) to form salts.

This distinction between metal oxides as basic and non-metal oxides as acidic has helped chemists in their classification of elements as either metal or non-metal (Chapter 1.10).

1 a) What are the main uses of oxygen?
   b) Why do rockets carry liquid oxygen?
2 What is meant by the following:
   a) basic oxide
   b) acidic oxide
   c) alkaline oxide?
3 Barium burns in air to form a solid oxide. This oxide reacts with water to give an alkaline solution.

   a) Is barium a metal or a non-metal?
   b) Write word equations for the reactions described above.
   c) Which of the following elements would react like barium?
      copper, sulfur, sodium, iron, nitrogen, calcium, carbon, potassium

2.7 Carbon dioxide

Carbon dioxide is an important simple molecular compound. It links respiration and photosynthesis, and is produced when carbon compounds burn. Carbon dioxide also has some important uses, which you will learn about here.

Figure 7.1 A firefighter demonstrates the use of a small carbon dioxide fire extinguisher.

■ Uses of carbon dioxide

Fire extinguishers

Liquid carbon dioxide and carbon dioxide gas at high pressure are used in fire extinguishers. When the extinguisher is used, carbon dioxide gas pours out and smothers the fire. Carbon dioxide is denser than air so it covers the fire and stops oxygen getting to it. The fire 'goes out' because carbon dioxide does not burn and substances will not burn in it.

Soda water and fizzy drinks

Solutions of carbon dioxide in water have a pleasant taste – the taste of soda water. Soda water and other fizzy drinks are made by dissolving carbon dioxide in them at high pressure. When a bottle of the drink is opened, it fizzes because the pressure falls and carbon dioxide gas can escape from the solution.

Refrigeration

Solid carbon dioxide is used for refrigerating ice-cream, soft fruit and meat. The solid carbon dioxide looks like ordinary ice, but it is colder and sublimes (solid to vapour) without going through a messy liquid stage. This is why it is called 'dry ice' or 'Dricold'.

Figure 7.2 'Dry ice' (solid carbon dioxide) creates a misty effect. Dry ice is so cold it will produce burns. Never touch it or try to pick it up with bare hands.

■ Making carbon dioxide

Carbon dioxide can be obtained from metal carbonate rocks such as calcium carbonate ($CaCO_3$) or copper carbonate ($CuCO_3$).

Reacting carbonates with acids

Strong acids, like hydrochloric acid, sulfuric acid and nitric acid, react with carbonates to form carbon dioxide and water.

$$\text{acid} + \text{carbonate} \rightarrow \text{salt} + \text{water} + \text{carbon dioxide}$$

Small amounts of carbon dioxide are usually prepared from marble chips (calcium carbonate) and dilute hydrochloric acid.

$$\begin{array}{ccccccccc} \text{calcium} \\ \text{carbonate} \end{array} + \begin{array}{c} \text{hydrochloric} \\ \text{acid} \end{array} \rightarrow \begin{array}{c} \text{calcium} \\ \text{chloride} \end{array} + \text{water} + \begin{array}{c} \text{carbon} \\ \text{dioxide} \end{array}$$

$$CaCO_3(s) + 2HCl(aq) \rightarrow CaCl_2(aq) + H_2O(l) + CO_2(g)$$

The carbon dioxide may be collected over water or by downward delivery, as carbon dioxide is denser (heavier) than air.

Heating a metal carbonate

Heating a metal carbonate strongly breaks the compound down to carbon dioxide and the metal oxide. Green copper carbonate changes into black copper(II) oxide and carbon dioxide gas.

$$\text{copper(II) carbonate} \rightarrow \text{copper(II) oxide} + \text{carbon dioxide}$$
$$CuCO_3(s) \rightarrow CuO(s) + CO_2(g)$$

This type of reaction where heating causes a compound to break down into two or more compounds is known as **thermal decomposition**.

Other metal carbonates also thermally decompose. Some are easier to decompose than others. You could try heating small samples of copper(II) carbonate, zinc carbonate and calcium carbonate to investigate which decompose easily. **Wear eye protection**.

Properties of
CARBON DIOXIDE

• colourless

• no smell

• denser than air

• slightly soluble
  in water

• does not burn

• substances will
  not burn in it

Figure 7.3 The properties of carbon dioxide.

■ The properties of carbon dioxide

Carbon dioxide is a typical non-metal oxide. It is acidic, gaseous and a simple molecular compound. Figure 7.3 shows some other properties of carbon dioxide. Notice that it is slightly soluble in water. The dissolved gas provides water plants, like seaweed, with the carbon dioxide they need for photosynthesis. About 1% of the gas which dissolves in water reacts to form carbonic acid (H_2CO_3).

$$H_2O + CO_2 \rightarrow H_2CO_3$$

The solution of carbonic acid is a very weak acid.

Carbon dioxide is a greenhouse gas

Carbon dioxide is one of a group of gases said to be greenhouse gases. Increasing levels of carbon dioxide and other greenhouse gases in the atmosphere means that the Earth becomes better at absorbing heat energy from the Sun. As a result the mean temperature of the Earth's atmosphere is increasing. As we burn more carbon-based fuels the concentration of carbon dioxide in the atmosphere has risen and may be contributing to climate change. The increase in temperature is leading to more extreme weather events, such as hurricanes and higher and lower rainfall. Less rainfall in some parts of the world is causing deserts to expand, while more rainfall in other areas is causing floods. Increasing temperature is causing the ice caps to shrink, leading to rises in sea levels. Other effects are that animal and plant habitats change and food crops fail.

Testing for carbon dioxide with limewater

The test for carbon dioxide uses its acidic property. Limewater is calcium hydroxide solution – a dilute alkali. When carbon dioxide is bubbled into limewater, the liquid goes milky as a white precipitate of calcium carbonate forms. Why does this precipitate form? First, the carbon dioxide reacts with OH^- ions in the alkali to form carbonate ions (CO_3^{2-}).

$$CO_2(g) + 2OH^-(aq) \rightarrow CO_3^{2-}(aq) + H_2O(l)$$

Then, CO_3^{2-} ions react with calcium ions in the limewater to form insoluble calcium carbonate.

$$Ca^{2+}(aq) + CO_3^{2-}(aq) \rightarrow CaCO_3(s)$$

STUDY QUESTIONS

1 Explain why carbon dioxide is used in:
   a) fizzy drinks
   b) fire extinguishers.
2 Give two reasons why 'dry ice' is better than ordinary ice for refrigeration.
3 Carbon dioxide can be poured from a gas jar onto a lighted candle and the candle goes out. What does this simple experiment show about the properties of carbon dioxide?
4 a) How is carbon dioxide obtained from a carbonate?
   b) Write an equation for the reaction in part (a).
   c) Why can the carbon dioxide be collected either by downward delivery or over water?
   d) How would you show that limestone is a carbonate?

2.8 The reactions of metals

Archaeologists excavating sites often find objects made from copper, gold and silver (Figure 8.1), but rarely iron. They find evidence of iron objects as areas of hydrated iron(III) oxide or rust. The evidence suggests that the inhabitants of the site could make and use iron implements, so why is only rust found? The answer is in the reactivity of the metals. Only gold, silver, copper and platinum are found naturally occurring in the ground. All the other metals are found in rocks that we call ores. The metal is joined with other elements as compounds – the metal has reacted.

Figure 8.1 These archaeological items are made from gold, silver and copper. Why are there no objects made from iron?

■ Metals and acids

The foods in Figure 8.2 contain acids that can react with most metals.

Table 1 shows what happens when different metals are added to dilute hydrochloric acid at room temperature (21 °C). This acid is more reactive than those in foods, but the results show how different metals are attacked by acids.

Notice in Table 1 that aluminium does not react at first. This is because its surface is protected by a layer of aluminium oxide. The oxide reacts slowly with the acid, but this then exposes aluminium, which reacts more vigorously.

Figure 8.2 All these foods contain acids that can react with metals.

Table 1 Reactions of metals with dilute hydrochloric acid.

Metal used	Reaction with dilute hydrochloric acid	Highest temperature recorded
aluminium	no reaction at first, but hydrogen is produced rapidly after a time	85 °C
copper	no reaction, no bubbles of hydrogen	21 °C
iron	slow reaction, bubbles of hydrogen produced slowly	35 °C
magnesium	very vigorous reaction, hydrogen is produced rapidly	95 °C
zinc	moderate reaction, bubbles of hydrogen are produced steadily	55 °C

Look at the results in Table 1. Use these results to draw up a 'reactivity series' for the five metals used. Put the metals in order from the most reactive to the least reactive.

Metal for cooking pans and cutlery

The metals used most commonly for pans and cutlery are aluminium, copper and iron (steel). Copper is the only one which does not react with the acids in food. But copper is so expensive that aluminium and steel are used for most of the saucepans sold today. A thin oxide coating on aluminium protects it from most of the weak acids in foods. However, acetic acid (ethanoic acid) in vinegar does react with aluminium and this 'cleans' the saucepan during cooking. Iron (steel) which is used in cutlery is also attacked very slowly by acids in food.

Storing food in metal cans

Foods containing acids are best stored in unreactive containers made of glass or plastic. Food cans ('tin cans') are also used to store acidic foods like pineapples and grapefruit. The cans are made of steel coated on both sides with tin and then covered on the inside with a thin layer of unreactive plastic between the tin and its contents.

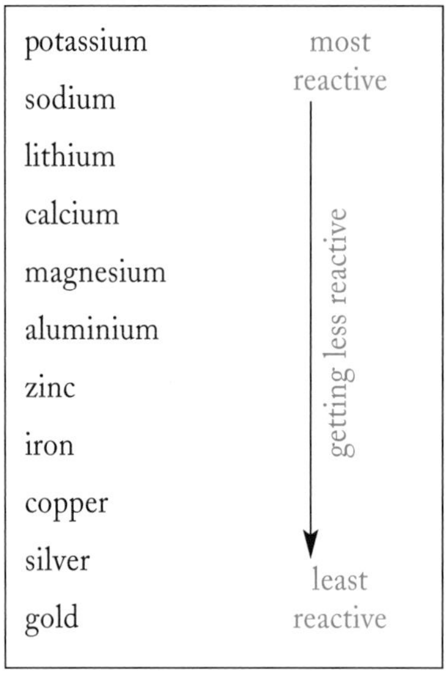

Metal reactions with hydrochloric acid

All the metals in Table 1 except copper react with dilute hydrochloric acid. The products of the reaction are hydrogen and the chloride of the metal.

metal + hydrochloric acid → metal chloride + hydrogen

Using M as a symbol for the metal and assuming M forms M^{2+} ions, we can write a general equation as:

$$M(s) + 2HCl(aq) \rightarrow MCl_2(aq) + H_2(g)$$

Metal reactions with sulfuric acid

A similar reaction occurs between metals and dilute sulfuric acid. This time the products are hydrogen and a metal sulfate.

| metal (above copper) | + | sulfuric acid | → | metal sulfate | + | hydrogen |

For example, when magnesium reacts with dilute sulfuric acid the products are magnesium sulfate and hydrogen.

$$Mg(s) + H_2SO_4(aq) \rightarrow MgSO_4(aq) + H_2(g)$$

potassium	most reactive
sodium	
lithium	
calcium	
magnesium	
aluminium	getting less reactive
zinc	
iron	
copper	
silver	
gold	least reactive

Figure 8.3 The reactivity series of metals.

Figure 8.4 What is the problem with using iron to make the water boiler in a steam train?

■ Using metal reactions to make a reactivity series

From these reactions of metals with dilute acids and from the reactions of metals with air (oxygen) and water, we can draw up an overall **reactivity series**. This is shown in Figure 8.3.

■ Summarising the reactions of metals

The order of reactivity of metals is the same with air (oxygen), with water and with acids. This is not really surprising because metal atoms react to form metal ions in each case. The higher the metal in the reactivity series, the more easily it forms its ions.

$$M \rightarrow M^{2+} + 2e^-$$

Reaction with air (oxygen)

Metals lose electrons to form metal ions. The electrons are taken by oxygen molecules (O_2) forming oxide ions (O^{2-}).

metal + oxygen → metal oxide

$$2M + O_2 \rightarrow 2M^{2+}O^{2-}$$

Reaction with water

The metals lose electrons to form positive ions. The electrons are taken by water molecules which form hydroxide ions (OH^-) and hydrogen (H_2).

metal + water → metal hydroxide + hydrogen

$$M + 2H_2O \rightarrow M^{2+}(OH^-)_2 + H_2$$

Reaction with acids

This time, the metals give up electrons to H^+ ions in the acids and hydrogen (H_2) is produced.

metal + acid → metal compound + hydrogen

$$M + 2H^+ \rightarrow M^{2+} + H_2$$

(above copper)

The reactivity series (Figure 8.3) is a very useful summary of the reactions of metals. Metals at the top of the series easily lose electrons and form ions. Metals at the bottom of the series are just the opposite. Ions of these metals more easily gain electrons and form atoms.

■ Oxidation and reduction

Gaining or losing oxygen

When elements react with oxygen, they form products called **oxides**. These reactions in which elements and other substances gain oxygen are called **oxidations**.

Sometimes, it is possible to remove oxygen from an oxide. For example, if mercury oxide is heated strongly, it will thermally decompose to mercury and oxygen.

$$\text{mercury oxide} \xrightarrow[\text{strongly}]{\text{heat}} \text{mercury} + \text{oxygen}$$

$$2HgO \longrightarrow 2Hg + O_2$$

reduction

Reactions like this in which a substance loses oxygen are called **reductions**.

So, oxidation is *gain* of oxygen, reduction is *loss* of oxygen.

Gaining or losing electrons

When magnesium reacts with oxygen, the product is magnesium oxide (MgO).

$$2Mg + O_2 \rightarrow 2Mg^{2+}O^{2-}$$

During this reaction, each magnesium atom (Mg) loses two electrons ($2e^-$) to form a magnesium ion Mg^{2+}. This means that four electrons are lost by the two magnesium atoms in the last equation.

$$2Mg \rightarrow 2Mg^{2+} + 4e^-$$

These four electrons are gained by the two oxygen atoms in the oxygen molecule (O_2) to form two oxide ions ($2O^{2-}$).

$$O_2 + 4e^- \rightarrow 2O^{2-}$$

Now we know that magnesium is oxidised in this reaction and oxygen is reduced. So, instead of defining oxidation in terms of oxygen, we can also define it in terms of electrons. Magnesium which loses electrons in the reaction is oxidised and oxygen which gains electrons is reduced.

In general, **oxidation** is the *loss* of electrons, **reduction** is the *gain* of electrons.

■ Redox reactions

By defining oxidation as the loss of electrons and reduction as the gain of electrons, it is easy to see that oxidation and reduction must always occur together. If one substance loses electrons in a reaction, then another substance must gain them.

Because **red**uction and **ox**idation always occur together, these reactions are often called **redox** reactions.

Redox is not just about oxygen

When oxidation and reduction are defined in terms of electrons, many more reactions can be classified and understood as redox reactions. These include the reactions of metals with water and with acids. When metals react with water, the products are the metal hydroxide and hydrogen.

$$M + 2H_2O \rightarrow M^{2+}(OH^-)_2 + H_2$$

In this reaction, the metal (M) loses electrons and is oxidised to its ions (M^{2+}). The water (H_2O) gains electrons and is reduced to hydroxide ions (OH^-) and hydrogen (H_2).

When metals react with acids containing hydrogen ions (H^+), the products are a metal compound containing ions of the metal (M^{2+}) and hydrogen (H_2).

$$M + 2H^+ \rightarrow M^{2+} + H_2$$

In this case, the metal (M) loses electrons again and is oxidised to its ions (M^{2+}). The hydrogen ions (H^+) in the acid gain electrons and are reduced to hydrogen (H_2).

- Substances such as O_2, H_2O, H^+ and Cl_2, which take electrons in redox reactions, are called **oxidising agents**.
- In contrast, metals that give up electrons in redox reactions are called **reducing agents**.

Therefore, oxidising agents are themselves reduced and reducing agents are oxidised in redox reactions.

■ Metal displacement reactions

Reactions between metals and metal oxides

When a powdered mixture of aluminium and iron(III) oxide is heated, an intensely exothermic reaction occurs producing aluminium oxide and molten iron which quickly solidifies.

$$2Al(s) + Fe_2O_3(s) \rightarrow Al_2O_3(s) + 2Fe(s)$$

The reaction involves redox. Atoms of Al have been oxidised to Al^{3+} ions by the loss of electrons, while Fe^{3+} ions have taken these electrons and have been reduced to Fe atoms.

$$Al \xrightarrow{\text{oxidation}} Al^{3+} + 3e^-$$

$$Fe^{3+} + 3e^- \xrightarrow{\text{reduction}} Fe$$

The reaction occurs because aluminium is more reactive than iron and more readily forms ions. So, aluminium has formed Al^{3+} ions at the expense of Fe^{3+} ions, which have been reduced to iron. The reaction can be regarded as a **displacement reaction** in which a more reactive metal, higher in the reactivity series, has displaced a less reactive metal lower in the reactivity series, from its oxide. Displacement reactions can be used to determine the reactivity of the two metals.

Reactions between metals and their compounds in aqueous solution

If a more reactive metal can displace a less reactive metal from its oxide, it is likely that a more reactive metal will also displace a less reactive metal from its aqueous solutions.

Figure 8.5 shows an experiment to investigate what happens when strips of magnesium ribbon are placed in solutions of sodium chloride, zinc sulfate and copper(II) sulfate.

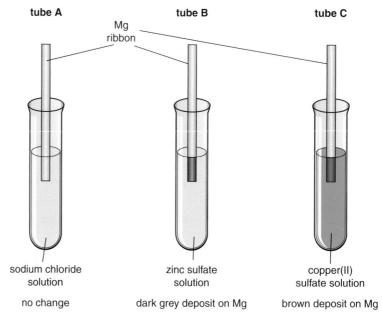

Figure 8.5 The reactions between magnesium and solutions of sodium chloride, zinc sulfate and copper(II) sulfate.

There is no change in tube A. In tube B, the magnesium ribbon turns dark grey and in tube C it turns pink-brown.

- In tube A, there is no reaction. Sodium is more reactive than magnesium and it's already present as a compound.
- In tube B, a dark grey deposit appears on the magnesium ribbon. This is zinc. Magnesium is more reactive than zinc. So magnesium has gone into solution as its ions. The electrons it gives up have been taken by zinc ions in the solution to form zinc atoms which have deposited on the magnesium ribbon as dark grey zinc metal.

This is the equation for the reaction:

$$Mg(s) + ZnSO_4(aq) \rightarrow MgSO_4(aq) + Zn(s)$$

This is how the atoms, ions and electrons change:

$$Mg(s) \rightarrow Mg^{2+}(aq) + 2e^-$$

$$Zn^{2+}(aq) + 2e^- \rightarrow Zn(s)$$

Remember, when interpreting the reaction of a metal with different metal compound solutions, if there is a reaction or change, then the metal is higher in the reactivity series than the metal in the compound. If there is no reaction, the metal is lower in the series than the metal in the compound.

■ In tube C, a similar reaction has occurred to that in tube B. This time it is brown copper that has deposited on the magnesium ribbon. Magnesium has displaced copper from copper sulfate solution:

$$Mg(s) + CuSO_4(aq) \rightarrow MgSO_4(aq) + Cu(s)$$

These displacement reactions between metals and their oxides and between metals and their compounds in aqueous solution can be used to work out the position of a metal within the reactivity series.

STUDY QUESTIONS

1 Look at the photograph of the steam train (Figure 8.4). Answer the question in the caption to the photo.

2 Plan an experiment that you could do to find the position of lithium in the reactivity series. Say what you would do and how you would ensure that your test is fair.

3 Metal P will remove oxygen from the oxide of metal Q, but not from the oxide of metal R. Write P, Q and R in their order in the reactivity series (most reactive first).

4 Write word equations and balanced symbol equations for the reactions of:
   a) copper with oxygen
   b) aluminium with oxygen
   c) calcium with water
   d) zinc with dilute hydrochloric acid
   e) iron with dilute sulfuric acid.

5 a) Why is copper better for saucepans than aluminium?
   b) Why is copper not used for most pans today?
   c) Why is aluminium less reactive than expected with acidic foods?
   d) How are tin cans protected from acids in their contents?

6 When a metal is added to copper(II) sulfate solution, the following reaction may occur:

   metal + copper(II) sulfate → metal sulfate + copper

a) What name is given to this type of reaction?
A student added different metals to copper(II) sulfate solution. He measured the temperature of the copper(II) sulfate solution before adding the metal and again 2 minutes after adding the metal.

b) State three variables that should be kept constant to make the experiment a fair test.

c) The student carried out the experiment three times for each metal and obtained the following results.

Metal	Temperature changes in the three experiments in °C		
iron	6.5	7.6	6.6
lead	3.2	3.6	3.4
nickel	4.5	5.1	4.8

i) Calculate the mean temperature change for each metal.

ii) Which metal has the least reliable results? Explain your answer.

iii) Why are the temperature changes different for the three metals?

iv) Write the three metals and copper in an order of reactivity (most reactive first).

2.9 Rusting

Figure 9.1 Steel parts on a bicycle rust more quickly when the bike is left out in the rain than when it is kept in a shed.

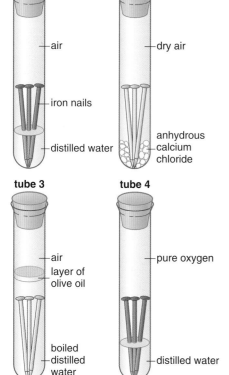

Figure 9.2 Investigating whether water and oxygen are involved in rusting.

Articles made of iron and steel rust much faster if they are left outside in wet weather (Figure 9. 1). This suggests that water plays a part in rusting.

When aluminium is exposed to air, it becomes coated with a layer of oxide. The metal has reacted with oxygen in the air. If rusting is similar to this, iron may also react with oxygen in the air.

■ What conditions are needed for rusting?

The apparatus in Figure 9.2 can be used to investigate whether water and oxygen are involved in rusting. Eye protection must be worn for this investigation. The test tubes are set up and left for several days. Tube 1 is the *control experiment*. It is the standard which we use to compare the results in the other tubes. It contains iron nails in moist air. Tube 2 contains iron nails and anhydrous calcium chloride which absorbs water vapour and keeps the air dry. Tube 3 contains nails covered with boiled distilled water. The water has been boiled to remove any dissolved air. The layer of olive oil prevents air dissolving in the water. Tube 4 contains iron nails in distilled water and pure oxygen.

The nails in tubes 1 and 4 rust, but those in tubes 2 and 3 don't rust.

1 Does iron rust if there is:
   (i) no water, (ii) no air, (iii) no oxygen?
2 What conditions are necessary for rusting?

■ What happens when iron rusts?

During rusting, iron reacts with oxygen to form brown iron(III) oxide.

iron + oxygen → brown iron(III) oxide

As the iron(III) oxide forms, it reacts with water to form hydrated brown iron(III) oxide. This is rust.

iron(III) oxide + water → hydrated iron(III) oxide (rust)

Substances, like rust, that have water as part of their structure are described as **hydrated** and we call them **hydrates**.

Iron will only rust if both oxygen and water are present.

Although iron and steel rust more easily than several other metals, steel is used for ships, cars, bridges and other structures because it is cheaper and stronger than other building materials.

■ How is rusting prevented?

In order to prevent the rusting of iron and steel, we must protect them from water and oxygen. There are a number of important ways of doing this.

Painting

This is the usual method of preventing rusting in ships, vehicles and bridges. Paint covers the iron (steel), but if the paint is scratched, then rusting starts.

Oiling or greasing

The moving parts of machines cannot be protected by paint which would get scratched off. Instead, they are oiled or greased. This also helps to lubricate the moving parts.

Covering with plastic

Steel is sometimes coated with plastic in articles such as garden chairs, dish racks, towel rails and food cans. The plastic is cheap and can be coloured to look attractive.

Coating (plating) with a more reactive metal

Zinc is often used to coat steel dustbins and gates. This process using zinc is described as **galvanizing**. Zinc is more reactive than iron, so oxygen in the air reacts with the zinc before it reacts with the iron (Figure 9.4). Other articles, like taps and kettles, are plated with chromium. This is more expensive than galvanizing and the chromium is only slightly more reactive than iron. So, the protection is poorer, but the chromium plating is more attractive.

Sacrificial protection

Another method of protecting iron from rusting is sacrificial protection. An example of this is attaching blocks of zinc to the steel hulls of ships. The more reactive zinc corrodes in preference to the iron. When the blocks have completely corroded they are replaced.

Another example is the sacrificial protection of underground pipelines. Sacks of magnesium are attached at intervals along the pipe. The more reactive magnesium corrodes in preference to the iron.

Figure 9.3 Food cans are made of steel and protected from water and dissolved oxygen in their contents by a very thin layer of plastic or an unreactive metal like tin. This is why they are often called 'tin' cans or 'tins'.

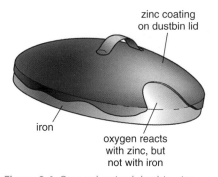

zinc coating on dustbin lid

iron

oxygen reacts with zinc, but not with iron

Figure 9.4 On a galvanized dustbin, zinc reacts before the iron, even when the zinc coating is scratched or broken.

STUDY QUESTIONS

1 a) What is rust?
   b) How does rust form?
2 What methods are used to stop rusting?
3 Explain the following statements.
   a) Iron objects rust away completely in time.
   b) The bottom parts of iron railings rust more quickly than the top.
   c) Iron on shipwrecks in deep seawater rusts very slowly.

4 What experiments would you do to find out whether:
   a) iron rusts more quickly in seawater or in distilled water
   b) steel rusts more quickly than iron?
   Draw a labelled diagram of the apparatus you would use in each case. What results would you expect?

2.10 Raw materials to metals

A few metals, like gold and silver, are very unreactive. They occur in the Earth as the metal itself (Figure 10.1). Most metals are too reactive to exist on their own in the Earth. They are usually found in rocks as compounds with non-metals and mixed with other substances.

Figure 10.1 Gold is so unreactive that it occurs in the Earth as the metal itself. You can see a vein of gold in this rock.

■ From rocks to metals

Rocks containing metals or metal compounds from which it is economic to extract the metal are called **ores**. To obtain a metal from its ore the first step is to mine and possibly concentrate the ore.

Figure 10.2 An aerial view of a copper mine in Arizona, USA. The ore being mined is copper pyrites, a mixture of copper(II) sulfide and iron(II) sulfide.

The second step is to try to reduce the ore to the metal. There are three ways that a metal ore can be reduced to the metal.

- If the metal is at the bottom of the reactivity series simply heating the ore in air may be sufficient to separate the metal from the rest of the ore.
- More reactive metals need their ores to be converted to the metal oxide and then heated with carbon or carbon monoxide to remove the oxygen.
- The most reactive metals are obtained by electrolysis of the molten ore.

Table 1 shows the reactivity series and which method is used to extract the metals.

Table 1 Summarising the methods used to extract metals.

Reactivity series	Method of extraction
potassium sodium lithium calcium magnesium aluminium	electrolysis of molten ore
zinc iron lead	reduction of ore with carbon or carbon monoxide
copper	heat ore in limited supply of air
silver gold	metals occur uncombined in the Earth

Reduction with carbon and carbon monoxide

Metals in the middle of the reactivity series, like zinc, iron and lead, cannot be obtained simply by heating their ores in air. They are obtained by reducing their oxides with carbon (coke) or carbon monoxide.

In these cases, carbon and carbon monoxide are more reactive than the metals. So, carbon or carbon monoxide can remove oxygen from the metal oxide, leaving the metal. For example:

zinc oxide + carbon → zinc + carbon monoxide
(coke)

$$ZnO + C \rightarrow Zn + CO$$

Figure 10.3 Abandoned tin mine buildings in Cornwall. Tinstone (tin(IV) oxide, SnO_2) was once mined in Cornwall and reduced to tin in furnaces near the mines. The tin ore is now virtually used up and the furnaces are derelict.

The reduction of iron(III) oxide to obtain iron is considered in the next chapter.

Sometimes, these metals exist as sulfide ores (Figure 10.2). These ores must be converted to oxides before reduction. This is done by heating the sulfides in air.

zinc sulfide + oxygen → zinc oxide + sulfur dioxide

$$2ZnS + 3O_2 \rightarrow 2ZnO + 2SO_2$$

Electrolysis of molten compounds

Metals at the top of the reactivity series, like sodium, magnesium and aluminium, cannot be obtained by reduction of their oxides with carbon or carbon monoxide. This is because the temperature needed to reduce their oxides is too high. These metals can be obtained from their ores using electricity in the process of **electrolysis**. But the process cannot use aqueous solutions. This is because electrolysis would decompose the water in the aqueous solution and *not* the metal compound.

Figure 10.4 Mining bauxite, impure aluminium oxide. Aluminium is extracted from the purified oxide using electrolysis.

The only way to extract these reactive metals is by electrolysis of their molten (melted) compounds. Potassium, sodium, calcium and magnesium are obtained by electrolysis of their molten chlorides. Aluminium is obtained by electrolysis of its molten oxide. This is described in Chapter 2.12.

■ Purifying the metal

Metals such as copper and iron are reduced with carbon in a furnace. The extracted metal often contains impurities. Copper which comes straight from the furnace contains about 3% impurities. Sheets of this copper are purified by electrolysis with copper(II) sulfate solution.

Similarly, iron obtained directly from the furnace contains about 7% impurities. The main impurity in iron is carbon, and this is removed by injecting oxygen into the molten iron.

STUDY QUESTIONS

1 List the three stages involved in extracting a metal from its ore.

2 Magnesium is extracted by electrolysis of molten magnesium chloride ($MgCl_2$).
   a) What ions are present in molten $MgCl_2$?
   b) Write an ionic half-equation to show the production of magnesium.
   c) Explain why this extraction of magnesium involves reduction.

3 Titanium is a transition metal with a relatively low density. It is resistant to corrosion and forms very strong alloys with aluminium. Titanium is extracted from the ore, rutile, which contains titanium(IV) oxide. This oxide is first converted to titanium(IV) chloride, $TiCl_4$. The $TiCl_4$ is then reacted with a more reactive metal, such as sodium, to form titanium metal. This reaction is carried out in an atmosphere of argon.
   a) Why are titanium alloys used for replacement hip joints?
   b) Suggest another possible use for titanium.
   c) Write the formula of titanium(IV) oxide.
   d) Write an equation for the reaction of titanium(IV) chloride with sodium to form titanium.
   e) Why is this reaction carried out in an atmosphere of argon?

2.11 Extracting iron from iron ore – a case study

There are blast furnaces like the one at Sestao, Spain, (shown in Figure 11.1) all over the world. They convert iron ore to iron metal. Iron is the most important metal. Most of it is made into steel and used for machinery, tools, vehicles and large girders in buildings and bridges.

The main raw material for making iron is iron ore (haematite). This ore contains iron(III) oxide. The best quality iron ore is found in Scandinavia, North America, Australia, North Africa and Russia.

Figure 11.1 Blast furnace at Sestao, Spain.

■ The blast furnace

Iron ore is converted to iron in special furnaces called **blast furnaces**, built as towers about 15 metres tall. The name blast furnace comes from the blasts of hot air that are blown into the bottom of the furnace.

The iron is extracted by heating iron ore with carbon in the form of coke made from coal. This is a cheap way to extract a metal. Limestone is added to the blast furnace to remove impurities as a slag. Fig 11.2 shows how the blast furnace works.

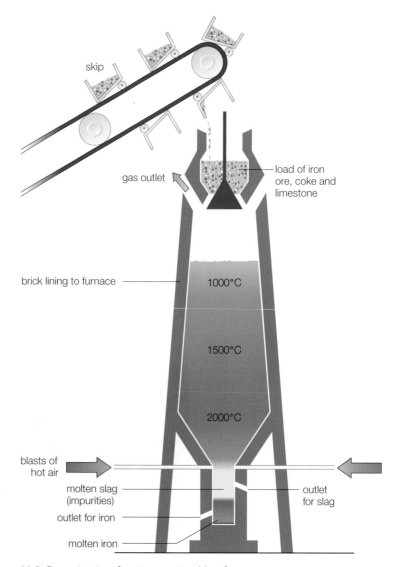

skip

gas outlet

load of iron ore, coke and limestone

brick lining to furnace

1000°C

1500°C

2000°C

blasts of hot air

molten slag (impurities)

outlet for iron

molten iron

outlet for slag

Figure 11.2 Extracting iron from iron ore in a blast furnace.

Blast furnaces work 24 hours a day. Raw materials are continually added at the top of the furnace and hot air is blasted in at the bottom. At the same time, molten slag and molten iron are tapped off from time to time as they collect. This process goes on all the time for about two years. After this time, the furnace has to be closed down so that the brick lining can be replaced.

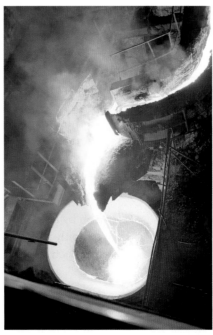

Figure 11.3 Molten iron being poured into a steel-making furnace.

Using carbon to extract other metals

Carbon can be used to extract other metals from their ores. This method of extraction is only used if the metal is less reactive than carbon in the reactivity series (see Chapter 2.8). Other metals extracted this way include lead, tin and zinc. Copper can also be extracted using carbon, but only if the copper produced can be prevented from reacting with oxygen in the air as it cools. Very pure copper, needed for electrical wiring, is then produced using electrolysis (see Chapter 2.12).

STUDY QUESTIONS

1 a) Why are the furnaces used to make iron called *blast* furnaces?
   b) Why are blast furnaces usually built near coal fields?
   c) What materials are added to a blast furnace?
   d) What materials come out of a blast furnace?

2 a) The prices of metals are given in the 'commodities' section of the more serious daily papers and on the internet. Look up the prices for iron (steel), aluminium, copper and zinc. How does the price of iron (steel) compare with other metals?
   b) Suggest three reasons why iron is the cheapest of all metals.
   c) Suggest three reasons why iron is used in greater quantities than any other metal.

2.12 Electrolysis – a case study

Aluminium has a relatively low density. It can also be made harder, stronger and stiffer by alloying with other metals, like titanium.

Figure 12.1 Aluminium alloys are used for the bodywork of aircraft.

■ Obtaining metals by electrolysis

Reactive metals, such as sodium and aluminium, cannot be obtained like iron by reducing their oxides to the metal with carbon (coke). These metals can only be obtained by electrolysis of their molten compounds. We cannot use electrolysis of their aqueous compounds because hydrogen (from the water), and not the metal, is produced at the cathode (see Chapter 1.25).

Metals low in the reactivity series, such as copper and silver, can be obtained by reduction of their compounds or by electrolysis of their aqueous compounds. When their aqueous compounds are electrolysed, the metal is produced at the cathode rather than hydrogen (from the water).

Manufacturing aluminium by electrolysis

Aluminium is manufactured by the electrolysis of aluminium oxide in molten cryolite. The aluminium oxide is obtained from bauxite (impure aluminium oxide, Figure 10.4 on page 140).

■ Which metal to use?

The Periodic Table is full of metals. How do we decide which metal to use for a particular job? We make car bodies out of steel, but aircraft out of aluminium alloys. In deciding which metal to use we have to consider the properties of the metal and compare these against what we want the item we make to be able to do (Figure 12.2).

Aluminium

Aluminium is a low density metal. It is a good conductor of heat and electricity and is resistant to corrosion. We use it for many purposes. Aircraft are made from aluminium alloys which are stronger than pure aluminium, do not corrode and have a low density like aluminium.

Figure 12.2 Uses of aluminium, iron and steel that depend on their chemical and physical properties.

Long distance electrical cables are made from aluminium as it is a good conductor of electricity and has a low density. If copper cables were used in the National Grid then the pylons would need to be at least three times stronger (and much costlier). Cooking pans are made from aluminium as the heat is quickly and easily conducted from the cooker to the food.

Copper

Copper has similar properties to aluminium except that it is much denser. Copper too is used for electrical cabling and cooking utensils. It is also anti-bacterial and is used where there is risk of bacterial transfer, such as risks of MRSA in hospitals and E. coli in kitchens. Copper is also used in plumbing where its unreactive nature and malleability at low temperatures are important.

Iron and steel

The method of producing iron and steel in the blast furnace (see Chapter 2.11) with carbon leaves considerable impurities of carbon in the metal. Table 1 shows the properties and uses of the different types of iron. Notice that steel is a purer form of iron than cast iron. Stainless steel is an alloy of iron with other metals such as manganese, vanadium or chromium.

Table 1 Reactions of metals with dilute hydrochloric acid.

Type of iron	Percentage of carbon	Properties	Uses
cast iron	2–4	hard, brittle, strong in compression	drain and man-hole covers, car engines
mild (low carbon) steel	0–0.25	easily shaped	car body panels, domestic goods
high carbon steel	1–2.5	hard	cutting tools
stainless steel	less than 2%	does not rust	cutlery, sink, tools

STUDY QUESTIONS

1 Suggest reasons for each of the following.
   a) Aluminium extraction plants are usually sited near hydroelectric power stations.
   b) Clay is the most abundant source of aluminium, but the metal is never extracted from clay.
2 Magnesium is manufactured by electrolysis of molten magnesium chloride.
   a) Give the symbols and charges on the ions in the electrolyte.
   b) Draw a circuit diagram to show the directions in which the ions and electrons move during electrolysis.
   c) The anode in this process is made of carbon and not steel, which would be cheaper. Why is this?

3 The use of a metal often depends on its properties. For each metal suggest the most likely property to explain the use given:
   a) steel, for girders to construct buildings
   b) aluminium, to make cooking pans
   c) aluminium, to make factory roofs
   d) steel, for tools such as hammer heads.

2.13 Extracting metals

Aluminium is the third most common element in the Earth's crust, measured by mass. It is so cheap that we use it to make drinks cans and often throw the empty cans away instead of recycling them.
We use aluminium to make cheap cutlery, but in the 1850s it was the most expensive metal in the world. Napoleon III, Emperor of France, boasted of his wealth to dinner guests by giving them aluminium knives, forks and spoons at banquets. King Christian X of Denmark had an aluminium crown. Why then was aluminium so precious?

Figure 13.1 Aluminium used to be so valuable it was used for royal jewelry, but now can be found in everyday household items.

■ Early attempts at aluminium extraction

There are three main ways to obtain a metal from its ore (see Chapter 2.10). Aluminium is too high up the reactivity series to be extracted from its ore by the use of carbon or carbon monoxide. Before the development of the modern electrolytic method of extraction (see Chapter 2.12) there were only two methods of producing aluminium.

Extraction with a more reactive metal

Aluminium was originally made by the reduction of aluminium oxide ore with pure sodium or potassium metal. In a violent explosion known as a thermit reaction small quantities were made:

$$Al_2O_3(s) + 6Na(s) \rightarrow 2Al(s) + 3Na_2O(s)$$

Figure 13.2 Reduction of aluminium oxide by sodium metal.

This reaction only made very small amounts of aluminium and was very costly. In 1853 in the USA 93000 kg of gold was purified, but only 93 kg of aluminium. Aluminium was the world's most costly metal.

Extraction by electrolysis

Aluminium can be obtained by electrolysis. Aluminium compounds do not dissolve easily so molten aluminium oxide has to be used. The problem with this is that the melting point of aluminium oxide is 2979 °C. A temperature this high is very costly and very hard to achieve. It was only in 1886 that C.M. Hall discovered that aluminium oxide could dissolve in molten cryolite at 950 °C, leading to the cheap production of aluminium.

■ Extracting other metals

Reactivity series

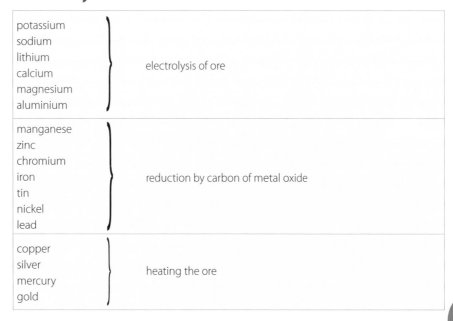

potassium sodium lithium calcium magnesium aluminium	electrolysis of ore
manganese zinc chromium iron tin nickel lead	reduction by carbon of metal oxide
copper silver mercury gold	heating the ore

Metal ores are compounds such as carbonates, sulfides and chlorides, as well as oxides. When a chemist is faced with a new ore to process to obtain the metal they need to select a suitable method for the extraction. The method they choose will be based on the chemistry, the costs, and health and safety.

The steps used to decide on the process are:

1 Identify the elements in the ore.
2 Select the method of extraction based the on the metal's position in the reactivity series.
3 Process the ore to produce a metal compound that can be used in the chosen extraction method:

- remove sulfur from sulfide ores by heating in air (roasting)
    metal sulfide + oxygen from air → metal oxide + sulfur dioxide
  for example nickel sulfide

$$2NiS(s) \quad + \quad 3O_2(g) \quad \rightarrow \quad 2NiO(s) \quad + \quad 2SO_2(g)$$

- remove carbon from carbonate ores by heating (thermal decomposition or calcination)
    metal carbonate → metal oxide + carbon dioxide

  for example copper carbonate

$$CuCO_3 \quad \rightarrow \quad CuO(s) \quad + \quad CO_2(g)$$

4 Extract the metal using the chosen method. Sometimes an ore might be reacted with an acid or other chemical to produce a different compound of the metal. This compound can then be more easily used for electrolysis or another process to reduce the metal.

Many ores can be reduced to the metal in a number of ways just like aluminium. The choice of method used depends on the cost of the method and also the waste compounds produced. With global warming, methods that produce greenhouse gases such as carbon dioxide will become more costly and will be avoided. Methods that produce useful waste products that can be sold, therefore reducing the cost of the method, will be favoured.

STUDY QUESTIONS

1 Name the three ways of extracting metals from their ores.

2 Describe how the reactivity series can be used to suggest a suitable method of extracting a metal.

3 Suggest how each of these metals should be extracted from their ore:
   a) mercury
   b) chromium
   c) nickel
   d) manganese
   e) calcium.

4 The equation shows the reduction of aluminium oxide by potassium metal:

$Al_2O_3(s) + 6K(s) \rightarrow 2Al + 3K_2O(s)$

   a) Name the element that is reduced.
   b) Name the element that is oxidised.
   c) Write half equations for the aluminium ion and the potassium atom.

5 Malachite is an ore of copper. It contains copper carbonate ($CuCO_3$). Before malachite can be converted into copper using carbon it is heated strongly in air.

a) Name the type of reaction caused by heating malachite strongly in air.

Copper can also be obtained from malachite by heating the ore whilst passing hydrogen gas over it.

   b) Explain, using chemical equations, how hydrogen can be used to reduce malachite to copper.
   c) Hydrogen can reduce the copper in copper(II) oxide to copper, but cannot reduce lead oxides to lead. Use this information to suggest where hydrogen might be placed in the reactivity series.
   d) Evaluate the two methods of copper production in terms of environmental problems each may cause.

6 Tin is produced from the mineral cassiterite (tin(IV) oxide, SnO_2) which also contains small amounts of tin sulfide (SnS). Tin is obtained from cassiterite by heating the ore in air before reducing the ore by heating with carbon.

   a) Explain why it is necessary to heat the ore in air. Write a balanced chemical equation for the reaction.
   b) Explain why reduction with carbon is preferred to the use of electrolysis.

2.14 Acids and their properties

The sharp taste of the lemon juice and vinegar shown in Figure 14.1 is caused by acids. Some acids can be identified by their sharp taste, but it would be highly dangerous to rely on taste to identify all acids.

Figure 14.1 Lemons and vinegar contain acids which give them their characteristic tastes.

■ Testing for acids in solutions

The most convenient method of testing for acids in solutions is to use **indicators**, like litmus and universal indicator. Indicators are substances which change colour depending on how acidic or how alkaline a solution is.

- Acidic solutions turn litmus red and give an orange or red colour with universal indicator (Figure 14.2).
- Alkaline solutions turn litmus blue and give a green, blue or violet colour with universal indicator.

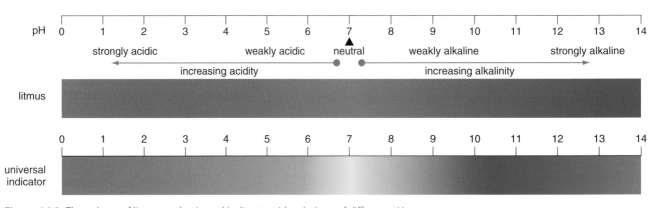

Figure 14.2 The colours of litmus and universal indicator with solutions of different pH.

■ The pH scale

It would be imprecise to just use the colour of an indicator to describe how acidic or how alkaline something is. So, chemists use a scale of numbers from about zero to 14, called the **pH scale**. The pH of a solution gives a measure of its acidity or alkalinity. On this scale:

- acidic solutions have a pH below 7
- alkaline solutions have a pH above 7
- neutral solutions have a pH of 7.

Measuring pH

Using universal indicator, it is possible to measure the approximate pH values of solutions. From these pH values, solutions can be classified as strongly acidic, weakly acidic, neutral, weakly alkaline or stongly alkaline (Figure 14.2). For example, battery acid containing sulfuric acid is strongly acidic, lemon juice containing citric acid is weakly acidic, water is neutral, and drain cleaner containing sodium hydroxide is strongly alkaline.

Other indicators include phenolphthalein and methyl orange (Figure 14.3).

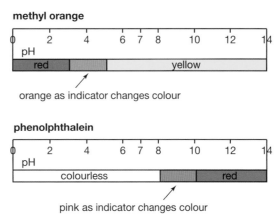

Figure 14.3 The colours of phenolphthalein and methyl orange indicators at different pH values.

■ Properties of acidic solutions

We have seen that acidic solutions have a sharp taste and they give characteristic colours with indicators. They also have a characteristic set of reactions.

Acids react with metals

Acids react with metals that are above copper in the reactivity series (Chapter 2.8) to form a **salt** and hydrogen.

metal + acid → salt + hydrogen

For example, $Zn + 2HCl \rightarrow ZnCl_2 + H_2$

Nearly all salts contain a metal and at least one non-metal. They are ionic compounds with a cation (e.g. Zn^{2+}, Cu^{2+}, Mg^{2+}) and an anion (Cl^-, SO_4^{2-}, NO_3^-). Sodium chloride (Na^+Cl^-) is known as common salt.

Acids react with bases

Acids react with bases (such as metal oxides and hydroxides) to form a salt and water. These reactions are called **neutralisations**. Neutralisation is studied in detail in Chapter 2.15.

base + acid → salt + water

For example, when black copper(II) oxide is added to warm dilute nitric acid, the black solid disappears and a blue solution of copper nitrate forms.

copper(II) oxide + nitric acid → copper(II) nitrate + water

$$CuO + 2HNO_3 \rightarrow Cu(NO_3)_2 + H_2O$$

Acids react with carbonates

Acids react with carbonates to give a salt plus carbon dioxide and water.

carbonate + acid → salt + CO_2 + H_2O

This explains why the sulfuric acid in acid rain 'attacks' buildings made of limestone (calcium carbonate).

$$\text{calcium carbonate} + \text{sulfuric acid} \rightarrow \text{calcium sulfate} + \text{carbon dioxide} + \text{water}$$

$$CaCO_3 + H_2SO_4 \rightarrow CaSO_4 + CO_2 + H_2O$$

Notice that carbonates neutralise acids like metal oxides and hydroxides. So, we must also classify carbonates as bases.

Figure 14.4 This gravestone is made from marble. The worn and pitted appearance has been caused by the action of sulfurous acid, sulfuric acid and nitric acid in 'acid rain'.

Acid solutions conduct electricity and are decomposed by it

Their conducting property shows that solutions of acids contain ions (Table 1). All acids produce hydrogen at the cathode during electrolysis (Chapter 1.25). This suggests that all acids contain H^+ ions.

Table 1 Some acids and the ions they form in solution.

Name of acid	Formula	Ions produced from acid
ethanoic acid	CH_3COOH	$H^+ + CH_3COO^-$
carbonic acid	H_2CO_3	$2H^+ + CO_3^{2-}$
hydrochloric acid	HCl	$H^+ + Cl^-$
nitric acid	HNO_3	$H^+ + NO_3^-$
sulfuric acid	H_2SO_4	$2H^+ + SO_4^{2-}$

■ The part of water in acidity

All these properties of acids apply to solutions of acids in water. But what happens when water is *not* present?

Dry hydrogen chloride (HCl) and pure *dry* ethanoic (acetic) acid have no effect on *dry* litmus paper or on magnesium. **So substances that we call acids do not behave as acids in the absence of water.** When a little water is added, they show acidic properties straight away. Blue litmus paper turns red and bubbles of hydrogen are produced with magnesium.

To study the part water plays with acids, we can compare a solution of hydrogen chloride in water (hydrochloric acid) with a solution of hydrogen chloride in methylbenzene (a solvent with properties like gasoline). Table 2 shows what happens. Look at it carefully. You will see that hydrochloric acid in methylbenzene has no acidic properties. It does not conduct electricity and therefore it contains no ions.

Table 2 Comparing solutions of HCl in water and HCl in methylbenzene.

Test	Solution of HCl in water	Solution of HCl in methylbenzene
colour of *dry* blue litmus paper in the solution	red	blue
add *dry* magnesium ribbon to the solution	bubbles of hydrogen are produced	no bubbles form
add *dry* anhydrous sodium carbonate to the solution	bubbles of carbon dioxide are produced	no bubbles form
does the solution conduct electricity?	yes	no

When hydrogen chloride in water (hydrochloric acid) is electrolysed, it produces hydrogen at the cathode and chlorine at the anode. This shows that it contains H^+ ions and Cl^- ions.

Chemists now know that it is the H^+ ions that cause the typical properties of acids with indicators, metals, metal oxides and carbonates.

This gives a definition for an acid.

An acid is a source of hydrogen ions, H^+, or a substance which can donate (give) H^+ ions.

Hydrogen chloride splits up into aqueous H^+ and Cl^- ions when it dissolves in water.

$$HCl(g) \xrightarrow{\text{water}} \underbrace{H^+(aq) + Cl^-(aq)}_{\text{hydrochloric acid}}$$

This explains why water is necessary for HCl to show acidic properties.

When acids are added to water, $H^+(aq)$ ions are produced and these cause the typical properties of acids.

■ Concentrated and dilute acids

Concentrated acids contain a lot of acid in a small amount of water. Concentrated sulfuric acid has 98% sulfuric acid and only 2% water.

Dilute acids have a small amount of acid in a lot of water. Dilute sulfuric acid has about 10% sulfuric acid and 90% water.

Concentration of a solution

Concentration tells us how much substance is dissolved in a certain volume of solution. It is usually given as the number of grams or the number of moles of solute per cubic decimetre (dm^3) of solution ($1\,dm^3 = 1000\,cm^3$).

Dilute acids usually have concentrations of 1.0 mol per dm^3 (mol/dm^3) of solution or less.

For example, a solution of sulfuric acid containing $1.0\,mol\,/\,dm^3$ has $1.0\,mol$ of sulfuric acid ($98\,g\ H_2SO_4$) in $1\,dm^3$ of solution.

$0.1\,M\ H_2SO_4$ contains $9.8\,g\ H_2SO_4$ in $1\,dm^3$ of solution.

Calculating the concentration of a solution

The following examples will help you to understand concentrations in $g\,/\,dm^3$ and $mol\,/\,dm^3$ of solution.

Example 1

Some vinegar contains $3\,g$ of ethanoic acid ($C_2H_4O_2$) in $100\,cm^3$ of the liquid. What is the concentration of ethanoic acid in the vinegar in:

a) $g\,/\,dm^3$ **b)** $mol\,/\,dm^3$?   ($C = 12$, $H = 1$, $O = 16$)

Answer

a) $100\,cm^3$ of the vinegar contains $3\,g$ ethanoic acid

$\Rightarrow 1\,cm^3$ of vinegar contains $3\,/\,100\,g$ ethanoic acid

$\Rightarrow 1000\,cm^3$ ($1\,dm^3$) of vinegar contains $0.03 \times 1000\,g$ ethanoic acid

$\therefore$ concentration of ethanoic acid in the vinegar $= 30\,g\,/\,dm^3$

b) The relative formula mass of ethanoic acid, $M_r(C_2H_4O_2)$
$= 2 \times A_r(C) + 4 \times A_r(H) + 2 \times A_r(O)$
$= (2 \times 12) + (4 \times 1) + (2 \times 16) = 60$
$\therefore$ molar mass of ethanoic acid $= 60\,g\,/\,mol$
concentration of the ethanoic acid $= 30\,g\,/\,dm^3$

$$= \frac{30\,g\,/\,dm^3}{60\,g\,/\,mol}$$

$$= 0.5\,mol\,/\,dm^3 \text{ or } 0.5\,M$$

Example 2

When $25\,cm^3$ of seawater was analysed, it contained $0.70\,g$ of sodium chloride. What is the concentration of sodium chloride in the seawater in:

a) $g\,/\,dm^3$ **b)** $mol\,/\,dm^3$?   ($Na = 23$, $Cl = 35.5$)

Answer

a) $25\,cm^3$ seawater contains $0.70\,g$ sodium chloride

$\Rightarrow 1000\,cm^3$ seawater contains $\dfrac{0.70}{25} \times 1000\,g = 28\,g$ of sodium chloride

$\therefore$ concentration of sodium chloride in seawater $= 28\,g\,/\,dm^3$

b) The relative formula mass of sodium chloride, $M_r(NaCl)$
$= A_r(Na) + A_r(Cl) = 23 + 35.5 = 58.5$
$\therefore$ molar mass of sodium chloride $= 58.5\,g\,/\,mol$

$\therefore$ concentration of sodium chloride in seawater $= \dfrac{28\,g\,/\,dm^3}{58.5\,g\,/\,mol}$

$$= 0.48\,mol\,/\,dm^3$$

EXAM TIP

The calculation of concentrations in terms of grams per decimetre cubed (g/dm^3) or moles per decimetre cubed (mol/dm^3) of solution can be applied to all solutions, not just acids.

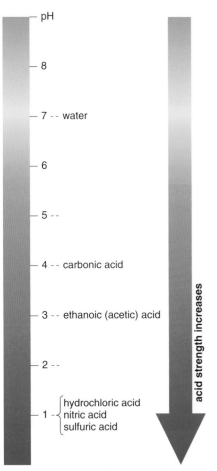

Figure 14.5 The pH of solutions of various acids (all solutions have a concentration of 0.1 mol / dm³).

■ Strong and weak acids

When different acids with the same concentration in moles per dm³ are tested with the same indicator, they give different pHs (Figure 14.5).

The different pH values mean that some acids produce H⁺ ions more readily than others. The results in Figure 14.5 show that hydrochloric acid, nitric acid and sulfuric acid produce more H⁺ ions in solution than the other acids. We say that they **ionise** (split up into ions) more easily. We call them **strong acids** and the others **weak acids**. Strong acids and weak acids also show a difference in their reactions with metals. Strong acids react much, much faster than weak acids.

We can show the difference between strong and weak acids in the way we write equations for their ionisation.

$$\text{hydrochloric acid:} \qquad HCl(aq) \rightarrow H^+(aq) + Cl^-(aq)$$
$$\text{ethanoic acid:} \qquad CH_3COOH(aq) \rightleftharpoons H^+(aq) + CH_3COO^-(aq)$$

A single arrow, as in the hydrochloric acid equation, shows that *all* the HCl has formed H⁺ and Cl⁻ ions in aqueous solution. The arrows in opposite directions for ethanoic acid show that some of the CH_3COOH molecules have formed H⁺ and CH_3COO^- ions, but most of it remains as CH_3COOH molecules.

- **Strong acids** are *completely* ionised in water.
- **Weak acids** are *only partly* ionised in water.

Concentration is not the same as strength

Notice the difference between the terms 'concentration' and 'strength'.

- **Concentration** tells us how much solute is dissolved in solution, and we use the words 'concentrated' and 'dilute'.
- **Strength** tells us the extent to which the acid is ionised and we use the words 'strong' and 'weak'.

We can distinguish between strong and weak acids by using the pH scale or by their rate of reaction with metals.

Figure 14.6 Formic acid is used to descale kettles. Notice the 'CORROSIVE' hazard label. Formic acid is a weak acid. Why is hydrochloric acid not used as a descaler?

STUDY QUESTIONS

1 Look carefully at Figure 14.3.
   a) Over what range of pH does methyl orange change colour?
   b) What colour is methyl orange in:
      i) dilute sulfuric acid
      ii) sodium hydroxide solution?
   c) What colour is phenolphthalein in:
      i) water
      ii) carbonic acid?
   d) A solution is colourless in phenolphthalein but yellow in methyl orange. What is its approximate pH?

2 Make a table to summarise the properties and chemical reactions of acids.

3 a) Why can vinegar (which contains ethanoic acid) be used to descale kettles?
   b) Why is sulfuric acid *not* used to descale kettles?
   c) Classify vinegar (1.0 M CH_3COOH) and battery acid (4.0M H_2SO_4) as:
      i) concentrated or dilute
      ii) strong or weak.

4 a) What part does water play in acidity?
   b) Why does dry HCl gas not act like an acid?
   c) What is an acid?

5 Write word equations and balanced equations for the following reactions:
   a) iron + sulfuric acid
   b) aluminium + hydrochloric acid
   c) sodium oxide + sulfuric acid
   d) zinc oxide + hydrochloric acid
   e) copper oxide + nitric acid
   f) copper carbonate + hydrochloric acid.

6 Concentrated sulfuric acid is 12.0 M. Acid in car batteries (battery acid) is 4.0 M sulfuric acid.
   a) What is the concentration of battery acid in:
      i) moles per dm^3
      ii) grams per dm^3
      of H_2SO_4?
   b) Battery acid can be made by diluting concentrated sulfuric acid with water. How much concentrated sulfuric acid and how much water are needed to make 6 dm^3 of battery acid?

2.15 Neutralisation

Adverts for indigestion cures usually mention 'acid stomach' or 'acid indigestion'. Medicines which ease stomach ache (such as Milk of Magnesia, Rennies and Gaviscon) are called antacids because they neutralise excess acid in the stomach.

- Substances which neutralise acids are called **bases**.
- Bases which are soluble in water are called **alkalis**.
- The reactions between acids and bases are called **neutralisations**.

The bases in indigestion tablets include magnesium hydroxide and calcium carbonate.

■ Examples of neutralisation

Making fertilisers such as ammonium nitrate ('Nitram')

This is a very important industrial application of neutralisation. Ammonium nitrate is manufactured by neutralising nitric acid (HNO_3) with ammonia (NH_3).

Dental care

Toothpaste neutralises the acids produced when food breaks down in the mouth (Figure 15.2). These acids react with the enamel on teeth when the pH falls below 5.5.

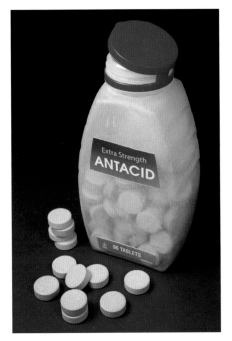

Figure 15.1 What substances in an antacid help to neutralise acids in the stomach?

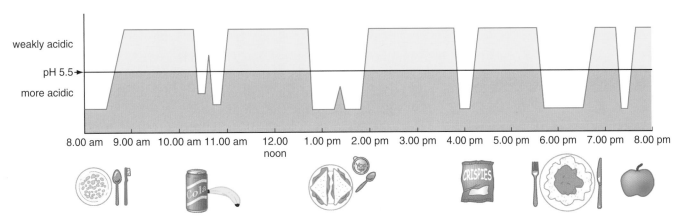

Figure 15.2 This shows how the pH in your mouth changes during the day. Notice how the pH becomes lower and more acidic during and just after meals. This is because sugars in your food are broken down into acids. These acids react with tooth enamel when the pH falls below 5.5.

Treating stings from plants and animals

The stings from certain plants and animals contain acids or bases, so they can be treated by neutralisation. For example, nettle stings and wasp stings contain complex bases like histamine. They are treated with acidic substances called antihistamines. Unlike wasp stings, bee stings are acidic. So, they are treated with bases.

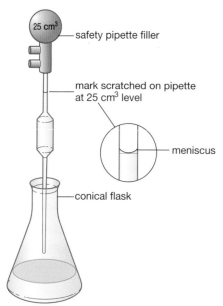

25 cm³ — safety pipette filler

mark scratched on pipette at 25 cm³ level

meniscus

conical flask

Figure 15.3 Measure 25.0 cm³ of 1.0 mol / dm³ NaOH(aq) using a pipette, showing correct use of the mark.

Table 1

Volume of 1.0 mol / dm³ HCl(aq) added in cm³	Colour of indicator
0	pink
5.00	pink
10.00	pink
15.00	pink
20.00	pink
21.00	pink
22.00	pink
23.00	pink
24.00	pale pink
25.00	colourless
26.00	
27.00	
28.00	
29.00	
30.00	

How much acid and base react?

When an acid is neutralised by a base, the pH of the solution changes. We can follow this pH change using an indicator to find out how much base just reacts with the acid to produce a neutral salt solution.

This method of adding one solution from a burette to another solution in order to find out how much of the two solutions will *just* react with each other is called a **titration**. When the two solutions just react and neither is in excess, we have found the **end point** of the titration.

How to carry out a titration

In this titration experiment, we will use phenolphthalein to determine how much hydrochloric acid just reacts with 25 cm³ of sodium hydroxide solution of concentration 0.1 mol / dm³. Eye protection must be worn for this experiment.

Before starting any titration you should:

- rinse the pipette with some of the solution to be used in it, and discard the rinsing.

- rinse the burette with some of the solution to be used in it, and discard the rinsing.

When taking measurements of the volume of a solution with the pipette and burette the surface of the solution inside the glass tube will form a curve as shown in fig 15.3 and 15.4. The volume is measured when the middle of the curve is exactly on the mark on the pipette or the graduation of the burette as shown in both diagrams.

1 Measure 25.0 cm³ of sodium hydroxide solution containing 0.1 mol / dm³ (0.1 M NaOH(aq)) into a conical flask using a pipette (Figure 15.3).
2 Add 3 drops of phenolphthalein and note the colour.
3 Place the conical flask on a white tile, so you can see the colour of the phenolphthalein indicator clearly. This will help you see exactly when the indicator turns colourless as the titration happens.
4 Add 5.00 cm³ of 0.1 mol / dm³ hydrochloric acid from a burette (Figure 15.4), mix well and record the colour again.
5 Record the colour also when 10.00, 15.00 and 20.00 cm³ of hydrochloric acid have been added.
6 Now add 1.00 cm³ of hydrochloric acid and record the colour again. Keep adding a further 1.00 cm³ of hydrochloric acid until the solution becomes colourless.
7 You now know roughly where the end point of the titration will be. This is a rough titration. Repeat the titration, only this time quickly add the hydrochloric acid until you are within 3.00 cm³ of your rough titration volume of hydrochloric acid.
8 Add more acid a drop at a time until the solution becomes colourless. Record the volume used to neutralise the sodium hydroxide. You should repeat the titration until you have obtained at least two values (titres) that are within 0.20 cm³ of one another. You should then calculate the mean of these results. Titres that are within 0.2 cm³ of one another are said to be **concordant**.

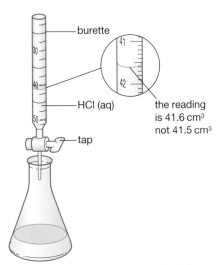

Figure 15.4 Adding 0.1 mol / dm³ HCl from a burette to 25.0 cm³ of 0.1 mol / dm³ NaOH.

Table 1 shows the results that you should get. Notice that the indicator is colourless when 25.00 cm³ of hydrochloric acid has been added. So, 25.00 cm³ of 0.1 mol / dm³ hydrochloric acid just neutralise 25.0 cm³ of 0.1 mol / dm³ sodium hydroxide.

∴ 0.0025 mol of HCl react with 0.0025 mol of NaOH

⇒ 1 mol of HCl reacts with 1 mol of NaOH

We can write the left-hand side of the reaction equation as:

$$HCl(aq) + NaOH(aq) \rightarrow$$

If all the water in the end-point solution is evaporated, the only product which remains is sodium chloride, NaCl(s). The complete equation is therefore:

$$HCl(aq) + NaOH(aq) \rightarrow NaCl(aq) + H_2O(l)$$

∴ 1 mol of HCl reacts with 1 mol of NaOH to give 1 mol of NaCl and 1 mol of H_2O.

Substances like sodium chloride which form when acids react with bases are called **salts**. Sodium chloride is usually known as common salt. Other important salts include copper sulfate ($CuSO_4$), potassium chloride (KCl) and ammonium nitrate (NH_4NO_3).

■ Naming salts

Look at Table 2. This shows how the name of a salt comes from its parent base and acid. So, magnesium oxide and nitric acid would produce magnesium nitrate.

Acids with names ending in '**–ic**' form salts with names ending in '**–ate**'. (Hydrochloric acid is an exception – its salts are called chlorides.)

Table 2 The names of salts.

Base	Name of salt
magnesium oxide	magnesium–
potassium hydroxide	potassium–
zinc oxide	zinc–

Acid	Name of salt
sulfuric	–sulfate
nitric	–nitrate
carbonic	–carbonate
hydrochloric	–chloride

STUDY QUESTIONS

1 **a)** What causes indigestion?
   b) How do indigestion cures like Rennies work?
2 Design an experiment to find out which indigestion tablets are the best at neutralising acid.
3 Copy and complete the following.
   a) magnesium oxide + sulfuric acid → ____ + ____
   b) potassium hydroxide + ____ →
       ____ nitrate + water
   c) ____ + hydrochloric acid → zinc ____ + ____

4 Explain the meaning of the following:
   base, indicator, titration, end point
5 30 cm³ of 2.0 mol / dm³ NaOH *just* reacts with 10 cm³ of 3.0 mol / dm³ H_2SO_4.
   a) How many moles of NaOH react?
   b) How many moles of H_2SO_4 react?
   c) How many moles of NaOH react with 1 mole of H_2SO_4?
   d) Write an equation for the reaction.

2.16 Bases and alkalis

The compounds shown in Figure 16.1 are all bases, but two of them are alkalis. How do we know which is which, and what is the difference?

Figure 16.1 White sodium oxide, green copper carbonate, black copper(II) oxide and white calcium hydroxide are all bases, but two are also alkalis.

■ Bases

> **Bases** are substances which neutralise acids. They accept the protons that acids donate. Bases are **proton acceptors**. They are the chemical opposites of acids.

The largest group of bases are metal oxides, hydroxides and carbonates, such as sodium oxide, copper(II) oxide, sodium hydroxide and copper carbonate.

■ Alkalis

> A special sub-set of bases are called **alkalis**. Alkalis are bases that are soluble in water. Their solutions have a pH above 7. They turn litmus blue and give a green, blue or purple colour with universal indicator. As alkalis neutralise acids by accepting an acid's proton, then they too are **proton acceptors.**

The most common alkalis are sodium hydroxide (NaOH), calcium hydroxide ($Ca(OH)_2$) and ammonia (NH_3). Calcium hydroxide is much less soluble than sodium hydroxide. A solution of calcium hydroxide in water is often called 'limewater'. Sodium oxide (Na_2O), potassium oxide (K_2O) and calcium

PRACTICAL

Generally, alkalis are more dangerous to the eyes than acids of the same concentration.
So, you must **always wear eye protection when using alkalis.**

oxide (CaO) react with water to form their hydroxides. So, the reactions of these three metal oxides with water produces alkalis. For example:

$$Na_2O(s) + H_2O(l) \rightarrow 2NaOH(aq)$$

$$CaO(s) + H_2O(l) \rightarrow Ca(OH)_2(aq)$$

Most other metal oxides and hydroxides are insoluble in water. These insoluble metal oxides and hydroxides are bases but *not* alkalis.

Like acids, alkalis can be classified by the extent of their ionisation in water.

- **Strong alkalis**, such as sodium hydroxide and calcium hydroxide, are completely ionised in water, for example:

$$NaOH(aq) \rightarrow Na^+(aq) + OH^-(aq)$$

- **Weak alkalis**, such as ammonia, are only partly ionised in water:

$$NH_3(aq) + H_2O(l) \rightleftharpoons NH_4^+(aq) + OH^-(aq)$$

All alkalis dissolve in water to produce hydroxide ions, OH^-. This has led to alkalis being defined as sources of hydroxide ions.

More about acids, bases and neutralisation

During the 19th century it was suggested that acids were substances which split up into ions (ionised) in water to produce hydrogen ions, H^+.

For example: $\qquad HCl \rightarrow H^+ + Cl^-$

At the same time, it was suggested that bases were substances which reacted with H^+ ions from acids to form water. For example:

base	+	**acid**	$\rightarrow$	**salt**	+	**water**
sodium hydroxide	+	hydrochloric acid	$\rightarrow$	sodium chloride	+	water
$NaOH(aq)$	+	$HCl(aq)$	$\rightarrow$	$NaCl(aq)$	+	$H_2O(l)$
copper oxide	+	sulfuric acid	$\rightarrow$	copper sulfate	+	water
$CuO(s)$	+	$H_2SO_4(aq)$	$\rightarrow$	$CuSO_4(aq)$	+	$H_2O(l)$

According to this theory, bases contained either oxide ions (O^{2-}) like copper oxide, or hydroxide ions (OH^-) like sodium hydroxide. During neutralisation, these ions react with H^+ ions in the acids to form water.

$$2H^+ + O^{2-} \rightarrow H_2O$$

So neutralisation can be summarised as the reaction of hydrogen ions from the acid with hydroxide ions from the base.

$$H^+(aq) + OH^-(aq) \rightarrow H_2O(l)$$

These ideas helped chemists to understand neutralisation and to see that bases were the chemical opposites of acids.

More recent definitions are that:

Acids are substances which donate H^+ ions and bases are substances which accept H^+ ions.

Using these definitions, carbonates can also be classified as bases by accepting H^+ ions.

$$CO_3^{2-} + 2H^+ \rightarrow CO_2 + H_2O$$
$$\text{carbonate} \quad \text{acid} \quad \text{carbon dioxide} \quad \text{water}$$

And the reaction between hydrogen chloride gas and ammonia gas is also an acid–base reaction.

$$HCl(g) + NH_3(g) \rightarrow NH_4^+Cl^-(s)$$

In this reaction, HCl has donated H^+ to NH_3 forming NH_4^+ and Cl^- ions.

So, these last two reactions are clearly acid–base reactions.

STUDY QUESTIONS

1 Suppose your best friend has missed the last few lessons on acids, bases and salts. How would you explain to him or her what the difference is between:
   a) acids and bases
   b) bases and alkalis
   c) bases and salts?

2 Explain the following:
   a) All alkalis are bases, but all bases are *not* alkalis.
   b) Limestone, slaked lime and quicklime are all bases, but only slaked lime is an alkali.

3 Write word equations and then balanced equations for the following reactions:
   a) the reaction of quicklime (calcium oxide) with water
   b) the reaction of zinc oxide with hydrochloric acid.

4 The labels on a tray of acids and alkalis have fallen off the bottles.
   a) Using only a pipette and a lump of calcium carbonate, describe how you could separate the acids from the alkalis.
   b) Write a balanced chemical equation for the reaction of the calcium carbonate with the hydrochloric acid.

5 A neutralisation reaction between any acid and any base or alkali can be written as:

$$H^+(aq) + OH^-(aq) \rightarrow H_2O(l)$$

Explain why this equation can be used to summarise the neutralisation reaction.

2.17 Salts

Across the world sodium chloride or 'salt' is obtained for our use. Sodium chloride is just one of an enormous number of compounds that chemists refer to as *salts*.

Figure 17.1 Sea salt is one example of common salt, sodium chloride.

What are salts?

Salts are formed when acids react with metals, bases or carbonates. Most salts contain a positive metal ion and a negative ion composed of one or two non-metals.

Salts have properties in common. They:

- are ionic compounds
- have high melting points and boiling points
- are electrolytes
- are often soluble in water.

Commonly occurring salts

The best known salt is sodium chloride, NaCl, which is often called 'common salt'. Many ores and minerals are composed of salts. These include chalk and limestone (calcium carbonate), gypsum (calcium sulfate) and copper pyrites ($CuFeS_2$).

Salt crystals, like those of sodium chloride, are often formed by crystallisation from aqueous solution. When this happens, water molecules sometimes form part of the crystal structure. This occurs in Epsom Salts ($MgSO_4.7H_2O$), gypsum ($CaSO_4.2H_2O$) and washing soda ($Na_2CO_3.10H_2O$). The water which forms part of the crystal structure is called **water of crystallisation**. Salts containing water of crystallisation are called **hydrates** or hydrated salts.

Figure 17.2 Purple cubic crystals of fluorite (calcium fluoride). Calcium fluoride is a salt. It is added to toothpaste so that we take in small amounts of fluoride. This helps to make our teeth and bones stronger.

Soluble and insoluble salts

If you are using a salt or making a salt, it is important to know whether it is soluble or insoluble.

163

Table 1 shows the solubilities of various salts in water at 20 °C. Notice the wide range in solubilities, from silver nitrate (217 g per 100 g water) to silver chloride (0.000 000 1 g per 100 g water).

Table 1 The solubilities of various salts.

Salt	Formula	Solubility (g per 100 g water at 20 °C)
barium chloride	$BaCl_2$	36.0
barium sulfate	$BaSO_4$	0.000 24
calcium fluoride	CaF_2	0.0018
calcium chloride	$CaCl_2$	74.0
calcium sulfate	$CaSO_4$	0.21
copper(II) sulfate	$CuSO_4$	20.5
lead(II) sulfate	$PbSO_4$	0.004
lead (II) nitrate	$Pb(NO_3)_2$	86.0
silver chloride	$AgCl$	0.000 000 1
silver nitrate	$AgNO_3$	217.0
sodium chloride	$NaCl$	36.0
sodium nitrate	$NaNO_3$	87.0

It is useful to divide salts into two categories – soluble and insoluble. Salts with a solubility greater than 1 g per 100 g water are classed as soluble; salts with a solubility less than 1 g per 100 g water are classed as insoluble.

Table 2 summarises the general rules for the **solubilities of common salts**.

Table 2 General rules for the solubilities of common salts.

all	sodium potassium ammonium	salts are soluble	
all	nitrates	are soluble	
all	sulfates	are soluble except	$CaSO_4$ $BaSO_4$, $PbSO_4$
all	chlorides	are soluble except	$AgCl$, $PbCl_2$
all	carbonates	are **insoluble** except those of	Na^+, K^+ and NH_4^+

The solubility of hydroxides is not included in Table 2 as they are bases. It is helpful to know that all hydroxides are insoluble except for sodium, and potassium. Calcium hydroxide is only slightly soluble.

You could try to predict if a salt is soluble and then make the salt to test your prediction. Choose an acid, then choose an alkali and name the salt they should form. For example, sulfuric acid and potassium hydroxide should make potassium sulfate. Now look at Table 2 and decide if potassium sulfate will be soluble or insoluble. Finally, mix equal volumes of the acid and alkali solutions together. If the salt is soluble there will be no precipitate, while an insoluble salt will precipitate out.

■ Preparing insoluble salts

The method used to prepare a salt depends on whether the salt is soluble or insoluble. Methods of preparing soluble salts are described in the next chapter. Insoluble salts, like lead chloride, silver chloride, calcium carbonate and barium sulfate, are prepared by **precipitation** – making the salt as a precipitate. If the solutions (or the insoluble salt) are hazardous, such as most lead, barium and silver salts, eye protection should be worn.

Preparing a sample of pure dry lead(II) sulfate

There are several things to consider when trying to make an insoluble salt such as lead(II) sulfate.

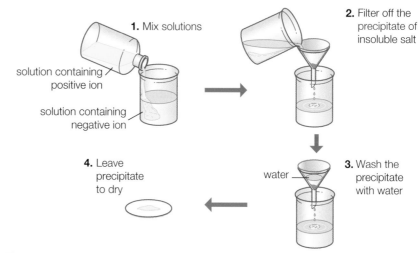

Figure 17.3 Preparing an insoluble salt.

How should the lead ions be obtained? Lead is low in the reactivity series and will not react directly with an acid such as sulfuric acid. Even if it did react, then the lead sulfate produced would coat the metal and prevent the reaction occurring. You need to use a soluble lead compound. There are only a few soluble lead compounds, but lead nitrate is one. To make a sulfate you need to provide a source of sulfate ions. The easiest source of sulfate ions is to use sulfuric acid. This is the reaction:

$$Pb(NO_3)_2(aq) + H_2SO_4(aq) \rightarrow PbSO_4(s) + 2HNO_3(aq)$$

Unfortunately this reaction produces nitric acid. A safer method would be to use sodium sulfate solution.

$$Pb(NO_3)_2(aq) + Na_2SO_4(aq) \rightarrow PbSO_4(s) + 2NaNO_3(aq)$$

Figure 17.3 shows the method.

Wear eye protection.

1 Mix $25\,cm^3$ of $1\,mol\,/\,dm^3$ lead(II) nitrate solution with $25\,cm^3$ of $1\,mol\,/\,dm^3$ sodium sulfate solution and stir.

2 Filter the mixture to separate the lead sulfate precipitate.

3 Whilst the filter paper is still in the filter funnel wash the precipitate thoroughly with de-ionised water.

4 Place the filter paper with the precipitate of lead sulfate in a warm oven to dry.

Great care should be taken with all lead compounds as they are toxic. If soluble lead(II) nitrate is not available, then lead(II) oxide can be dissolved in warm nitric acid using the method described in the next chapter (see Figure 18.2). After filtering (step 2 in Figure 18.2), this method will make a solution of lead(II) nitrate.

You could calculate your percentage yield for preparing lead sulfate.

1 Calculate the number of moles of lead nitrate in $25\,cm^3$ of $1\,mol\,/\,dm^3$ solution.

2 Looking at the balanced equation, 1 mole of lead nitrate makes 1 mole of lead sulfate. Using the number of moles of lead nitrate you used, work out the mass of this number of moles of lead sulfate. This is the theoretical yield.

3 Weigh the mass of lead sulfate you made in your experiment. This is the actual yield.

4 Use this equation to find the percentage yield:

$$\text{Percentage yield} \quad = \quad \frac{\text{actual yield}}{\text{theoretical yield}} \quad \times \quad 100$$

STUDY QUESTIONS

1 Explain the following terms: *hydrated, water of crystallisation, precipitation, insoluble.*

2 What units are used for:
   a) concentration
   b) solubility?

3 a) Summarise the stages in preparing an insoluble salt.

   b) Describe how you would prepare a pure sample of insoluble barium sulfate.
   c) Write an equation for the reaction which occurs.

4 Make a table to show whether the following salts are soluble or insoluble.
   $Pb(NO_3)_2$, $CuCO_3$, K_2SO_4, NH_4Cl, $FeSO_4$

5 Epsom Salts have the formula $MgSO_4.\,7H_2O$. What does this tell you about Epsom Salts?

2.18 Preparing soluble salts

Figure 18.1 The bright yellow substance in 'no parking' lines is lead chromate, an insoluble salt.

Lead chromate is used to paint yellow lines on roads as it is so bright. It is a salt that does not dissolve in water, unlike common salt or sodium chloride. Lead chromate is insoluble. It has to be, otherwise it would just wash off the road whenever it rained!

■ Soluble or insoluble?

When you are making a salt, the first question to ask is 'Is the salt soluble or insoluble?'.

> If the salt is **insoluble**, it is usually prepared by **precipitation**, described in the last chapter.
> If the salt is **soluble**, it is usually prepared by **reacting an acid with a metal, a base or a carbonate**.

$$metal + acid \rightarrow salt + H_2$$
$$base + acid \rightarrow salt + H_2O$$
$$carbonate + acid \rightarrow salt + CO_2 + H_2O$$

■ Preparing soluble salts

Method 1: Using metals, insoluble bases or insoluble carbonates

Figure 18.2 shows the main stages in this method.

REQUIRED PRACTICAL

This required practical relates to spec point 2.39. **Wear eye protection if you try any of the experiments in this chapter.**

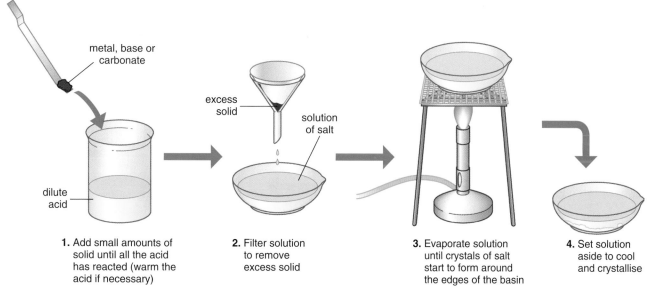

1. Add small amounts of solid until all the acid has reacted (warm the acid if necessary)

2. Filter solution to remove excess solid

3. Evaporate solution until crystals of salt start to form around the edges of the basin

4. Set solution aside to cool and crystallise

Figure 18.2 The preparation of soluble salts using metals, insoluble bases or insoluble carbonates

This method can be used to prepare a sample of pure hydrated copper(II) sulfate crystals from copper(II) oxide.

Wear eye protection.

1 Pour dilute sulfuric acid into a conical flask. Warm it gently, by standing the flask in a beaker of boiling water.
2 Add a spatula of copper(II) oxide to 25 cm³ of the warm dilute sulfuric acid.
3 Stir the solution until the copper(II) oxide has all reacted.
4 Add another spatula of copper(II) oxide and stir.
5 Continue adding copper(II) oxide until no more dissolves.
6 Use indicator paper to confirm that that there is no acid left, i.e. that the solution is neutral. If it is still acidic, you may need to warm the mixture gently so that the copper oxide continues to react. You may even need to add more copper oxide.
7 Filter the warm mixture into an evaporating basin.
8 Evaporate the contents of the basin until you see blue crystals appearing around the edge of the solution. Take care not to allow the solution to boil dry. If you see any fumes, switch off the Bunsen burner at once.
9 Put the basin and solution aside to cool.
10 When cold, filter the solution and allow the blue crystals to dry in a low temperature oven or the air.

Method 2: Using soluble bases (alkalis) or soluble carbonates

In method 1, we can tell when the acid has been used up because unreacted metal, base or carbonate remains in the liquid as undissolved, *insoluble* solid. When we use more of a substance such as copper oxide than is necessary to use up all the dilute sulfuric acid we say that we have used excess copper oxide. Using an excess of one substance means that all of the other substance used has reacted. There is none that is unreacted. To remove the excess copper oxide the mixture is filtered in part 5. But, if the base is *soluble* (like sodium hydroxide), we cannot tell when the acid has been used up because any excess solid will dissolve even after the acid has been neutralised. To get round this, we must use an indicator to tell us when we have added just enough base to neutralise the acid. Figure 18.3 shows the main stages involved.

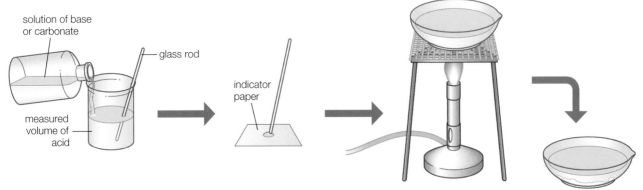

solution of base or carbonate

glass rod

measured volume of acid

indicator paper

1. Add base or carbonate a little at a time to the acid. Stir well
2. Check pH after each addition by transferring a drop of the solution to indicator paper
3. When the acid is just neutralised, evaporate the salt solution to crystallising point
4. Set solution aside to cool and crystallise

Figure 18.3 Preparing soluble salts using soluble bases or soluble carbonates. **Wear eye protection.**

Alternatively, a titration as shown in chapter 2.15, Figure 15.4 could be done. The burette would contain the acid.

- After finding the volume of acid required to neutralise 25cm³ of the alkali, then 25cm³ of fresh alkali would be mixed with the neutralising volume of acid.

- To obtain dry crystals of the salt you would boil the mixture and reduce the volume to one-third of the original volume, and allow to cool. Take care not to allow the solution to boil dry. If you see any fumes, switch off the Bunsen burner at once.

- When cool the salt crystals will be in the mixture and can be obtained by filtration and then drying in a warm oven.

Potassium chloride can be made by this method using hydrochloric acid with either potassium hydroxide or potassium carbonate.

$$KOH + HCl \rightarrow KCl + H_2O$$

$$K_2CO_3 + 2HCl \rightarrow 2KCl + CO_2 + H_2O$$

Method 2 is used to make the salts of sodium, potassium and ammonium because the bases and carbonates containing sodium, potassium and ammonium are all soluble. Other soluble salts are usually made by method 1.

Figure 18.4 on the next page is a flowchart showing how you can prepare a particular salt.

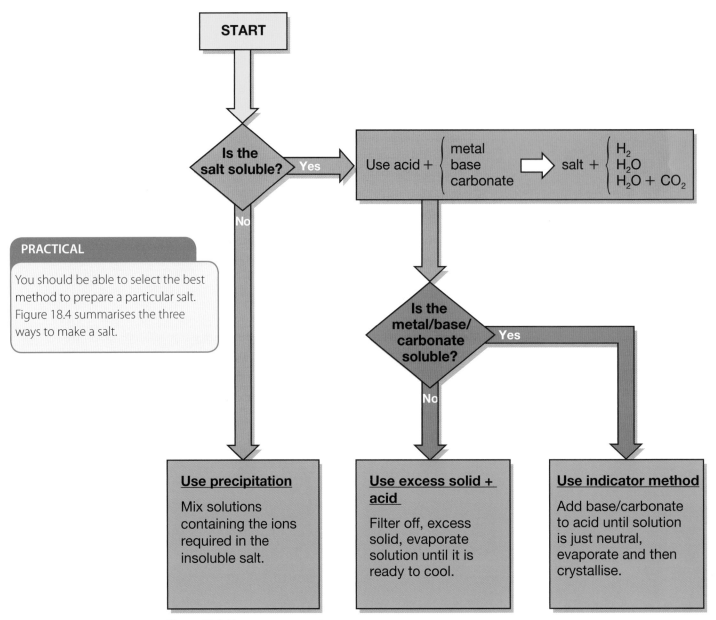

Figure 18.4 How to prepare a salt.

PRACTICAL

You should be able to select the best method to prepare a particular salt. Figure 18.4 summarises the three ways to make a salt.

STUDY QUESTIONS

1 Look at method 1 for preparing soluble salts (Figure 18.2).
   a) Why is this method not used with sodium?
   b) How can you tell when all the acid is used up if the solid is:
      i) zinc:
      ii) copper(II) oxide:
      iii) copper carbonate?
   c) Why is the salt produced not contaminated with:
      i) the acid used:
      ii) the solid added?
   d) Why is method 1 no good for insoluble salts?
   e) Why is method 1 no good if the solid added dissolves in water?

2 Look at method 2 for preparing salts (Figure 18.3).
   a) Why is the pH of the solution tested using indicator paper rather than putting indicator solution into the acid?
   b) Describe how you would make sodium nitrate by this method.
   c) Write a word equation and a balanced symbol equation for the reaction in (b).

2.19 Tests for ions, gases and water

Figure 19.1 In 2012 every Olympic medal winner was tested for banned performance-enhancing drugs.

Scientists need to be able to test substances to find out what they are. In sport, to make sure that competition for medals is fair, urine samples from athletes are tested to see if they contain performance-enhancing drugs that are banned. These tests are very sophisticated and more substances can be identified every year.

How do we identify simple compounds? We can identify different substances using tests for the atoms and ions in them. The best way to identify a substance is to find a property or a reaction which is shown only by that substance and is easy to see.

■ Testing for positive ions

Positive ions, or cations, can be tested for using three different methods. The method you choose depends on what you suspect the cation to be.

Flame tests

When substances are heated strongly, the electrons in them absorb extra energy. We say that the electrons are **excited**. The excited electrons soon release this excess energy as radiation and they become stable again. For some cations, the radiation is emitted as coloured light which colours the flame. The cations that produce these flame colours are listed in Table 1.

You can check the flame test for a potassium or a copper compound using the following method.

Wear eye protection. Dip a nichrome wire in concentrated hydrochloric acid and then heat it in a roaring Bunsen flame until it gives no colour to the flame. The wire is now clean. Dip it in hydrochloric acid again, and then in the substance to be tested. Heat the wire in a non-roaring, non-luminous Bunsen flame and note the flame colour.

Table 1 The flame colours from some cations.

Cation present in substance	Flame colour
K^+	lilac
Na^+	yellow
Li^+	red
Ca^{2+}	orange-red
Cu^{2+}	blue-green

PRACTICAL

This suggested practical relates to spec point 2.44. You need to know all the tests in this chapter and how to interpret the results from them.

Figure 19.2 Carrying out a flame test for potassium. **If you do a flame test, wear eye protection.**

Better flame tests

Chemists have developed special instruments called emission spectroscopes which can measure the wavelengths of radiation emitted during flame tests. This allows them to identify the substance under test. Emission spectroscopes enable chemists to identify certain ions very accurately and very rapidly, even when the amount of substance to be tested is very small.

Emission spectroscopes are used to monitor substances in the environment, in the water we drink and in the food we eat.

Using sodium hydroxide solution

Table 2 shows what happens when a little sodium hydroxide solution, NaOH(aq) is added to solutions of some common cations.

Table 2 Testing for cations with sodium hydroxide solution. **Wear eye protection**.

Cation in solution	3 drops of NaOH(aq) added to 3 cm³ of solution of cation
Fe^{2+}	a green precipitate of $Fe(OH)_2$ forms $Fe^{2+} + 2OH^- \rightarrow Fe(OH)_2$
Fe^{3+}	a brown precipitate of $Fe(OH)_3$ forms $Fe^{3+} + 3OH^- \rightarrow Fe(OH)_3$
Cu^{2+}	a blue precipitate of $Cu(OH)_2$ forms $Cu^{2+} + 2OH^- \rightarrow Cu(OH)_2$

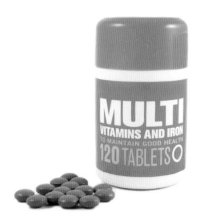

Figure 19.3 What tests would you carry out to see whether iron tablets contain Fe^{2+} or Fe^{3+} ions?

Testing for ammonium ions, NH_4^+

The ammonium cation, NH_4^+, can be identified by adding sodium hydroxide solution and then warming the mixture. If ammonium ions are present this produces ammonia gas (NH_3), which turns damp red litmus paper blue. **Wear eye protection**.

■ Testing for negative ions

Negative ions are sometimes referred to as anions. To identify anions successfully there are three different tests you can try. **Wear eye protection**.

Identifying compounds containing carbonates

Add a few drops of dilute hydrochloric acid to the substance you are testing. If it is a carbonate there will be a reaction. The compound will produce bubbles of clear odourless gas, which is carbon dioxide. To prove the gas contains carbon dioxide you should do the test for carbon dioxide described later in this chapter (page 174).

Identifying compounds containing sulfates

Add dilute hydrochloric acid to a solution of the substance. Then add barium chloride solution. If the substance contains sulfate (SO_4^{2-}), a thick white precipitate of barium sulfate ($BaSO_4$) forms.

$$Ba^{2+}(aq) + SO_4^{2-}(aq) \rightarrow BaSO_4(s)$$

Identifying compounds containing chlorides, bromides or iodides

Add dilute nitric acid to a solution of the substance. Then add silver nitrate solution.

■ Chlorides (Cl^-) give a white precipitate of silver chloride.

$Ag^+(aq) + Cl^-(aq) \rightarrow AgCl(s)$

■ Bromides (Br^-) give a cream precipitate of silver bromide.

$Ag^+(aq) + Br^-(aq) \rightarrow AgBr(s)$

■ Iodides (I^-) give a yellow precipitate of silver iodide.

$Ag^+(aq) + I^-(aq) \rightarrow AgI(s)$

In both the sulfate and halide tests, the acid is added to remove any carbonate ions that might produce a precipitate that would give a false-positive result.

■ Testing for gases

Hydrogen

Wear eye protection. Collect a sample of the gas you suspect is hydrogen in a test tube. Light a thin wooden splint and place the lighted splint into the test tube. If the gas is hydrogen you will hear a loud 'pop' as the hydrogen burns with oxygen from the air.

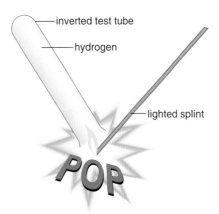

inverted test tube

hydrogen

lighted splint

POP

Figure 19.4 The 'pop' test for hydrogen.

Oxygen

Wear eye protection. Collect a sample of the gas you suspect is oxygen in a test tube. Light a thin wooden splint and blow it out. Place the glowing splint into the test tube. If the gas is oxygen the splint will burst into flame.

Carbon dioxide

Wear eye protection. Bubble the gas you suspect is carbon dioxide through some limewater. Figure 19.5 shows a metal carbonate reacting with dilute hydrochloric acid in the test for a carbonate. The suspected carbon dioxide is being bubbled through limewater. If the gas contains carbon dioxide the limewater will turn milky or cloudy white with a precipitate of calcium carbonate. If more carbon dioxide is bubbled through, then the limewater will become clear.

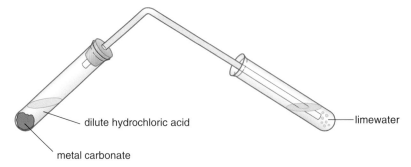

dilute hydrochloric acid

limewater

metal carbonate

Figure 19.5 Testing the gas released by a metal carbonate for carbon dioxide.

Ammonia and chlorine

Both ammonia and chlorine produce a reaction with damp litmus paper (or solution) and with universal indicator.

Wear eye protection. Bubble the gas through the solution, or direct the gas at the damp paper.

- If the gas contains ammonia red litmus paper or solution will turn blue. Universal indicator paper or solution will also turn blue.

- If the gas is chlorine blue litmus paper or solution will turn red and then be bleached. Universal indicator paper or solution will also turn red and then be bleached.

■ Testing for water

Testing that water is present

When blue copper(II) sulfate crystals are heated, steamy water vapour is given off and the blue crystals change to a white powder. Experiments show that the blue crystals contain both copper(II) sulfate and water combined together. Substances like this, which contain water as part of their structure, are described as hydrated, and we call them hydrates. So, blue copper(II) sulfate is often called hydrated copper(II) sulfate.

When the blue crystals are heated, they decompose, losing water vapour and leaving behind pure white copper(II) sulfate. This copper(II) sulfate without water is called anhydrous copper(II) sulfate.

$$\text{hydrated copper(II) sulfate} \underset{}{\overset{\text{heat}}{\rightleftharpoons}} \text{anhydrous copper(II) sulfate + water}$$
$$\text{(blue)} \qquad\qquad\qquad \text{(white)}$$

If water is now added to the white anhydrous copper(II) sulfate, synthesis takes place and blue hydrated copper(II) sulfate re-forms.

anhydrous copper(II) sulfate + water $\rightleftharpoons$ hydrated copper(II) sulfate
(white)   (blue)

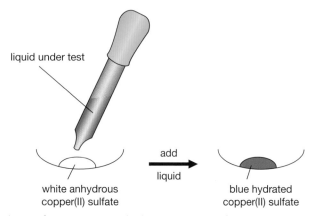

Figure 19.6 The test for water using anhydrous copper(II) sulfate.

This reaction provides a simple chemical test for water. Just add a little of any liquid to white anhydrous copper(II) sulfate and if it turns blue then water is present. But note that this test only indicates the presence of water. It does not mean that the liquid tested is pure water.

Testing if a liquid is pure water

Place a small sample of the liquid you suspect is water into a boiling tube with a thermometer. Heat the liquid until it boils and then measure its boiling point. If the boiling point is 100 °C then you can be sure the liquid is pure water.

1 a) How would you carry out a flame test on a sample of calcium carbonate
   b) What colour should the flame test give?
   c) Why must eye protection be worn during flame testing?
   d) What causes flame colours from certain cations?
2 a) A garden pesticide is thought to contain copper sulfate. Describe two tests that you would do to find out whether it contains Cu^{2+} ions.
   b) How would you show that the pesticide contains sulfate?
3 Sodium chloride and sodium iodide are both white crystals. You have two bottles of white crystals labelled X and Y. Describe how you would show that X

contained sodium chloride and Y contained sodium iodide.
4 You have a white powder you have been told is ammonium chloride.
   a) Describe how you could show that the compound contains both ammonium ions and chloride ions.
   b) When you heat a small sample of the white powder it gives off a gas. You think it may be chlorine gas. What test would you perform on the gas given off to find out if it is chlorine?
5 You have three unlabelled boiling tubes of gas. One tube contains hydrogen, the second oxygen, the third carbon dioxide. Describe how you can identify which tube has which gas in it.

Summary

I am confident that:

✓ **I know the positions of metals and non-metals in the Periodic Table and understand the meaning of groups and periods**

✓ **I understand why elements in the same group have similar chemical properties**
- The atoms of each element in a group has the same number of outer electrons.

✓ **I am able to classify elements as metallic or non-metallic, from:**
- Their electrical conductivity
- the pH of their oxides.

✓ **I can explain why the noble gases (Group 0) are unreactive**
- Their atoms do not easily lose, gain or share electrons.

✓ **I am able to describe the reactions of lithium, sodium and potassium:**
- with water
- with oxygen.

✓ **I can describe and explain the relative reactivity of the Group 1 elements**
- As the atoms get larger down the group, the distance of the outer electrons from the nucleus increases.
- There is a weaker attraction of the outer electron to the nucleus as the atom size increases.
- Therefore the outer electrons are more easily lost.

✓ **I know the physical states and colours of Group 7 elements, chlorine, bromine and iodine at room temperature, and can predict the properties of the other two halogens**

✓ **I can describe and explain the relative reactivity of the Group 7 elements**
- As the atoms get larger down the group, the distance of the outer electrons from the nucleus increases.
- There is a weaker attraction of extra electrons to the nucleus as the atom size increases.
- Therefore extra electrons are less easily gained.

✓ **I can describe and predict the result of halogen displacement experiments**
- A more reactive halogen element displaces a less reactive halogen from a solution of one of its salts.
- These reactions are redox reactions.

✓ **I know the percentage composition of gases in the air**

✓ **I can describe experiments to show the percentage volume of oxygen in the air**

✓ **I can describe the reactions of magnesium, carbon and sulfur with oxygen and the pH of the oxides formed**
- The pH of the oxide identifies the elements as metal or non-metal.

✓ **I know how some metal carbonates thermally decompose to make metal oxides and carbon dioxide gas**

✓ **I understand that carbon dioxide is a greenhouse gas and that it may contribute to global warming**

✓ **I can describe the reactions of dilute hydrochloric acid and sulfuric acid**
- with magnesium, aluminium, zinc and iron
- and can describe how to test the hydrogen gas they may produce in these reactions.

✓ **I can describe tests to show whether:**
- water is present in a liquid
- the liquid is pure water.

✓ **I can describe how the reactions of metals and their compounds can be used to make a reactivity series**
- The reactivity series of metals is: potassium, sodium, lithium, calcium, magnesium, aluminium, zinc, iron, copper, silver, gold.
- Displacement reactions between metals and their oxides, and between metals and their salts in aqueous solutions, determine the position of a metal in the reactivity series.
- I can explain how the method of metal extraction is related to the metal's position in the reactivity series. Metals high in the reactivity series are extracted by electrolysis. Metals lower in the reactivity series are extracted by reduction with carbon.
- I can describe the main features of the extraction of aluminium and iron. Aluminium uses electrolysis, with molten aluminium oxide dissolved in cryolite. Iron is extracted using coke and limestone in a blast furnace.

✓ **I can describe oxidation and reduction**
- Oxidation is the addition of oxygen, or the loss of electrons.
- Reduction is the removal of oxygen, or the gain of electrons.

- Reactions involving oxidation and reduction are known as redox reactions.
- The substance being reduced is the oxidising agent, and the substance being oxidised is the reducing agent.

✓ **I understand the conditions needed for rusting**
- Rusting of iron needs both water and oxygen to take place.
- The use of galvanizing and sacrificial metals in rust prevention is explained by the reactivity series.

✓ **I can describe tests and the positive results for cations:**
- Li^+, Na^+, K^+, Ca^{2+} using flame tests
- NH_4^+, Cu^{2+}, Fe^{2+}, Fe^{3+} using sodium hydroxide solution.

✓ **I can describe tests and the positive results for anions:**
- Cl^-, Br^-, I^- using silver nitrate solution and nitric acid
- SO_4^{2-} using barium chloride and hydrochloric acid
- CO_3^{2-} using hydrochloric acid and limewater.

✓ **I can describe tests and the positive results for these gases: hydrogen, oxygen, carbon dioxide, ammonia and chlorine**

Sample answers and expert's comments

1 Copper was first extracted by reduction from copper ores containing copper(II) carbonate in the Middle East. The copper(II) carbonate was heated in fires with wood charcoal to produce impure copper.

   a) Copy and complete the chemical equation. (2)

   $$\_\_\_\ CuCO_3(s) + C(s) \rightarrow _____ + _____$$

   b) Calculate the mass in grams of 1 mol of copper carbonate. (2)

   c) Use the equation to:

   i)   give the state of the carbon at the start (1)

   ii)   state the number, in moles, of carbon dioxide molecules released when 1 mol of copper is made (1)

   iii) calculate the mass of carbon dioxide released by the reaction of 1 mol of copper carbonate with carbon. (3)

   (Total for question = 9 marks)

Student response Total 8/9	Expert comments and tips for success
a) $2CuCO_3(s) + C(s) \rightarrow 2Cu(s) + 3CO_2(g)$ ✔✔	The formulae for the products are correct and the balancing is correct.
b) $CuCO_3$ i $63.5 + 12 + (3 \times 16)$ ✔ i 123.5 ✔	The formula is given in the question. 1 mark for correct substitution of relative atomic masses and 1 mark for correct addition.
c) i) solid ✔	The state symbol provided in the question gives the answer.
ii) 3 mols ○	This answer comes from the equation in part (a), but 3 mols of carbon dioxide are produced for every 2 mols of copper, not 1 mol of copper. Half the copper means half the carbon dioxide, so divide the 3 mols by 2 to get 1.5 mols.
iii) CO_2 is 44, ✔ so 3×44 ✔ i 132 g ✔	1 mark for correctly stating the relative formula mass of carbon dioxide as 44. The number of moles in part (c) ii) is wrong, but the error is carried forward. The working gains 1 mark for showing the 3 mols multiplied by the formula mass of CO_2. The final mark is gained for correct calculation. If you do not show your working, you will miss out on these marks.

2 A student wanted to make some copper(II) sulfate. Copper(II) sulfate is a soluble salt. The student had some copper(II) oxide and reacted it with dilute sulfuric acid.

a) Describe the steps needed for the student to obtain a pure neutral sample of copper(II) sulfate crystals. (4)

b) Describe how the student could obtain some dry copper(II) sulfate crystals from the copper(II) sulfate solution. (2)

c) Describe a chemical test the student could do to show that the crystals obtained contained sulfate ions. (3)

(Total for question = 9 marks)

Student response Total 7/9	Expert comments and tips for success
a) Heat 25 cm³ of dilute sulfuric acid in a beaker over a Bunsen burner. Add a spatula at a time of copper(II) oxide. ✔ Stir between each addition and keep adding until no more will dissolve ✔. The solution will look blackish, but the liquid will be blue. Filter the hot liquid, ✔ and place the filtrate in an evaporating dish. Heat until one-third is left, then allow to cool. ✔	This is the standard of answer you should aim for. You should remember there are three methods for making a salt. You either use precipitation for insoluble salts, and wash and filter the precipitate, titration for alkalis or react a solid with an acid. Metals, metal carbonates and metal oxides all react with the acid.
b) Filter to obtain the crystals. ✔	Filtering is correct but the question asked for dry crystals. Make sure you read the question carefully.
c) Add the crystals to some dilute hydrochloric acid and barium chloride solution. ✔ It should give a white precipitate. ✔	You need to remember all the steps in a test. For this test the crystal should first be dissolved, so 1 mark is lost.

Exam-style questions

1   Use the Periodic Table on page 273 to help you answer these questions.

   a) In 1869, Mendeléev produced a Periodic Table. His Periodic Table had the elements in order of increasing relative atomic mass.

   Find the elements potassium and argon in the Periodic Table.

   i) What problem is caused if relative atomic mass is used to place these elements in order?   [1]

   ii) How is this problem solved for potassium and argon in a modern Periodic Table?   [1]

   The table below gives information about some elements in Period 3 of the Periodic Table.

Element	Symbol	Electronic configuration	Formulae of chloride
sodium	Na		NaCl
magnesium	Mg	2, 8, 2	
aluminium	Al		AlCl$_3$
silicon	Si		SiCl$_4$
phosphorus	P		PCl$_5$

   b) There is a pattern in the electronic configurations of the elements in this period.

   i) Copy and complete the missing electronic configurations in the table.   [3]

   ii) What is the connection between the electronic configuration and the position of an element in the Periodic Table?   [1]

   c) There is a pattern in the formulae of chlorides in Period 3. State the formula for magnesium chloride.   [1]

   d) Potassium is in the same group of the Periodic Table as sodium.

   i) Write down the electronic configuration in a potassium atom.   [1]

   ii) Explain, in terms of electron structure, why potassium is more reactive than sodium.   [3]

2   a) Some of the properties of titanium are listed below.

   • It has a high melting point.
   • It is solid at room temperature.
   • It conducts electricity.
   • It is a good conductor of heat.
   • It forms coloured compounds.
   • It forms crystalline compounds.
   • It forms compounds that are catalysts.

   Select **three** properties, from the list, which are **not** typical of a Group 1 metal.   [3]

   b) 80 g of an oxide of titanium was analysed and found to contain 48 g of titanium. Calculate the empirical formula of this titanium oxide. Show your working. (Ti = 48, O = 16)   [4]

3   a) i) Describe what is seen when a small piece of sodium is dropped onto water.   [3]

   ii) Write a chemical equation for the reaction.   [2]

   iii) Give **one** observation that will be different if rubidium is used in place of sodium.   [1]

   b) Sodium reacts readily with oxygen to form the ionic compound sodium oxide.

   i) The diagram shows the electronic configuration of an atom of sodium and an atom of oxygen.

   Describe how sodium atoms and oxygen atoms form sodium ions and oxide ions.   [3]

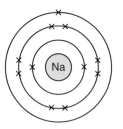 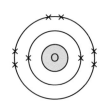

   ii) Sodium oxide has a melting point of 1275 °C. Explain why sodium oxide has a high melting point.   [3]

   iii) Magnesium oxide, MgO, has a melting point of 2852 °C. Suggest why magnesium oxide has a higher melting point than sodium oxide.   [2]

4 The diagram below summarises the reactions of sodium, an element in Group 1.

Products in the reactions are labelled, **X**, **Y** and **Z**.

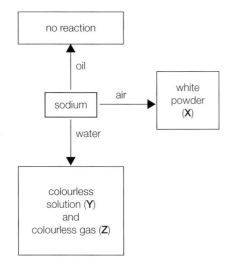

a) i) State the chemical names of the products **X**, **Y** and **Z**. [3]

ii) Copy, complete and balance the chemical equation for the reaction that occurs when sodium burns in air. Include state symbols.

.... Na + ... → .... Na₂O [2]

iii) Which reaction, in the diagram above, helps to explain why sodium is described as an alkali metal? Explain your answer. [2]

b) Explain, **in terms of electronic configuration**, why Group 1 elements become more reactive as relative atomic mass increases. [2]

5 This question is about the halogen elements in Group 7 of the Periodic Table.

The reactivity of the elements in Group 7 decreases down the group.

a) Write down the name and symbol of the **most** reactive element in Group 7. [1]

b) The table gives information about three elements in Group 7.

Element	Colour	Melting point in °C	Boiling point in °C	State at room temperature and pressure
chlorine	pale green	−101	−34	gas
bromine	red-brown	−7	60	liquid
iodine	dark grey	114	185	solid

Astatine (At) is in Group 7 of the Periodic Table. It is below iodine.

Use the information in the table above and your knowledge to answer the following questions.

i) Predict the state of astatine at room temperature and pressure. [1]

ii) Suggest a melting point for astatine. Explain your answer. [1]

iii) Predict the colour of astatine. [1]

iv) Suggest the name and formula of the compound formed by sodium and astatine. [2]

6 Use the Periodic Table on page 273 to help you answer this question.

a) Suggest the most reactive metallic element in the Periodic Table. [1]

b) Give the formula of the compound formed between sodium and the most reactive element in Group 7. [1]

c) All of the metals in Group 1 react with water. There are similarities between the reactions. Write out **three** of the following statements which apply to the reactions of **all** Group 1 metals with water.

- a flame is seen
- a solution of the metal hydroxide is formed
- a solution of the metal oxide is formed
- carbon dioxide is formed
- hydrogen is formed
- the metal sinks
- the solution formed is acidic
- the solution formed is alkaline. [3]

d) The elements in Group 0 were originally thought to be totally unreactive. However, in 1962 the first compound of xenon was made, but it was not until 2000 that the first compound of argon was made.

What does this order of discovery suggest about the trend in reactivity of the elements in Group 0? [1]

7 Air contains about 20% oxygen. When a fuel burns in air, it reacts with the oxygen. A student investigated the length of time a candle burns when it is covered by an upturned beaker. The diagram shows the apparatus she used.

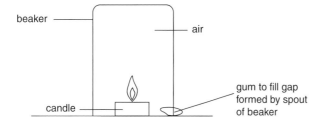

beaker

air

candle

gum to fill gap formed by spout of beaker

She repeated the experiment using different sizes of beaker.

a) Before she started the experiment, the student sketched a graph to show how she thought the length of time the candle would burn would depend on the volume of air in the beaker.

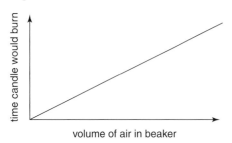

time candle would burn

volume of air in beaker

i)   Describe the relationship shown in her sketch graph.   [2]

ii) Suggest why she thought the graph was this shape.   [2]

iii) Why is it important to seal the spout of the beaker with gum?   [1]

The results the student obtained are shown in the table.

Beaker	Volume of air in beaker in cm³	Time for which candle burned in seconds			Mean time in seconds
		Run 1	Run 2	Run 3	
A	240	14	16	18	16
B	460	27	28	29	28
C	700	59	61	66	62
D	1020	68	69	73	70
E	1250	95	96	91	

b) Suggest a method the student could use to measure the volume of the beaker used in each run accurately.   [1]

c) Calculate the mean time for beaker E.   [1]

d) i) Draw a graph of the mean time for which the candle burned (vertically) against the volume of air in the beaker (horizontally).   [4]

ii) Which one of the points on your graph is anomalous?   [1]

iii) Suggest and explain what may have happened in the experiment to produce this anomalous point.   [2]

iv) The student was not sure whether or not the graph line went through (0, 0). What further practical work should she do to help her decide?   [1]

e) Another student repeats the experiment using pure oxygen in place of air. She finds the candle burns for about five times longer than when air is used.

i)   Explain why the candle burns about five times longer in pure oxygen than in air.   [1]

ii) Use your graph to help you calculate how long a candle would burn in a beaker containing 600 cm³ of oxygen. You must show your working.   [2]

8   a) i) What percentage of the air is oxygen?   [1]

ii) Write a word equation for the reaction which occurs when copper is heated strongly in air.   [1]

b) Copy and complete the table below to:

i)   name **two** gases present in the air other than oxygen

ii) give the percentage, by volume, of each of these gases present in a sample of unpolluted, dry air   [4]

Name of gas	Percentage in dry air

9   By observing their reactions with water and dilute sulfuric acid it is possible to put metals in order of their reactivity.

A, **B**, **C** and **D** are four metals.

Metal	Reaction with water	Reaction with dilute sulfuric acid
A	no reaction	reacts slowly
B	no reaction	no reaction
C	little reaction	reacts quickly
D	vigorous reaction	violent reaction

a) Put metals **A**, **B**, **C** and **D** in order of their reactivity from most reactive to least reactive. [3]

b) The metals used were copper, magnesium, sodium and zinc. Which of these metals was **A**, **B**, **C** and **D**? [3]

10 a) Chlorine is an element in Group 7 of the Periodic Table. Chlorine reacts with hydrogen to form hydrogen chloride gas. Hydrogen chloride gas dissolves in water to form hydrochloric acid.

  i) What common name is used for the elements of Group 7? [1]

  ii) Name an element in Group 7 that is a dark-coloured solid at room temperature. [1]

  iii) The table shows some information about chlorine, hydrogen chloride and hydrochloric acid.

  Copy and complete the table. [6]

Name of substance	Colour	State symbol	Effect on damp blue litmus paper
chlorine	pale green		
hydrogen chloride		g	
hydrochloric acid			paper turns red

b) A student adds chlorine to a solution of sodium bromide. The solution changes from colourless to orange.

  i) Write a word equation for the reaction that occurs. [1]

  ii) State the type of reaction that occurs. [1]

c) Another student adds bromine to a solution of sodium chloride. Why does no reaction occur? [1]

11 Most of the cans used for drinks are made from aluminium.

a) i) Aluminium is an element. What does this mean? [1]

  ii) Metals are malleable and this makes them suitable to make drinks cans. What is meant by 'malleable'? [1]

b) The reaction between aluminium and iron(III) oxide is used to join lengths of railway track. It is called the thermit reaction.

$$Fe_2O_3(s) + 2Al(s) \rightarrow Al_2O_3(s) + 2Fe(l)$$

  i) Why does aluminium react with iron(III) oxide [1]

  ii) What does the (l) after Fe in the chemical equation mean? [1]

  iii) Suggest why the thermit reaction can be used to join lengths of railway track. [1]

12 Use information from the table to answer this question.

	Name of metal	Colour of solid metal	Colour of a solution of the metal(II) sulfate
	magnesium	grey	colourless
	zinc	grey	colourless
	iron	dark grey	green
increasing activity	copper	pink-brown	blue

(increasing activity ↑)

a) When zinc is added to magnesium sulfate solution, no reaction occurs. Explain why. [1]

b) When iron filings are added to copper(II) sulfate solution, a reaction takes place.

  i) Write a chemical equation for this reaction. [2]

  ii) Describe the colour changes during this reaction:

    • colour change of solid [2]

    • colour change of solution. [2]

c) When copper is added to dilute sulfuric acid, no reaction occurs. When iron is added to dilute sulfuric acid, hydrogen gas and iron(II) sulfate solution are formed. What does this show about the reactivity of hydrogen compared to the reactivity of copper and the reactivity of iron? [2]

13 A student tests a solution to see if it contains CO_3^{2-} ions. The first part of the test involves this reaction:

$$2H^+(\ldots) + CO_3^{2-}(aq) \rightarrow H_2O(\ldots) + CO_2(\ldots)$$

a) One state symbol is given in the equation. Copy and complete the equation by writing the other state symbols in the spaces provided. [1]

b) Name a reagent that can provide the H^+ ions in the reaction. [1]

c) Give the name for each of the following formulae:

    i) CO_3^{2-} **ii)** CO_2 [2]

d) The second part of the test involves using $Ca(OH)_2$ to detect the CO_2.

    i) What is the chemical name for $Ca(OH)_2$? [1]

    ii) The $Ca(OH)_2$ is dissolved in water to make a solution when doing the test for CO_2. What is the common name for this solution? [1]

    iii) What is *seen* during the test for CO_2? [1]

    iv) Copy and complete the chemical equation for the reaction between these two substances:

$$Ca(OH)_2 + CO_2 \rightarrow \underline{\quad\quad} + \underline{\quad\quad}$$ [2]

14 A student has four solutions labelled **A**, **B**, **C** and **D**.

Each solution contains one compound from the following list.

    KNO_3 $FeCl_2$ $Fe(NO_3)_3$ $CuSO_4$ NH_4Cl

The student does some simple tests to identify the compounds present. The table shows the tests and observations.

Solution	Colour	Add sodium hydroxide solution	Add dilute nitric acid and silver nitrate solution
A	colourless	pungent gas given off	white precipitate
B	blue	blue precipitate	no change
C	colourless	no change	no change
D	green	green precipitate	white precipitate

a) i) What is the pungent gas formed by solution **A**? [1]

    ii) Which ion must be present in **A** for the white precipitate to form? [1]

    iii) Which ion must be present in **B** for the blue precipitate to form? [1]

    iv) Which ion must be present in **D** for the green precipitate to form? [1]

b) i) Which compound in the list can be identified using barium chloride solution? [1]

    ii) State **one** compound in the list than can be identified using a flame test. State the colour of the flame. [2]

c) Silver nitrate solution, $AgNO_3(aq)$, is added to a solution of lithium iodide, LiI.

    i) Describe what is seen. [1]

    ii) Write the chemical equation, including state symbols, for the reaction. [3]

15 a) Iron is produced by the reduction of iron(III) oxide with carbon making iron and carbon dioxide gas.

    i) Why is this reaction described as a reduction reaction? [1]

    ii) Explain why iron(II) oxide can be reduced to iron by carbon? [2]

b) Aluminium is another important metal. It is extracted by electrolysis.

    i) Unlike iron, aluminium cannot be extracted from its ore using carbon. Explain why it is extracted using electrolysis. [2]

    ii) State one large scale use of aluminium. Give a property of aluminium on which this use depends. [2]

16 Covellite (CuS) is a rare ore of copper. A student had a sample of covellite and wanted to make some copper from it. The flow chart shows what he did.

Stage 1: Powdered the ore

Stage 2: Heated the ore in lots of oxygen

Stage 3: Mixed the residue with lots of charcoal

Stage 4: Heated it strongly in a boiling tube

Stage 5: Allowed it to cool, before pouring out his copper sample.

a) Why did the student powder the ore? [1]

b) Complete the equation to show what happened in stage 2.

$$2CuS(s) + 3O_2\,(g) \rightarrow 2CuO(s) + 2\,\underline{\quad\quad}$$ [1]

c) What does stage 3 suggest about the reactivity of copper? [1]

d) In stage 4 the charcoal reacted with the copper(II) oxide and made copper. Name the gas given off. How would you test for it? [3]

e) When the student emptied the boiling tube there was only a black powder. Another student suggested that a better method would have been to tip the contents of the hot boiling tube (end of stage 4) into some cold water. Suggest why this would be more likely to produce some copper metal? [2]

17 Acids and bases are commonly found around the home.

a) Baking powder contains sodium hydrogencarbonate mixed with an acid.

 i) When water is added, the mixture reacts producing carbon dioxide. How could you show it is carbon dioxide? [2]

 ii) Copy out, complete and balance the chemical equation for the reaction of sodium hydrogencarbonate with sulfuric acid.

$$NaHCO_3 + H_2SO_4 \rightarrow \ldots + \ldots + \ldots$$ [2]

b) Indigestion tablets contain bases which cure indigestion by neutralising excess stomach acid.

 i) One type of indigestion tablet contains magnesium hydroxide. This base neutralises stomach acid by the following chemical equation.

$$Mg(OH)_2 + 2HCl \rightarrow MgCl_2 + 2H_2O$$

 Write a balanced ionic equation for the neutralisation reaction. [1]

 ii) How does the pH in the stomach change after taking the tablets? [1]

c) Ammonium sulfate is an important lawn fertiliser. Describe how you would prepare some ammonium sulfate using ammonia solution. [4]

18 a) A solution was made by dissolving 1.62 g of hydrogen bromide, HBr, in 250 cm³ of water.

 i) Calculate the relative formula mass of hydrogen bromide. (H = 1, Br = 80) [1]

 ii) Calculate the amount, in moles, of hydrogen bromide in a 1.62 g sample. [2]

 iii) Calculate the concentration, in mol / dm³, of the hydrogen bromide solution. [2]

 iv) Calculate the concentration, in g / dm³, of the hydrogen bromide solution. [2]

b) Hydrogen bromide solution can be neutralised by adding sodium hydroxide solution.

 A 20.0 cm³ sample of a solution of hydrogen bromide had a concentration of 0.200 mol / dm³.

 i) Write a chemical equation for this neutralisation reaction. [1]

 ii) Explain why this reaction is described as a neutralisation reaction. [2]

 iii) Calculate the amount, in moles, of hydrogen bromide in 20.0 cm³ of 0.200 mol / dm³ solution [2]

 iv) Calculate the volume of 0.100 mol / dm³ sodium hydroxide solution needed to neutralise this sample of hydrogen bromide solution. [2]

 v) Suggest the name of an indicator (other than litmus), and its colour change, that could be used to check when neutralisation was complete. [3]

19 a) Magnesium chloride is a soluble salt that can be made by reacting magnesium carbonate with dilute hydrochloric acid. Magnesium carbonate is insoluble in water.

 Describe how you could make a dry sample of magnesium chloride crystals from magnesium carbonate and dilute hydrochloric acid. [5]

b) 25.0 cm³ of dilute sulfuric acid are placed in a conical flask. A few drops of phenolphthalein indicator are added. The acid requires 8.70 cm³ of sodium hydroxide solution of concentration 0.150 mol / dm³ for neutralisation.

 The chemical equation for the reaction is:

$$H_2SO_4 + 2NaOH \rightarrow Na_2SO_4 + 2H_2O$$

 i) What colour change is seen when the acid is neutralised? [2]

 ii) Calculate the amount, in moles, of sodium hydroxide used. [2]

 iii) Calculate the amount, in moles, of sulfuric acid used. [1]

 iv) Calculate the concentration, in mol / dm³, of sulfuric acid. [1]

20 Calcium sulfate can be prepared using a precipitation reaction between calcium chloride solution and dilute sulfuric acid.

$$CaCl_2(aq) + H_2SO_4(aq) \rightarrow CaSO_4(s) + 2HCl(aq)$$

a) State **three** steps needed to produce a pure dry sample of calcium sulfate from the mixture formed in this reaction. [3]

b) A 5.55 g sample of calcium chloride ($M_r = 111$) is dissolved in water to make a solution.

  i) Calculate the amount, in moles, in the sample of calcium chloride. [2]

  ii) What amount, in moles, of sulfuric acid is needed to react completely with the calcium chloride solution? [1]

  iii) Calculate the relative formula mass of calcium sulfate.
  (Ca = 40, S = 32, O = 16) [1]

  iv) Calculate the mass, in grams, of calcium sulfate formed. [2]

c) The following equation represents a reaction used to prepare the salt lead(II) nitrate.

$$PbCO_3(s) + 2HNO_3(aq) \rightarrow Pb(NO_3)_2(aq) + H_2O(l) + CO_2(g)$$

In this experiment the amount of nitric acid used was 0.0400 mol.

  i) The concentration of the dilute nitric acid used was 0.500 mol / dm³. Calculate the volume, in cm³, of dilute nitric acid used. [3]

  ii) In this experiment, 0.0200 mol of carbon dioxide gas was produced. Calculate the volume, in cm³, that this amount of carbon dioxide occupies at room temperature and pressure (r.t.p.).

  (molar volume of any gas = 24 000 cm³ at r.t.p.) [1]

21 Potassium chloride can be prepared from potassium hydroxide solution and hydrochloric acid. A titration is used to find the volumes of the solutions which just react with each other. In this titration the hydrochloric acid is added to the potassium hydroxide solution.

a) Name the **two** items of equipment used to measure the volumes of solutions precisely in a titration. [2]

b) The reaction is complete when all the potassium hydroxide has been neutralised by hydrochloric acid. How can you tell this point is reached? [2]

c) The equation for the reaction is:

$$KOH + HCl \rightarrow KCl + H_2O$$

Calculate the maximum theoretical mass of potassium chloride which can be obtained from 16.8 g of potassium hydroxide.

(K = 39, O = 16, H = 1, Cl = 35.5) [4]

EXTEND AND CHALLENGE

Using trends in the Periodic Table

Dmitri Mendeléev used predictions when devising his Periodic Table. These predictions helped his version of the arrangement of the elements become accepted.

Mendeléev suggested that gaps should be left for elements that had not as yet been discovered. He made several predictions about these missing elements. His predictions were based on what was already known about other elements. At first his predictions were dismissed as guesses by other scientists.

Eka-silicon was the name given by Mendeléev to one undiscovered element. Table 1 gives some details about the elements surrounding eka-silicon that Mendeléev knew.

Table 1 Some data on elements near to eka-silicon in the Periodic Table.

silver-coloured solid metal mass 27	dark grey-coloured solid non-metal mass 28	white-coloured solid non-metal mass 31
dull silver-coloured metal mass 70	? eka-silicon	grey-coloured semi-metal mass 75
silver-coloured metal mass 115	silver-coloured metal mass 119	grey-coloured semi-metal mass 122

1 Use the trends shown by the information about the other eight elements to suggest:
   a) the colour of eka-silicon
   b) if eka-silicon is a metal, semi-metal or non-metal
   c) the possible atomic mass of eka-silicon.
2 Now use the Periodic Table to find the name of eka-silicon. You could check your predictions on the internet.

The chemical element astatine is a strange member of the halogen family of elements. Unlike fluorine, chlorine, bromine and iodine, all its isotopes are radioactive. As such it has very limited uses. Each radioactive isotope exists for only a few hours before changing into a different isotope of astatine or bismuth, polonium or radon. It has been estimated that at any moment there is no more than 30 g of astatine on Earth. It is produced by the radioactive decay of other elements.

Since there is so little astatine, and it is also radioactive, many of the properties of astatine were at first estimated.

The early investigators of astatine knew it was a halogen element. They knew the physical properties of the other halogens shown in Figure 1 and Table 2, and they used these to predict the likely properties of astatine.

Table 2 Some physical properties of the halogens

Element	Atomic number	Atomic mass	Melting point in °C	Boiling point in °C	Density in g / cm³
fluorine	9	19	53	85	1.1
chlorine	17	35.5	172	239	1.56
bromine	35	80	266	331	3.12
iodine	53	127	387	456	4.94
astatine	85				

Rather than guess, they plotted graphs of atomic number against each physical property, extrapolated (extended the trend line), and then read off the likely value for astatine (atomic number 85) from the graph.

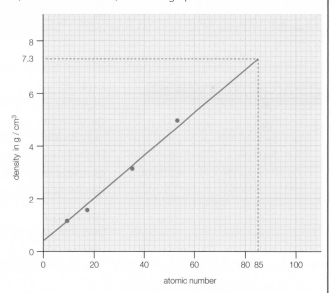

Figure 1 Graph of atomic number against density for the halogens.

3 Use graphs to estimate
   a) the atomic mass of astatine
   b) the melting point of astatine
   c) the boiling point of astatine.

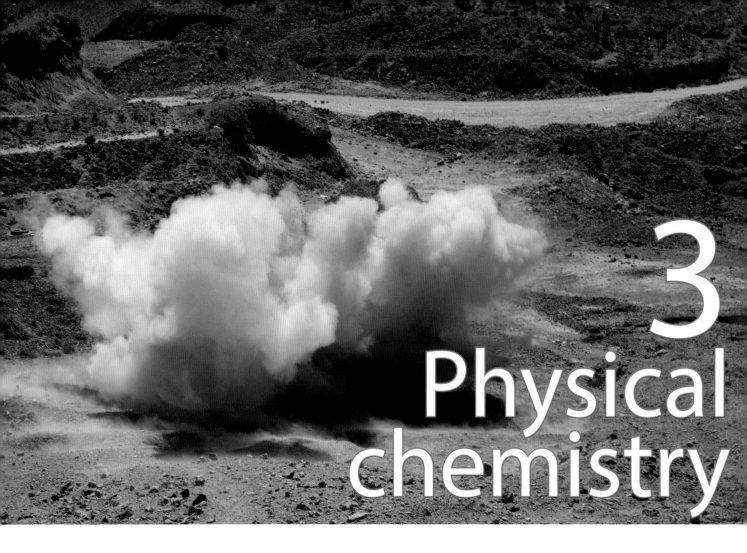

3
Physical chemistry

DISCUSS · PRESENT

1 Products for use around the home for cleaning often suggest that you soak the surface to be cleaned with the product before attempting to clean it. Suggest reasons why this is good for the manufacturer, the consumer and the environment.
2 Microwave cookers have several heat settings. Discuss with a friend why this is and how it can be used to control the chemical reactions in food when cooking.
3 The explosive used in the picture to break up the rock is placed into small holes that are then sealed up. Explain how this might make the explosion more effective.

Explosions are good examples of the use of reaction rates. Gunpowder can be either very destructive or just a disappointment. An open container of gunpowder when ignited just burns, producing some smoke, but if the gunpowder is ignited in a sealed container the effects are spectacular – the reaction happens in a very short time and is far more useful. So gunpowder can drive rockets into the sky, propel bullets and cannonballs a long way, or just do very little.

For many chemical reactions in industry, the rate of reaction is a critical factor in whether the process is competitive and can make the company money. 'How fast?' and 'How far?' are questions often asked about a chemical reaction.

By the end of this section you should:
· know that chemical reactions can produce heat energy, or need heat energy to occur, and how chemists describe these reactions
· know the factors that affect the rate of a reaction, and how they can be controlled
· understand that some reactions are reversible
· know that some reversible reactions make a mixture of products and reactants and are in equilibrium when the ratio of reactants to products becomes stable
· be able to predict how changes in temperature and pressure affect the ratio of reactants to products in an equilibrium.

3.1 Energy changes and enthalpy changes

Burning a fuel such as gas is a chemical reaction. The reaction of the gas with the oxygen in the air releases heat energy, which is the reason why the gas is burned. We do not need the carbon dioxide or water vapour made, just the heat energy. The study of heat energy changes during reactions is called *thermodynamics*, from *thermo* meaning heat and *dynamics* meaning changes.

Figure 1.1 Using the energy change of a chemical reaction to heat water.

■ Energy changes

The study of energy changes during chemical reactions is important. By measuring the energy changes that occur in chemical reactions, chemists can calculate the strength of chemical bonds.

The term 'system' is important in studying energy changes in reactions and it has a precise meaning. The 'system' means only the materials or the chemicals being studied. Everything around the system (the container, any other apparatus, the air in the laboratory, etc.) is called 'the surroundings'.

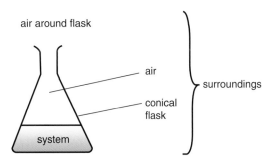

Figure 1.2 A system and its surroundings.

■ Exothermic and endothermic reactions

When chemical reactions occur, there is almost always a temperature change. The temperature change occurs because energy in the form of heat energy is either given out to the surroundings or taken in from the surroundings as the substances react.

Exothermic reactions

Most chemical reactions are **exothermic**, giving out heat energy to the surroundings as substances in the system react. Burning fuels are obvious examples of exothermic reactions. Fuels provide most of the heat and energy we use in our homes and industries. Respiration is another exothermic reaction, in which food substances are oxidised, providing the energy for living things to grow, move and keep warm.

Endothermic reactions

A smaller number of reactions take in heat energy from their surroundings and these are described as **endothermic** reactions. Melting is an obvious endothermic change (although not a chemical reaction), as heat energy is taken in by a substance as it changes from solid to liquid. Photosynthesis is an endothermic chemical change. In this reaction, plants take in energy (light) from the Sun in order to produce glucose from carbon dioxide and water.

Figure 1.4 shows the difference between exothermic and endothermic processes.

Figure 1.3 Hot packs in self-warming cans involve exothermic reactions.
The heat energy produced from a reaction in a separate sealed compartment heats up the contents.

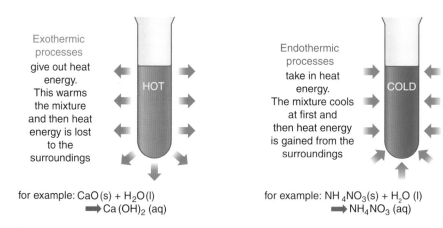

Exothermic processes give out heat energy. This warms the mixture and then heat energy is lost to the surroundings

for example: CaO (s) + H₂O (l) $\longrightarrow$ Ca (OH)₂ (aq)

Endothermic processes take in heat energy. The mixture cools at first and then heat energy is gained from the surroundings

for example: NH₄NO₃(s) + H₂O (l) $\longrightarrow$ NH₄NO₃ (aq)

Figure 1.4 Exothermic and endothermic processes.

When 1 mol of solid calcium oxide reacts with water to form a solution of calcium hydroxide, 1070 kJ of energy are given out. The system (solid calcium oxide + water) loses energy in the form of heat. At first, this warms the mixture well above room temperature. Then heat energy is lost to the surroundings, and the system (calcium hydroxide solution) cools down to room temperature. The reaction is exothermic.

When ammonium nitrate dissolves in water, the separation of the ammonium ion and nitrate ion requires energy. At first this causes the temperature of the solution to fall, then energy is taken in from the surroundings. This is an endothermic process.

■ Enthalpy changes and ΔH

The heat energy transferred between a system and its surroundings in a chemical reaction is described as an **enthalpy change**. Enthalpy means 'heat content' so an enthalpy change is a measure of the change in the heat content of reactants as they form products. The enthalpy change for a reaction is given the symbol ΔH and its units are kilojoules per mole (kJ / mol).

For an exothermic reaction, the sign of ΔH is *negative* because heat energy is *lost* to the surroundings when the temperature *rises* as a reaction takes place, and the products eventually come to the same temperature as the initial reactants.

For an endothermic reaction, ΔH is *positive* because the system needs heat energy for the reaction to occur; the temperature *drops* and the system *gains* heat energy from the surroundings.

Scientists use the Greek capital letter delta, Δ, for the change in a physical quantity. So, ΔH means change in enthalpy (heat content).

So, for the exothermic example in Figure 1.4 we can write:

$$CaO(s) + H_2O(l) \rightarrow Ca(OH)_2(aq) \qquad \Delta H = -1070 \, kJ / mol$$

And, for the endothermic example we can write:

$$NH_4NO_3 (aq) \rightarrow NH_4^+ (aq) + NO_3^- (aq) \quad \Delta H = +25 \, kJ / mol$$

When an enthalpy change relates to one mole of a particular reactant, as in the equations above, it is sometimes described as a **molar enthalpy change**. So the molar enthalpy change of solution for ammonium nitrate is $+25 \, kJ / mol$.

■ Energy level diagrams

The energy changes in chemical processes can be summarised in **energy level diagrams**. Figure 1.5 shows the energy level diagram for the reaction of calcium oxide with water. Heat energy is lost to the surroundings as the reactants form the product, so the product is at a lower energy level.

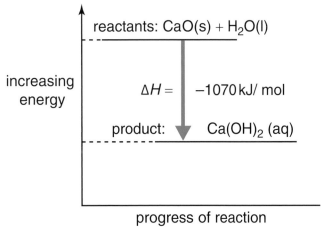

Figure 1.5 An energy level diagram for the reaction of calcium oxide with water.

Endothermic reactions take in heat energy from the surroundings, so the energy content of the products is greater than that of the reactants. This means that the products are at a higher energy level than the reactants in the energy level diagram for an endothermic process (Figure 1.6).

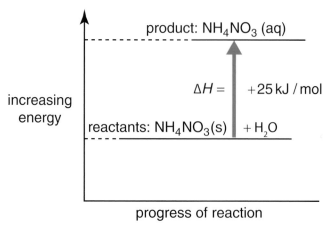

Figure 1.6 An energy level diagram for dissolving ammonium nitrate in water.

STUDY QUESTIONS

1 Which of the following changes are exothermic and which are endothermic?:
   a) boiling water
   b) burning coal,
   c) forming icicles.

2 When 1 mol of methane, CH_4, burns completely, 880 kJ of heat energy is given out.
   a) Write an equation for the reaction with state symbols and show the enthalpy change.
   b) Draw an energy level diagram for the reaction showing the enthalpy change.

3 The energy change for the manufacture of lime (CaO) from calcium carbonate ($CaCO_3$) can be written as:
   $CaCO_3(s) \rightarrow CaO(s) + CO_2(g)$ $\Delta H = +178$ kJ / mol
   a) Is the reaction exothermic or endothermic?

   b) Do the products contain more or less energy than the reactants?
   c) Draw an energy level diagram for the reaction.

4 When 1 g of carbon (charcoal) burns completely in a barbecue, 33 kJ of heat energy are produced.
   a) Write an equation for the reaction when carbon burns completely.
   b) How much heat energy is produced when 1 mol of carbon burns completely?
   c) What is the molar enthalpy change of combustion for carbon?
   d) Draw an energy level diagram for the reaction including the enthalpy change.

3.2 Measuring enthalpy changes

The amount of heat energy given out or taken in by a chemical reaction can be measured simply by recording the temperature change of the system. In Figure 2.1, however, the full temperature change is not being measured, as some energy has been lost to the surroundings. Scientists have devised sophisticated methods to reduce the heat losses to the environment, or to find out how much heat energy has been lost in this way.

■ Enthalpy changes of combustion

It is useful to know how much heat energy is produced when different fuels burn. Figure 2.2 shows the simple apparatus that can be used to measure the heat energy given out from a liquid fuel like ethanol.

In the experiment, we will assume that all the heat energy produced from the burning ethanol warms the water in the metal can. The results of one experiment are shown in Table 1.

Table 1 The results of an experiment to measure the heat energy produced when ethanol burns.

mass of burner + ethanol at start of experiment = 271.8 g	
mass of burner + ethanol at end of experiment = 271.3 g	
∴ mass of ethanol burned = 0.5 g	
volume of water in can = 250 cm³	
∴ mass of water in can = 250 g	
rise in temp. of water = 10 °C	

Figure 2.1 Measuring the temperature change of a chemical reaction.

The amount of energy released can be calculated using the formula:

$$Q = mc\,\Delta T$$

where Q = heat energy change

m = mass of substance

c = specific heat capacity of the substance and

ΔT = temperature change of the substance

This equation can also be written as:

energy change (J) = mass of water (g) × specific heat capacity of water (J / g / °C) × temperature rise (°C)

Calculating the enthalpy change of combustion

From the mass of water in the can (250 g), its temperature rise (10 °C) and its **specific heat capacity** (4.2 J / g / °C), we can work out the heat energy produced from the burning ethanol using the formula:

$$\text{heat energy produced (J)} = \text{mass of water (g)} \times \text{specific heat capacity (J / g / °C)} \times \text{temp. change (°C)}$$

So, heat energy produced = $250 \times 4.2 \times 10$

$$= 10\,500\,\text{J}$$

From the loss in mass of the liquid burner, we can find the mass of ethanol which has burned (0.5 g).

So, 0.5 g of ethanol produces 10 500 J of heat energy

$$\therefore \ 1\,\text{g of ethanol produces } 10\,500 \times \frac{1}{0.5} = 21\,000\,\text{J of heat energy, or } 21\,\text{kJ}$$

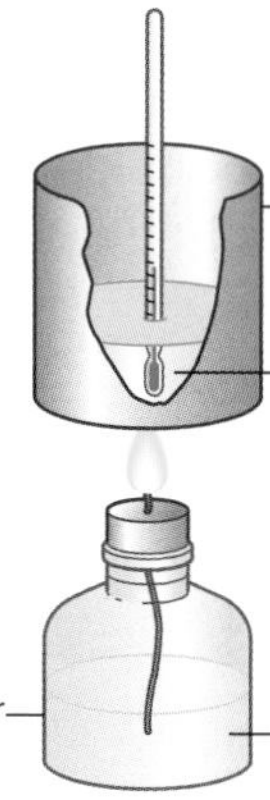

Ethanol has a relative formula mass of 46, so:

heat energy produced when 1 mol of ethanol burns = $46 \times 21\,\text{kJ} = 966\,\text{kJ}$

So we can write:

$$C_2H_5OH(l) + 3O_2(g) \rightarrow 2CO_2(g) + 3H_2O(l) \qquad \Delta H = -966\,\text{kJ / mol}$$

This means that the molar enthalpy change of combustion of ethanol is −966 kilojoules per mole.

If we know the mass of fuel burnt we can calculate how much heat energy is released per g of fuel burnt, or more usefully per mole of fuel burnt. This allows us to compare the heat energy released by different fuels. You could try this for a range of alcohols in Chapter 4.6 using this method.

Figure 2.2 Measuring the heat energy given out when ethanol burns. **Wear eye protection if you try this experiment** and remember that liquid fuels are highly flammable.

■ Enthalpy changes in solution

The enthalpy changes of reactions in solution can be measured using insulated plastic containers like the polystyrene cup in Figure 2.4. Polystyrene is ideal because it is an excellent insulator. Its specific heat capacity is also very low, which means that any heat energy lost or gained from the polystyrene cup can be ignored compared to that transferred to or from the reaction mixture.

If a reaction is exothermic very little heat energy escapes because polystyrene is such an excellent insulator. So, the heat energy produced warms up the reaction mixture. If a reaction is endothermic very little heat energy gets in from the surroundings, so it is taken from the reaction mixture which cools down.

If the solutions in the reaction mixture are dilute, the enthalpy changes can be calculated by assuming that the solutions have the same density and specific heat capacity as water. So, it can be assumed that 1 cm³ of each solution has a mass of 1 g and that 4.2 J raises the temperature of 1 g of solution by 1 °C (1 K).

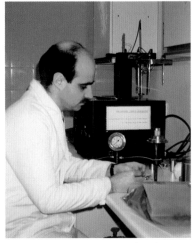

Figure 2.3 Scientists use bomb calorimeters like the one in this photo to measure the heat energy produced by different fuels and foods.

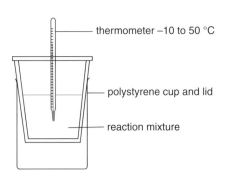

thermometer −10 to 50 °C

polystyrene cup and lid

reaction mixture

Figure 2.4 Measuring the enthalpy change for a reaction in solution.

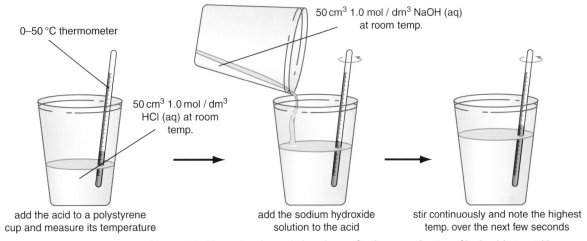

0–50 °C thermometer

50 cm³ 1.0 mol / dm³ HCl (aq) at room temp.

50 cm³ 1.0 mol / dm³ NaOH (aq) at room temp.

add the acid to a polystyrene cup and measure its temperature

add the sodium hydroxide solution to the acid

stir continuously and note the highest temp. over the next few seconds

Figure 2.5 Measuring the enthalpy change for the neutralisation of hydrochloric acid by sodium hydroxide solution. **Wear eye protection for this experiment.**

Measuring an enthalpy change of neutralisation

The enthalpy change for the neutralisation of hydrochloric acid by sodium hydroxide solution was carried out using the method shown in Figure 2.5.

Results

Temperature of hydrochloric acid before reaction	= 23.5 °C
Temperature of sodium hydroxide solution before reaction	= 23.5 °C
Highest temperature of mixture after reaction	= 29.5 °C
Increase in temperature from reaction	= 6 °C
Volume of mixture after reaction	= 100 cm³

REQUIRED PRACTICAL

This required practical relates to specification point 3.8. In the experimental method for determining the enthalpy change for a reaction, you need to know that *the mass of water (in grams) × 4.2 (specific heat capacity of water in joules per gram per degree) × the temperature change (°C)* can be used to find the energy released by the reaction. If you know the mass of the reactant, you can then use the energy value to work out the enthalpy change per mole of reactant.

Calculation

The equation for the reaction is:

$$HCl(aq) + NaOH(aq) \rightarrow NaCl(aq) + H_2O(l)$$

$$\text{Amount of HCl reacting} = \frac{50}{1000} \text{ dm}^3 \times 1.0 \text{ mol} / \text{dm}^3 = 0.05 \text{ mol}$$

$$\text{Amount of NaOH reacting} = \frac{50}{1000} \text{ dm}^3 \times 1.0 \text{ mol} / \text{dm}^3 = 0.05 \text{ mol}$$

We can assume that the solution after reaction has the same density and specific heat capacity as water. So,

Mass of the solution after mixing = 100 g

$\quad$ 4.2 J raises the temperature of 1 g of the solution by 1 °C

and so $\quad 4.2 \times 100 \times 6$ J raises the temperature of 100 g of the solution by 6 °C

So, when 0.05 mole of HCl reacts with 0.05 mole of NaOH,

$$\text{heat energy given out} = 4.2 \times 100 \times 6 \text{ J} = 2520 \text{ J}$$

When 1 mole of HCl reacts with 1 mole of NaOH,

$$\text{heat energy given out} = \frac{2520 \text{ J}}{0.05 \text{ mol}} = 50\,400 \text{ J} / \text{mol} = 50.4 \text{ kJ} / \text{mol}$$

So, $HCl(aq) + NaOH(aq) \rightarrow NaCl(aq) + H_2O(l) \qquad \Delta H = -50.4 \text{ kJ} / \text{mol}$

The heat energy produced during this reaction is usually described as an enthalpy change of neutralisation.

Measuring an enthalpy change of displacement reaction

If you add an excess of zinc to a solution of copper sulfate a displacement reaction takes place.

$$Zn(s) + CuSO_4(aq) \rightarrow ZnSO_4(aq) + Cu(s)$$

The reaction is exothermic and produces a temperature rise.

In an experiment using apparatus similar to Figure 2.4, an excess of 0.5 g of zinc was added to 25 cm³ of 0.2 mol / dm³ of copper sulfate solution. The temperature rise was 35 °C.

Calculation

$$\text{Amount of CuSO}_4 \text{ reacting is} = \frac{25 \text{ dm}^3}{1000 \text{ dm}^3} \times 0.2 \text{ mol} = 0.005 \text{ mol}$$

Again we assume that before and after the reaction the density and specific heat capacity of the solution is the same as that of water.

energy released (J) = mass (g) × specific heat capacity of the solution
(J / g / °C) × temperature change of the solution (°C)

The mass of the solution is 25 g, the specific heat capacity of water is 4.2 J / g / °C and the temperature rise is 35 °C,

∴ energy released = 25 × 4.2 × 35 = 3675 J

When 1 mole of $CuSO_4$ reacts with 1 mole of zinc the heat energy given out will be $\dfrac{3675}{0.005}$ = 735 000 J / mol

$$735\,000\,J / mol = 735\,kJ / mol$$

So $\Delta H = -735\,kJ / mol$

This value is slightly less than the actual value as no account has been taken of the heat losses to the polystyrene cup, the thermometer, losses due to conduction, convection or radiation, the unreacted zinc present, or the copper produced.

STUDY QUESTIONS

1 The simple apparatus in Figure 2.2 does not give reliable results. The actual value for the heat energy produced when ethanol burns is significantly higher than 21 kJ / g.
   a) Why do you think the apparatus in Figure 2.2 gives inaccurate results?
   b) How would you modify the apparatus to obtain more accurate results?

2 Draw a diagram of the apparatus you would use to find the heat energy produced when 1 g of a firelighter burns.

3 When 11.1 g of powdered calcium chloride ($CaCl_2(s)$) dissolves in 25 cm^3 of water, the temperature rises by 7 °C.
   a) What mass of solution is warmed up? (Assume 1 cm^3 of solution has a mass of 1 g.)
   b) How many joules of heat energy are given out as the $CaCl_2$ dissolves? (Assume 4.2 J raise the temperature of 1 g of solution by 1 °C.)
   c) What is the amount in moles of $CaCl_2$ that dissolves?

   d) How much heat energy is given out when 1 mol of $CaCl_2$ dissolves? (This is called the molar enthalpy change of solution of calcium chloride.)

4 a) A student suggested that the accuracy of the experiment in Figure 2.2 would be improved if the mass and specific heat capacity of the metal can was included in the calculation (see pages 193–194). The can was made of 250 g of copper. Copper has a specific heat capacity of 0.381 joules per gram per degree. Use this additional data to find how much heat energy was absorbed by the can. The temperature rise was 10 °C.
   b) Use your answer to part (a) to work out a more accurate value for ΔH for the combustion of ethanol. You need to refer to page 194 to find the amount of energy released by 1 g ethanol.

3.3 Enthalpy changes and bonding

The atoms in methane and oxygen molecules have to split apart and rearrange themselves as water and carbon dioxide when methane burns. Somehow this change in the arrangement of the atoms produces the useful heat energy change. The only change is to the way the bonds are organised, so the change in the bonding must be providing the change in the heat energy.

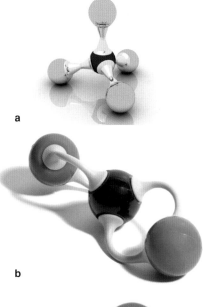

a

b

c

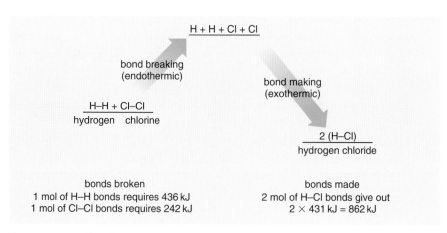

d

Figure 3.1 The molecules involved in burning methane (CH_4).

■ Explaining the heat energy changes in reactions

When most chemical reactions occur, bonds in the reactants must *break* before new bonds can be *made* as the products form. Breaking bonds involves pulling atoms apart and this requires heat energy. Making bonds helps to make atoms more stable and this gives out heat energy.

- ■ Bond *breaking* is endothermic.
- ■ Bond *making* is exothermic.

Figure 3.2 shows the bond breaking and bond making that takes place when hydrogen reacts with chlorine to form hydrogen chloride.

H + H + Cl + Cl

bond breaking (endothermic)

bond making (exothermic)

H–H + Cl–Cl
hydrogen   chlorine

2 (H–Cl)
hydrogen chloride

bonds broken
1 mol of H–H bonds requires 436 kJ
1 mol of Cl–Cl bonds requires 242 kJ

bonds made
2 mol of H–Cl bonds give out
2 × 431 kJ = 862 kJ

Figure 3.2 Bond breaking and bond making when hydrogen and chlorine react.

The bonds between hydrogen atoms in H_2 molecules and those between chlorine atoms in Cl_2 molecules must first break. These bond-breaking processes are endothermic, requiring heat energy.

New bonds are then made between H atoms and Cl atoms as they form hydrogen chloride. This process makes the H and Cl atoms more stable and heat energy is given out.

Calculating the enthalpy changes from bond energy values

Chemists have been able to determine the energy needed to break the bonds between atoms in various molecules such as those between hydrogen atoms in H_2 and chlorine atoms in Cl_2. The energy is usually calculated for one mole of bonds and the term **mean bond energy** is used for this measurement. So, the mean bond energy for one mole of H—H bonds is 436 kJ / mol. This value and a few other mean bond energies are listed in Table 1. Mean bond energies are sometimes called bond dissociation energies.

> The **mean bond energy** tells us the average amount of heat energy taken in or given out when one mole of bonds are broken or made.

We can use the bond energies in Table 1 to work out the heat energy changes involved in the reaction shown in Figure 3.2.

From Figure 3.2:

total heat energy required for bond breaking $= 436 + 242 = 678\,kJ$
total heat energy given out on bond making $= 862\,kJ$
$\therefore$ overall heat energy change $= 184\,kJ$ given out
$\therefore \Delta H = -184\,kJ / mol$

Calculating enthalpy changes from bond energies is very helpful when the practical you would have to carry out to measure the enthalpy change is very dangerous.

Showing ΔH on energy level diagrams

An energy level diagram for the reaction of hydrogen with chlorine is shown in Figure 3.3. In an exothermic reaction such as this, the heat energy released in forming new bonds in the product is greater than the heat energy needed to break original bonds in the reactants.

In endothermic reactions, the opposite is true. The heat energy needed to break existing bonds is greater than the heatenergy released in forming new bonds and ΔH has a positive value.

Table 1 Mean bond energies.

Bond	Mean bond energy / kJ / mol
H—H	436
Cl—Cl	242
H—Cl	431
C—H	413
C—C	347
O=O	498
C=O	805
H—O	464

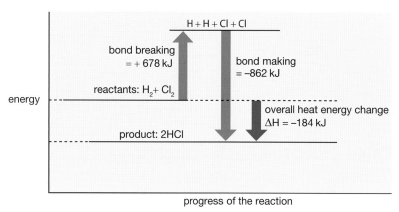

Figure 3.3 An energy level diagram for the reaction of hydrogen with chlorine. This is exothermic: ΔH is negative.

Figure 3.4 Photosynthesis is very endothermic with a large positive ΔH. It cannot occur spontaneously and needs the input of energy in the form of sunlight for it to occur. The energy needed to break bonds in the reactants CO_2 and H_2O is greater than that released as new bonds form in the products – carbohydrates and O_2.

STUDY QUESTIONS

1 a) Write a balanced equation with state symbols for the reaction of hydrogen with oxygen to form water vapour.

b) Re-write your equation showing displayed formulae for the reactants and products. (Remember that O_2 is O=O.)

c) Draw a bond-breaking and bond-making diagram for the reaction similar to that in Figure 3.2.

d) Calculate the heat energy input for bonds broken in your diagram and the heat energy given out when bonds are made. (Refer to Table 1.)

e) Calculate ΔH for the reaction.

2 The burning of natural gas, mainly methane, can be summarised by the equation:
$$CH_4(g) + 2O_2(g) \rightarrow CO_2(g) + 2H_2O(g)$$
For the reaction in this equation, use the data in Table 1 to calculate:

a) the heat energy input for bonds broken in the reactants

b) the heat energy given out when bonds form in the products (remember the bonding in CO_2 is O=C=O)

c) the overall enthalpy change.

3 The reaction which occurs in the Haber process for the manufacture of ammonia is:
$$N_2(g) + 3H_2(g) \rightarrow 2NH_3(g) \qquad \Delta H = -x \text{ kJ / mol}$$

a) An energy level diagram has been started for the reaction, shown in the figure below. Copy and complete the figure showing the products and the enthalpy change for the reaction.

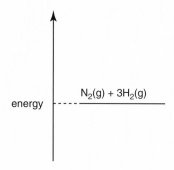

b) The table below shows the values of some mean bond energies.

Bond	N≡N	H—H	N—H
Bond energy kJ / mol	944	436	388

Use the values in the table to calculate the enthalpy change in the equation for the manufacture of ammonia.

3.4 Studying reaction rates

When two cars collide (Figure 4.1) there are many changes to their structure. The main body changes shape and some parts of the structure are separated. The amount of damage depends on the energies of the two cars. Cars which collide at slow speeds (little energy) have no damage. At a greater speed they can show some damage, but not enough to prevent them from working. At high speed the damage is so great the car is changed and cannot be driven afterwards. Chemical reactions are like this.

Figure 4.1 The collision of these two cars has caused many changes to their structure.

■ Chemical reactions and collisions

A chemical reaction cannot happen unless particles in the reacting substances collide with each other.

This statement explains why reactions between gases and liquids usually happen faster than reactions involving solids. Particles in gases and liquids can mix and collide much more easily than particles in solids. In a solid, only the particles on the surface can react.

■ Measuring reaction rate

During a reaction, reactants are being used up and products are forming. The amounts of the reactants fall as the amounts of the products rise. So, we can measure reaction rates by measuring how much of a reactant is used up or how much of a product forms in a given time.

$$\text{reaction rate} = \frac{\text{change in amount of the substance}}{\text{time taken}}$$

For example, when 0.1 g of magnesium was added to dilute hydrochloric acid, the magnesium reacted and disappeared in 10 seconds.

$$\therefore \quad \text{reaction rate} = \frac{\text{change in mass of magnesium}}{\text{time taken}}$$

$$= \frac{0.1\,\text{g}}{10\,\text{s}} = 0.01\,\text{g magnesium used up per second}$$

$$= 0.01\,\text{g}/\text{s}$$

Strictly speaking, this is the *mean* reaction rate over the 10 seconds for all the magnesium to react. Although reaction rates are usually measured as changes in mass or volume with time, we can also use changes in concentration, pressure and colour with time.

Using loss of mass to measure the effect of surface area on the rate of reaction

When marble chips (calcium carbonate) react with dilute hydrochloric acid, carbon dioxide is produced.

calcium carbonate	+	hydrochloric acid	$\rightarrow$	calcium chloride	+	water	+	carbon dioxide

$$CaCO_3(s) + 2HCl(aq) \rightarrow CaCl_2(aq) + H_2O(l) + CO_2(g)$$

The carbon dioxide escapes from the flask and so the mass of the flask and its contents decrease.

The rate of the reaction can be studied using the apparatus in Figure 4.2. Figure 4.3 shows how you could follow such a reaction using data logging equipment.

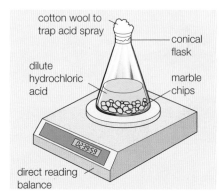

Figure 4.2 Measuring the rate of reaction between marble chips and hydrochloric acid.

Figure 4.3 Data logging equipment to follow the mass loss in an experiment.

The effect of surface area on the rate of a reaction can be investigated using marble chips of different sizes. The same mass of large marble chips has a smaller surface area than the same mass of small marble chips.

1 Measure 250 cm³ of 1 mol / dm³ dilute hydrochloric acid into a conical flask. Put the cotton wool stopper in and weigh the flask and its contents. Record the mass.

2 Weigh out approximately 8–10 g of large marble chips. Record the mass.

3 Remove the cotton wool, add the marble chips to the flask, replace the cotton wool, start a stop watch, and place the flask back on the balance.

4 Weigh the flask and its contents every minute for 10 minutes.

5 Repeat the experiment using a similar mass of small marble chips and fresh dilute hydrochloric acid. Make sure you know the mass of small marble chips you use.

Table 1 shows the results of an experiment done by two students. They calculated the mass at time zero by adding the mass from step 1 to the mass of 5g of marble chips they used (recorded in either step 2 or step 5).

Table 1 The results from an investigation into the effect of surface area on the rate of reaction.

Time (min)	Large marble chips		Small marble chips	
	Mass of flask and contents (g)	Decrease in mass since start (g)	Mass of flask and contents (g)	Decrease in mass since start (g)
0	278.00	0.00	278.00	0.00
1	277.75	0.75	276.50	1.50
2	276.60	1.40	275.50	2.50
3	276.10	1.90	274.95	3.05
4	275.70	2.30	274.60	3.40
5	275.35	2.65	274.41	3.59
6	275.02	2.98	274.33	3.59
7	274.75	3.25	274.30	3.70
8	274.50	3.50	274.30	3.70
9	274.30	3.70	274.30	3.70
10	274.30	3.70	274.30	3.70

During the first minute there is a decrease in mass of 1.5 g for the small chips as carbon dioxide escapes.

∴ mean rate of reaction in the first minute

$$= \frac{\text{change in mass}}{\text{time taken}} = \frac{1.5}{1} = 1.5 \text{ g of carbon dioxide per minute}$$

During the first minute (for the large chips), 0.75 g of carbon dioxide escapes.

∴ mean rate of reaction in the first minute

$$= \frac{0.75}{1} = 0.75 \text{ g of } CO_2 \text{ per minute}$$

Using a graph to interpret the results

The results of the experiment are plotted on a graph in Figure 4.4. Notice that the rate of reaction is fastest at the start of the reaction when the slopes of the graphs in Figure 4.4 are steepest. The small marble chips have the steepest curve and after 6 minutes the graph flattens as the calcium carbonate is used up. The start of the flattened section shows the end of the reaction. The large marble chips also finish reacting but after 9 minutes. So, the larger surface area of the small marble chips reacts faster than the smaller surface area of the large marble chips.

The greater the surface area of a solid then the greater the rate of reaction.

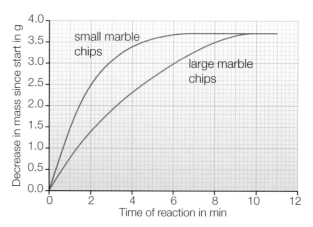

Figure 4.4 A graph showing the effect of surface area on rate of reaction

Notice the mass of carbon dioxide released is the same in both trials. This is because both trials used almost the same mass of calcium carbonate and the same volume and concentration of dilute hydrochloric acid.

Measuring the rate of reaction from the graph.

Another method to find the rate of the reaction involves using the graph to find the gradient of the curve at any time. This has the advantage of measuring the rate of reaction at a specific time. The method above measures the mean rate over a minute.

Look at Figure 4.5. If you want to find the rate of reaction after 2.5 minutes for the small marble chips, then you draw a tangent to the curve at the 2.5 minute point as shown. Using the tangent line as the hypotenuse, you then draw a right angle triangle and measure the two legs using the scales of the graph.

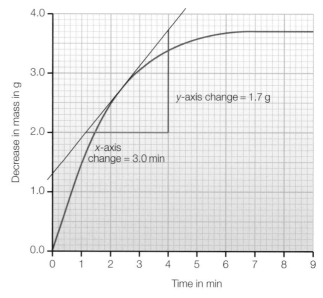

Figure 4.5 Using tangents to calculate the rate of reaction.

Divide the y-axis change by the x-axis change to obtain the gradient of the curve at 2.5 minutes.

$$\text{gradient at time 2.5 min} = \text{rate of reaction at 2.5 min} = \frac{1.7\,g}{3.0\,\text{min}}$$

$$= 0.57\,g \text{ per min}$$

STUDY QUESTIONS

1 Look at the results in Table 1 and the graph in Figure 4.4.
   a) What mass of carbon dioxide is lost from the large chip flask in:
      i)   the third minute (time 2 to 3 minutes);
      ii) the fourth minute (time 3 to 4 minutes);
      iii) the fifth minute (time 4 to 5 minutes)?
   b) What is happening to the reaction rate as time passes?
   c) Explain the change in reaction rate with time.
   d) Why does the graph become horizontal after a while?

   e) Calculate the rate of reaction using the tangent method for small chips at time three minutes.

2 a) When magnesium reacts with dilute hydrochloric acid, does the magnesium react faster at the start of the reaction or at the finish?
   b) Give two reasons for your answer in part (a).

3 a) Weedkillers can be added to a lawn either as solid pellets or as aqueous solutions. Which method will affect the weeds faster? Explain your answer.
   b) The selective weedkiller 2,4-D kills dandelions in a lawn, but not the grass. Suggest how it might work.

3.5 Making reactions go faster

Carbon dioxide is a gas that dissolves in rainwater making the rain acidic. In rural areas, where there is little carbon dioxide in the rain, marble tombstones dissolve slowly. In industrial areas, where factories release extra carbon dioxide into the atmosphere, the marble tombstones dissolve faster. The concentration of the acid in the rain is greater in industrial areas.

Figure 5.1 Why do headstones in industrial areas decay faster than headstones in rural areas?

REQUIRED PRACTICAL

This required practical relates to specification point 3.15. **Wear eye protection for this practical.**

■ Concentration and reaction rates

Some students used the reaction between marble chips (calcium carbonate) and dilute hydrochloric acid to study the effect of concentration on reaction rate.

$$CaCO_3(s) + 2HCl(aq) \rightarrow CaCl_2(aq) + H_2O(l) + CO_2(g)$$

The students used 0.35 g of small calcium carbonate chips and 50 cm³ of hydrochloric acid. Figure 5.2 shows their apparatus.

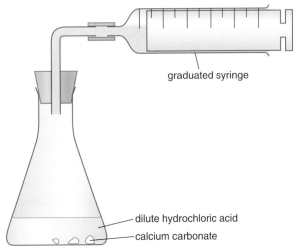

graduated syringe

dilute hydrochloric acid

calcium carbonate

Figure 5.2 Investigating the effect of concentration on reaction rate.

During the reaction the carbon dioxide escaped from the conical flask into the graduated gas syringe. They measured the volume of gas produced every ten seconds. They did two trials with different concentrations of hydrochloric acid. Trial 1 used 1.0 mol / dm³ of hydrochloric acid, trial 2 used 0.5 mol / dm³ of hydrochloric acid. Figure 5.3 shows their results.

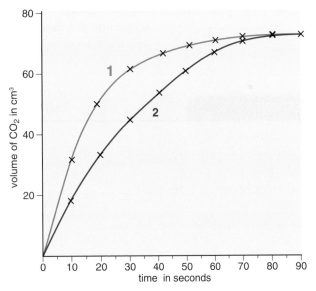

Figure 5.3 A graph to show the results of the effect of concentration on reaction rate.

On both occasions when the reaction had finished there were no calcium carbonate chips left in the flask. This told the students that there was more than enough hydrochloric acid to react with all the calcium carbonate in both trials. When more of a substance is present in a reaction than necessary we say the substance is in **excess**. The hydrochloric acid was in excess.

Look at the results of the experiments in Figure 5.3.

1 Why is the final volume of carbon dioxide the same in both experiments?
2 Why do the graphs become horizontal?
3 Which graph shows the larger volume of CO_2 produced per minute at the start of the experiment?
4 Which experiment begins at the faster rate?
5 Why is the reaction rate different in the two experiments?

Reactions need collisions

Chemical reactions occur when particles of the reacting substances collide with each other.

When the concentration of one substance is increased there are more particles of that substance present in the same volume. The particles of the two reactants will collide more frequently with each other, leading to more reactions between the reacting particles in the same time, so the reaction rate is increased. Lowering the concentration of one reactant will reduce the rate of reaction as there will be fewer collisions between the particles in the same length of time.

> In general, reactions go faster when the concentration of reactants is increased.

In reactions between gases, the concentration of each gas can be increased by increasing pressure. Increasing the pressure gives more particles in the same volume, so increasing the pressure increases the rate of the reaction.

STUDY QUESTIONS

1 It takes about 10 minutes to fry chips, but about 20 minutes to cook them in boiling water. Whole potatoes take even longer to boil.
   a) Why can chips be cooked faster than boiled potatoes?
   b) Why do larger potatoes take longer to cook than small ones?
   c) In a pressure cooker water boils at 121 °C. Why can boiled potatoes be cooked faster in a pressure cooker?
2 Why do gaseous reactions go faster if the pressure of the reacting gases is increased?
3 Which of the following will affect the rate at which a

candle burns: the temperature of the air; the shape of the candle; the air pressure; the length of the wick? Explain your answer in each case.
State two other factors that will affect the rate at which a candle burns.
4 Limestone (calcium carbonate) weathers (wears away) owing to the action of dilute nitric and sulfuric acids as well as carbonic acid in rainwater. Design an experiment to investigate the effect of acid concentration on the weathering of limestone.

Do not carry out your experiment unless it has been checked by your teacher.

3.6 Temperature and reaction rates

Milk will keep for days in a cool refrigerator, but it turns sour very quickly if it is left out on a hot, sunny day. Other perishable foods, like strawberries and cream, also go bad more quickly at higher temperatures. This is because chemical reactions go faster at higher temperatures.

Figure 6.1 Fish, meat and soft fruit can be kept for long periods in a freezer where the temperature is about -18°C. (The temperature in a fridge is about 5°C).

■ The effect of temperature

Chemical reactions can be speeded up by increasing the temperature, or slowed down by reducing the temperature. This effect of temperature on reaction rates can be studied using the reaction between sodium thiosulfate solution, $Na_2S_2O_3(aq)$, and dilute hydrochloric acid.

$$\begin{array}{c}\text{sodium} \\ \text{thiosulfate}\end{array} + \begin{array}{c}\text{hydrochloric} \\ \text{acid}\end{array} \rightarrow \begin{array}{c}\text{sodium} \\ \text{chloride}\end{array} + \text{water} + \begin{array}{c}\text{sulfur} \\ \text{dioxide}\end{array} + \text{sulfur}$$

$$Na_2S_2O_3(aq) + 2HCl(aq) \rightarrow 2NaCl(aq) + H_2O(l) + SO_2(g) + S(s)$$

When the reactants are mixed, a fine precipitate of sulfur starts to form. The solution turns cloudy and slowly becomes more and more yellow.

A toxic gas is produced in solution but gradually escapes. Take care not to inhale it. Dispose of the cloudy mixture as soon as you have finished timing by pouring into sodium carbonate solution, preferably in a fume cupboard. (Figure 6.2).

PRACTICAL

This experiment is sometimes called 'the disappearing cross' experiment. You can probably guess why. It is important to keep control variables the same throughout the experiment. Always use the same cross and piece of paper, and also the same eye. You could control the variables by using data logging. Can you think how?

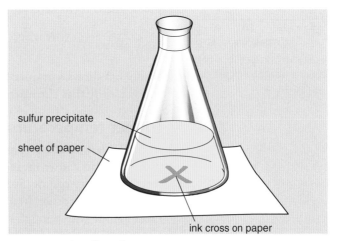

sulfur precipitate

sheet of paper

ink cross on paper

Figure 6.2 Investigating the effect of temperature on reaction rate. **Wear eye protection.**

As the precipitate forms, the ink cross on white paper below the flask slowly disappears. We can study the reaction rate by mixing 5 cm³ of dilute hydrochloric acid with 50 cm³ of sodium thiosulfate solution and then measuring the time it takes for the cross to disappear. Table 1 shows the results obtained when the reaction was carried out at five different temperatures between 23 and 44 °C.

Table 1 Studying the reaction between sodium thiosulfate solution and dilute hydrochloric acid at different temperatures.

Temperature in °C	Time for cross to disappear in s	$\dfrac{1}{\text{Time for cross to disappear}}$
23	132	0.0076
29	90	0.0111
34	65	0.0154
39	46	0.0217
44	33	0.0313

Interpreting the results

The results in Table 1 show that the cross disappears more quickly at higher temperatures. This means that the reaction goes faster at higher temperatures. If the temperature rises by 10 °C, the reaction rate is about twice as fast. For example, at 29 °C the cross disappears in 90 seconds, while at 39 °C it disappears in about half that time (46 seconds).

Calculating the reaction rate

Using the equation for reaction rate in Chapter 3.4, we can say,

$$\text{reaction rate} = \frac{\text{change in amount of sulfur}}{\text{time taken}}$$

$$= \frac{\text{amount of sulfur precipitated}}{\text{time taken}}$$

If other variables are controlled, the cross disappears at the same thickness of precipitate each time. So, when the cross disappears, the amount of sulfur precipitated is the same at each temperature.

$$\therefore \quad \text{reaction rate} \propto \frac{1}{\text{time for cross to disappear}}$$

Figure 6.3 shows a graph of this reciprocal against temperature. The graph shows clearly that the reaction rate increases as temperature increases.

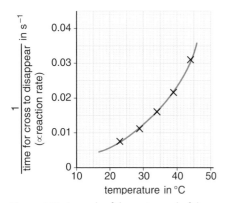

Figure 6.3 A graph of the reciprocal of the time for the cross to disappear ($\propto$ reaction rate) against temperature.

Higher temperatures and collisions

At higher temperatures, particles move about faster. So they collide more often and this causes more reactions every second. But particles don't always react when they collide. Some collisions are so soft that the particles simply bounce off each other. In order to react, particles (molecules, atoms or ions) must collide with enough energy for bonds to stretch and break. At higher temperatures, this is more likely because the particles have more energy.

At higher temperatures particles collide with more energy, so more collisions result in a reaction.

The collisions between reacting particles can be compared to the collisions between cars. If particles collide with little energy, bonds cannot break to form new substances. If cars collide at slow speeds (with low energy), they hardly dent each other. But, if cars collide at high speeds (with high energy), they bend and break.

■ Collision theory

We can explain the effects of changing surface area, concentration or temperature using the kinetic theory (Chapter 1.2). In any reaction mixture, the particles are continually moving about and colliding with each other. And, when they collide, there is a chance that a reaction will occur. This is sometimes called the **collision theory**.

Concentration, pressure and collision theory

Increasing the *concentration* of reactants in solution means there are more particles in the same volume. There are more collisions per second and therefore the reaction rate increases. Increasing the *pressure* of a gaseous mixture also results in more particles in the same volume with a similar effect on the reaction rate.

Particle size, surface area and collision theory

When a solid reacts with a liquid or a gas, the reaction rate increases if the solid is broken up into smaller pieces. Breaking up the solid increases its *surface area*. This allows more collisions per second between the reacting particles (Figure 6.4) and so the rate of reaction increases.

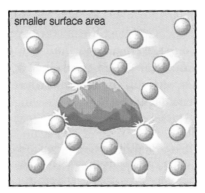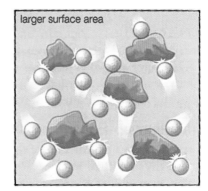

Figure 6.4 Breaking up a solid increases its surface area, so more collisions between the reacting particles take place.

Temperature, activation energy and collision theory

When the temperature of a reaction increases, the particles move around faster, colliding more frequently and with more energy. So, more particles have enough energy for bonds to break when they collide and the reaction rate increases. Figure 6.5 shows an energy profile for a successful collision resulting in reaction. Chemists use the term **activation energy** for the minimum energy that reactants must possess if they are to react.

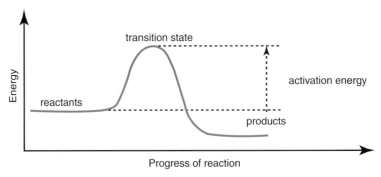

Figure 6.5 The reaction profile for a typical exothermic reaction showing the activation energy of the reaction.

The energy profile in Figure 6.5 shows the mean energy level of reactants and products for a typical exothermic reaction. Some reactant particles which are moving faster will have more energy than the mean level shown and others will have less energy than the mean. The red curve, which shows the course of the reaction, indicates the activation energy. This is the minimum energy that colliding particles must have if they are to collide with sufficient energy to react. At this point, bonds in the reactants will have broken, allowing new bonds to form in the products with the release of energy.

Activation energies explain why reactions go more slowly than you might expect if every collision led to a reaction. At room temperature, only a small proportion of molecules have sufficient energy to react.

STUDY QUESTIONS

1 The curves in the graph in Figure 6.6 show the volume of hydrogen produced during different experiments to investigate the reaction between magnesium and hydrochloric acid. Curve X is obtained when 1 g of magnesium ribbon reacts with 100 cm³ (excess) hydrochloric acid at 30 °C. Which of the curves A, B, C or D would you expect to obtain when:
   a) 1 g of magnesium ribbon reacts with 100 cm³ of the same acid at 50 °C?
   b) 1 g of magnesium ribbon reacts with 100 cm³ of the same acid at 15 °C?
   c) 0.5 g of magnesium ribbon reacts with 100 cm³ of the same acid at 30 °C?

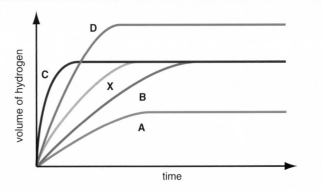

Figure 6.6 The volume of hydrogen produced during different experiments to investigate the reaction between magnesium and hydrochloric acid.

3.7 Catalysts and reaction rates

Mention catalysts today and everyone thinks of catalytic converters on vehicles. But catalysts are used in many places. Adhesives that are very strong often need two different substances to be mixed together before the adhesive can work. One tube is the glue, the other a catalyst to make it harden quickly. So what are catalysts, and how do they work on a reaction rate?

■ Investigating catalysts

Hydrogen peroxide solution, $H_2O_2(aq)$, decomposes very slowly into water and oxygen at room temperature.

$$2H_2O_2(aq) \rightarrow 2H_2O(l) + O_2(g)$$

Some substances can increase the rate of this reaction.

1 Put six test tubes in a test tube rack. **Wear eye protection**.
2 Add 1 level spatula of:
       manganese(IV) oxide to tube 1,
       copper(II) oxide to the second test tube 2,
       zinc oxide to the third test tube 3,
       sodium chloride to tube 4
       a 1 cm³ cube of peeled potato to tube 5
       a 1 cm³ cube of sliced liver to tube 6
3 Add 2 cm³ of 20 volume hydrogen peroxide solution to each test tube in turn. ('20 volume' refers to the volume of oxygen gas the hydrogen peroxide can release. 1 litre of 20 volume hydrogen peroxide will release 20 litres of oxygen gas.)
4 Observe the rate of production of oxygen bubbles in each tube. Arrange the tubes in order of rate of reaction.
5 You could test the gas to see that it is oxygen. Place a glowing splint on the top of each tube in turn (see Chapter 2.19).

If you weigh the spatula of manganese(IV) oxide before you add it, and at the end of the experiment filter the solution, dry the recovered manganese(IV) oxide and weigh it, the two masses should be the same.

Catalysts are substances which increase the rate of chemical reactions without being used up during the reaction.

Transition metal compound catalysts

Transition metal compounds which act as catalysts, such as manganese(IV) oxide with hydrogen peroxide, work by forming an intermediate compound

Figure 7.1 The most common use of a catalyst.

REQUIRED PRACTICAL

This required practical relates to specification point 3.16. The decomposition of hydrogen peroxide by manganese(IV) oxide is a good example of catalysis in the laboratory.

with one or more of the reactants. This product then reacts further to form the product and release the catalyst, which can be used again.

◼ Catalysts and activation energy

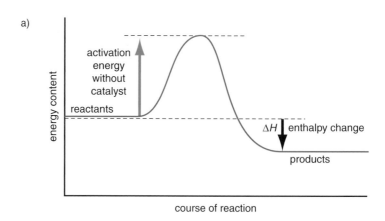

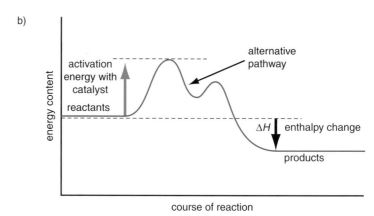

Figure 7.2 The reaction profiles for a typical exothermic reaction a) without a catalyst and b) with a catalyst. The dip in the profile with a catalyst shows the formation of either an intermediate or adsorbed reactants.

Catalysts work by providing an alternative route or pathway for the reaction with a lower activation energy (Figure 7.2). Lowering the activation energy increases the proportion of molecules with enough energy to react and this increases the rate of the reaction.

The catalyst can change the reaction pathway by adsorbing reactants onto its surface or by forming a distinct intermediate. Once the adsorbed products are released or the intermediate breaks down, the catalyst is released. This frees the catalyst to interact with further reactant molecules and the reaction continues.

■ The importance of catalysts

The use of catalysts in chemical reactions can be compared to the use of motorways for journeys. Catalysts provide a faster, easier pathway for reactions in the same way that motorways provide a faster, easier route for journeys. With catalysts, less energy is required for the reaction in the same way that less gasoline (petrol) is needed for motorway journeys compared to routes through winding, narrow roads.

Catalysts play an important role in the chemical industry. They are used, for example, in the production of gasoline (Chapter 4.3), sulfuric acid and ammonia (Chapter 3.9). Catalysts speed up these industrial processes and the products are obtained more quickly. They also allow the processes to take place at lower temperatures, so saving on energy costs.

STUDY QUESTIONS

1 The catalysts in many reactions are transition metals or their compounds. Make a list of five reactions catalysed by transition metals or their compounds.

2 Describe an experiment that you could carry out to show that manganese(IV) oxide is not used up when it catalyses the decomposition of hydrogen peroxide.

3 Explain why a catalyst can lower the activation energy for a chemical reaction. Sketch reaction profiles for an exothermic reaction with and without a catalyst.

3.8 Reversible reactions

When you bake a cake, chemical reactions take place in the cake mixture. Once the cake is baked, it is impossible to turn it back into flour, margarine, eggs and sugar.

Figure 8.1 Baking a cake is an irreversible reaction.

■ Irreversible changes

Once you have burned charcoal in a barbecue, you can never get back the original materials. The charcoal, which is mainly carbon, reacts with oxygen in the air forming carbon dioxide.

$$\text{carbon (charcoal)} + \text{oxygen} \rightarrow \text{carbon dioxide}$$
$$C(s) + O_2(g) \rightarrow CO_2(g)$$

No matter what you do, the carbon dioxide which has formed cannot be turned back into charcoal and oxygen.

> Reactions like this which cannot be reversed are called **irreversible reactions**.

■ Some reversible changes

Most of the chemical reactions that we have studied so far are also irreversible. But there are some processes that can be reversed. For example, ice turns into water on heating (Figure 8.2).

$$\text{ice} \xrightarrow{\text{heat}} \text{water}$$
$$H_2O(s) \xrightarrow{\text{heat}} H_2O(l)$$

If the water is now cooled, ice re-forms.

$$\text{water} \xrightarrow{\text{cool}} \text{ice}$$
$$H_2O(l) \xrightarrow{\text{cool}} H_2O(s)$$

Figure 8.2 Ice melts as it warms up in a drink. If the drink is cooled, ice will re-form. This is a reversible process.

These two parts of this reversible process (not a reaction) can be combined in one equation as:

$$H_2O(s) \underset{\text{cool}}{\overset{\text{heat}}{\rightleftharpoons}} H_2O(l)$$

This shows that the reaction can go in both directions.

Dehydration of hydrated copper(II) sulfate

When blue hydrated copper sulfate is heated, it decomposes to white anhydrous copper sulfate and water vapour.

$$\text{hydrated copper sulfate} \xrightarrow{\text{heat}} \text{anhydrous copper sulfate} + \text{water}$$
$$\underset{\text{(blue)}}{CuSO_4.5H_2O(s)} \xrightarrow{\text{heat}} \underset{\text{(white)}}{CuSO_4(s)} + 5H_2O(g)$$

If water is now added, the change can be reversed and blue hydrated copper sulfate re-forms.

$$\underset{\text{(white)}}{CuSO_4(s) + 5H_2O(l)} \rightarrow \underset{\text{(blue)}}{CuSO_4.5H_2O(s)}$$

These two processes can be combined in one equation as:

$$CuSO_4.5H_2O(s) \underset{\text{mix reactants}}{\overset{\text{heat}}{\rightleftharpoons}} CuSO_4(s) + 5H_2O(l)$$

Reactions like this which can be reversed are called **reversible reactions**.

Effect of heat on ammonium chloride

Figure 8.3 shows an experiment to show the effect of heat on ammonium chloride. Many ammonium compounds turn directly into a gas from their solid state; this change is called **sublimation**. When ammonium chloride is heated in an evaporating basin it decomposes into ammonia gas and hydrogen chloride gas. When the two mixed gases rise to hit the cooler glass filter funnel, the reaction is reversed and ammonium chloride powder is deposited, as shown:

$$NH_4Cl(s) \rightleftharpoons HCl(g) + NH_3(g)$$

The decomposition of ammonium chloride into hydrogen chloride and ammonia, as shown from left to right in the equation, is termed the **forward reaction**. The re-combination, from right to left in the equation, of the hydrogen chloride and ammonia to ammonium chloride is termed the **backward reaction**.

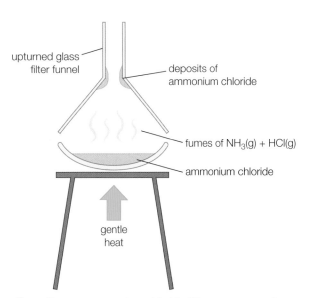

upturned glass filter funnel

deposits of ammonium chloride

fumes of $NH_3(g) + HCl(g)$

ammonium chloride

gentle heat

Figure 8.3 The effect of heat on ammonium chloride. **Wear eye protection**.

Making ammonia is a reversible reaction

The reaction between nitrogen and hydrogen to form ammonia is also reversible. This can be demonstrated using the apparatus in Figure 8.4. You **should not attempt** the experiment yourself. It should only be demonstrated by your teacher.

Using the syringes, the mixture of hydrogen and nitrogen is pushed to and fro over the heated iron wool. The gases in the syringes are then ejected onto damp red litmus paper. The litmus paper turns blue showing that ammonia has been produced. Ammonia is the only common alkaline gas.

$$\text{nitrogen} + \text{hydrogen} \rightarrow \text{ammonia}$$
$$N_2(g) + 3H_2(g) \rightarrow 2NH_3(g)$$

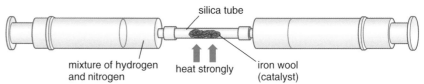

Figure 8.4 The reaction between nitrogen and hydrogen to form ammonia. **Wear eye protection**.

The experiment can be repeated, starting with ammonia in the syringes. This time, nitrogen and hydrogen are produced when the gas is pushed to and fro over the heated iron wool (which acts as a catalyst).

$$2NH_3(g) \rightarrow N_2(g) + 3H_2(g)$$

These experiments show that the reaction between nitrogen and hydrogen to form ammonia is reversible. In fact, this reaction is the basis of the Haber process to manufacture ammonia shown in the next chapter.

Coming to equilibrium

During a reversible reaction, the reactants are sometimes *completely* changed to the products. But, in other cases, the reactants are *only partly* converted to the products. Think again about the analogy of ice and water. If ice and water are kept at $0\,°C$, neither the ice nor the water seems to change. We say the two substances are in **equilibrium**.

So, at $0\,°C$,
$$\text{ice} \rightleftharpoons \text{water}$$
$$H_2O(s) \rightleftharpoons H_2O(l)$$

In the same way, nitrogen and hydrogen will come to equilibrium with ammonia in the apparatus shown in Figure 8.4.

$$N_2(g) + 3H_2(g) \rightleftharpoons 2NH_3(g)$$

> When equilibrium is reached in any reaction, the amounts and concentrations of the reactants and products do not change any more. However, both the forward reaction and the backward reaction are still going on.

So, in the equilibrium just described, nitrogen and hydrogen are still reacting to form ammonia, while ammonia is decomposing to re-form nitrogen and hydrogen. These two processes, the forward reaction and the backward reaction, are taking place at the same rate. So, there is no change in the overall amounts of any substance and their concentrations.

This is described as a **dynamic equilibrium** to indicate that substances are 'moving' (reacting) in both directions at equilibrium. A dynamic equilibrium can only be established if the reaction is reversible, and the system is closed, i.e. nothing can enter or leave the system.

STUDY QUESTIONS

1 Explain the following terms: *irreversible reaction; reversible reaction; dynamic equilibrium.*
2 Figure 8.5 shows what happens when ammonium chloride is heated to form ammonia and hydrogen

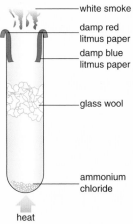

- white smoke
- damp red litmus paper
- damp blue litmus paper
- glass wool
- ammonium chloride
- heat

Figure 8.5 Heating ammonium chloride.

chloride. The red litmus first turns blue, then both pieces of litmus turn red.
   a) Write an equation for the decomposition of ammonium chloride.
   b) Why do the gases produced separate as they pass up the tube through the glass wool?
   c) Which gas is detected first and why?
   d) Why does white smoke form above the tube?
3 When purple hydrated cobalt chloride ($CoCl_2.6H_2O$) is heated, it changes to blue anhydrous cobalt chloride.
   a) Write an equation for this reaction.
   b) How is the reaction reversed?
   c) How is this reaction used as a test for water?

3.9 Dynamic Equilibria

Changing the conditions of temperature and gas pressure of a reversible reaction can have a big impact on the proportions of each substance in a dynamic equilibrium. Industrial chemistry needs to produce materials quickly and cheaply, and energy efficiently. Chemists often use equilibria to help them do just that, by altering the temperature and pressure. One such reaction is the production of ammonia gas from nitrogen and hydrogen.

Figure 9.1 Fritz Haber (1868–1934). In 1904, Haber began studying the reaction between nitrogen and hydrogen. By 1908, he had found the most economic conditions to make ammonia (NH₃). The ammonia could then be used to make ammonium salts and nitrates for fertilisers.

■ How changing conditions effects equilibria

The reaction between nitrogen and hydrogen to make ammonia can be summarised as:

$$N_2(g) + 3H_2(g) \rightleftharpoons 2NH_3(g) \; \Delta H = -92 \text{ kJ / mol}$$

The reaction shown by the equation can produce a dynamic equilibrium. The forward reaction is exothermic – heat energy is released when ammonia is made from nitrogen and hydrogen (and so ΔH is negative). The reverse or backward reaction is endothermic – heat energy is taken in when ammonia is being converted to nitrogen and hydrogen. Changing either the temperature or the pressure inside the reaction vessel will alter the proportions of ammonia, nitrogen and hydrogen at equilibrium.

The effect of a catalyst on the position of equilibrium

The addition of a catalyst increases the rate of both the forward and backward reactions. However, it increases the rates of both reactions to the same extent. For example, if it doubles the rate of the forward reaction, it will also double the rate of the backward reaction. The catalyst, therefore, has no effect on the position of equilibrium, which will not alter. However, equilibrium will be reached more quickly.

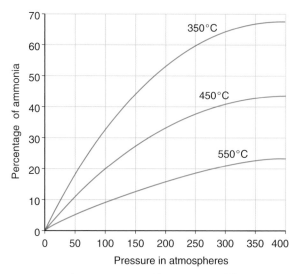

Figure 9.2 The percentage of ammonia at equilibrium under different temperatures and pressures.

■ Predicting the effects of changing pressure on equilibria

Look at Figure 9.2. As the pressure increases, the yield of ammonia at equilibrium also increases. So, if the system is in equilibrium at 50 atm pressure and the pressure is suddenly raised to 100 atm, the system will respond by forming more ammonia. In general, experiments with gaseous equilibria show that when the pressure is increased, systems move (if they can) in a direction which produces fewer molecules. Figure 9.2 shows that when the pressure is reduced, the yield of ammonia at equilibrium decreases. In this case, the system responds by forming more nitrogen and hydrogen, increasing the number of molecules.

■ Predicting the effects of changing temperature on equilibria

A similar situation arises when the temperature is changed. The reaction forming ammonia is exothermic.

$$N_2(g) + 3H_2(g) \rightleftharpoons 2NH_3 (g) \ \Delta H = -92 \text{ kJ} / \text{mol}$$

Now look at Figure 9.2 again. You will see that, if the pressure stays constant, when the temperature increases, the yield of ammonia decreases. So when the temperature increases, the system above moves to the left, in the endothermic direction. Similarly, when the temperature of the $N_2 / H_2 / NH_3$ system is reduced, more ammonia is produced. The system responds by moving in the exothermic direction.

■ Responses of dynamic equilibria to changes in the conditions of reaction.

All dynamic equilibria react according to the same simple rules shown by the reaction of nitrogen and hydrogen to make ammonia.

If forward reaction is exothermic, then carrying out the reaction at a higher temperature will shift the position of equilibrium in the direction of the endothermic reaction, i.e. to the left. The yield of the product decreases. If the reaction is carried out a lower temperature, the position of equilibrium shifts to the right, i.e. in the direction of the exothermic reaction, and the yield of product increases.

If the forward reaction is endothermic, the opposite changes occur. Carrying out the reaction at a higher temperature will increase the yield of the products, whereas carrying out the reaction at a lower temperature will decrease the yield of the products.

When a reaction involving gases is carried out at a higher pressure, the position of equilibrium will shift the position in the direction that produces fewer moles of gas. Carrying out the reaction at a lower pressure will shift the position of equilibrium in the direction that produces more moles of gas.

STUDY QUESTIONS

1 What are the main factors that affect the rate of a chemical reaction?

2 The key reaction in the manufacture of sulfuric acid involves the contact process:

$$2SO_2(g) + O_2(g) \rightleftharpoons 2SO_3(g) \quad \Delta H = -197 \text{ kJ / mol}$$

a) Will high pressure or low pressure give the highest yield of SO_3?

b) Will high temperature or low temperature give the highest yield of SO_3?

3 Hydrogen is produced for the production of ammonia by reacting natural gas (methane) with steam.

$$CH_4(g) + H_2O(g) \rightleftharpoons CO(g) + 3H2(g)$$
$$\Delta H = +210 \text{ kJ / mol}$$

The reaction is carried out at about 750 °C and a pressure of 30 atm.

a) What conditions (high or low) of temperature and pressure favour the highest yield of hydrogen in this reaction?

b) Explain the choice of temperature and pressure for the industrial process.

Summary

I am confident that:

✓ **I know the difference between an exothermic reaction and an endothermic reaction, and can describe the enthalpy changes between the products and reactants**
- ΔH represents the enthalpy (heat energy) change in exothermic and endothermic reactions.
- ΔH for an exothermic reaction is negative.
- ΔH for an endothermic reaction is positive.
- The overall enthalpy change is the difference in heat energy between the heat energy required to break the bonds of the reactants (an endothermic process) and the heat energy released by the formation of the products bonds (an exothermic process).

✓ **I can calculate the enthalpy change for a reaction, when given bond energy data and a balanced equation for a reaction**

✓ **I can describe experiments to measure the heat energy changes in:**
- combustion reactions
- displacement reactions
- dissolving
- neutralisation reactions.

✓ **I am able to calculate the molar enthalpy change from heat energy changes for measured masses of reactants, using:**
- the mass of the reactants and the temperature change
- the mass of water heated, the specific heat capacity of water and the temperature change.

✓ **I can describe experiments to investigate how the rate of a reaction is affected by:**
- surface area of reactants
- concentration of reactants
- temperature
- use of a catalyst.

✓ **I can use the particle collision theory to explain how these variables affect the rate of reaction**
- This explains the likelihood of reaction in terms of the number, speed and colliding force of the reactant particles.

✓ **I understand the term activation energy, and can show it on a reaction profile diagram**
- A catalyst provides an alternative pathway with a lower activation energy.

✓ **I know that some reactions are reversible and can happen in either direction**
- These reactions use ⇌ instead of an arrow in their equations.
- Examples are the effect of heat on ammonium chloride and the dehydration of hydrated copper(II) sulfate.
- Reversibe reactions can come to dynamic equilibrium.

✓ **I can predict the effect of changing the concentration, pressure or temperature on the equilibrium position when given the balanced chemical equation, and whether the reaction is exothermic or endothermic.**

Sample answers and expert's comments

Working with graphs
Example

1 A student wanted to find out how changing the temperature, concentration and particle size affects the rate of a chemical reaction.

The student decided to react excess sodium carbonate with hydrochloric acid. He measured the volume of carbon dioxide gas produced against time. He did one reaction, and used this to compare with his other reactions. Graph B shows his original experiment. Graphs A, C and D show his other experiments.

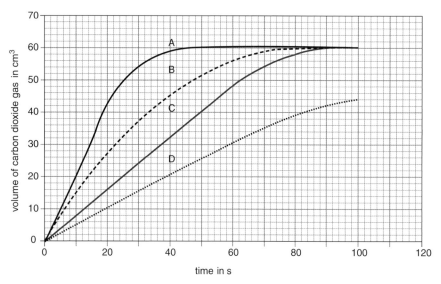

a) Explain why lines A, B and C all rise to a maximum but then do not change.

(2)

b) Explain which graph represents the greatest rate of reaction.

(2)

c) Explain which graph could show the reaction taking place at a lower temperature than the original experiment.

(2)

d) Explain which graph shows a reaction that has not completed.

(2)

(Total for question = 8 marks)

Student response	Total 7/8	Expert comments and tips for success
a) _At the maximum point all the sodium carbonate has reacted._		No mark. Make sure you know which substance is in excess. Here the substance in excess is sodium carbonate, so it is the hydrochloric acid that has run out.
b) _A ✔ as it has the steepest curve. ✔_		Correct. Remember that in rate graphs, the steepest curve has the fastest reaction.
c) _C ✔ as the reaction is slower. ✔_		Correct. You need to know how temperature affects the rate of a reaction. Curve C is less steep and therefore slower than B, so it is the most likely lower temperature reaction. As D does not reach the same height as A, B, or C, it is likely to be at a different concentration rather than temperature.
d) _D ✔ as the reaction line has not flattened out. ✔_		Correct. The flat part of the graph shows that the reaction has stopped. If it does not become flat, then the reaction is still happening.

Data analysis
Example

1 Hydrogen peroxide (H_2O_2) decomposes to water and oxygen. A student investigated adding manganese(IV) oxide to hydrogen peroxide by measuring the volume of oxygen gas given off over a period of ten hours by 50 cm³ of hydrogen peroxide. Here are the results:

	Volume of oxygen gas in cm³		
Time (hours)	No manganese(IV) oxide	With 1 g of manganese(IV) oxide	With 2 g of manganese(IV) oxide
0	0	0	0
2	5	495	505
4	10	785	775
6	15	945	935
8	20	985	975
10	25	990	985

a) What do we call a substance that increases the rate of a chemical reaction and is unchanged at the end? (1)

b) Use data from the table to describe the difference, if any, between the reaction with 1 g of manganese(IV) oxide and without manganese(IV) oxide. (2)

c) Use data from the table to describe the difference, if any, between the reaction with 1 g of manganese(IV) oxide and with 2 g of manganese(IV) oxide. (2)

d) What conclusion should the student make about using manganese(IV) oxide on the effect of the rate of the reaction from the table? (2)

(Total for question = 7 marks)

Student response	Total 6/7	Expert comments and tips for success
a) catalyst ✔		Correct. Make sure you know the correct scientific terms.
b) After every time there is far more oxygen ✔ made with the manganese(IV) oxide than without.		1 mark for stating that more oxygen is made with manganese(IV) oxide. To gain the second mark the answer needs to refer to data from the 1 g column of the table.
c) Although all the figures are different they are in the <u>same sort of area</u> ✔, and they both seem to slow up towards the end. I think there is <u>no real difference</u> between the effect. ✔		Poorly expressed but right. Remember that experimental data will have random errors. You should concentrate on the trends rather than the exact figures. Saying 'no real difference' is quite correct from the data.
d) It increases the rate of reaction. ✔ It probably doesn't matter how much you use. ✔		A good conclusion made by comparing the data about the effect of the catalyst, and the mass of catalyst used.

Exam-style questions

1 The equation for the combustion of hydrogen is:

$$2H_2(g) + O_2(g) \rightarrow 2H_2O(g)$$

The reaction gives out a lot of heat.

a) What term is used for reactions that give out heat? [1]

b) Explain why hydrogen and oxygen are gases at room temperature. [2]

c) The table below shows the values of three mean bond energies.

bond	H–H	O=O	O–H
bond energy in kJ / mol	436	498	464

Use the values in the table to calculate the energy change for the combustion of hydrogen. [3]

d) Draw an energy level diagram for the combustion of hydrogen. [3]

e) On cooling, $H_2O(g)$ produced during the combustion of hydrogen condenses to $H_2O(l)$. How does the speed of and distance between H_2O molecules change during this process? [2]

2 Excess solid sodium hydrogencarbonate was added to $50\,cm^3$ of $1.0\,mol / dm^3$ ethanoic acid in a polystyrene container. The temperature of the mixture fell from $25\,°C$ to $17\,°C$ as the products formed.

a) Copy and complete the following equation for the reaction.

$$CH_3COOH(aq) + NaHCO_3(s) \rightarrow \ldots + \ldots + \ldots \quad [2]$$

b) The solid $NaHCO_3$ was added in small portions to the acid. Why was this? [1]

The heat energy change of a reaction can be calculated using this equation:

heat energy change = mass of solution (g)
× 4.2 J /g / °C ×
temperature change (°C)

c) Calculate the heat energy change during the reaction (assume the density of the final solution is $1.0\,g / cm^3$). [3]

d) Calculate the amount, in moles, of ethanoic acid used. [2]

e) Calculate the enthalpy change of the reaction for 1 mol of ethanoic acid. Show the correct sign and units. [2]

3 Hydrogen peroxide decomposes into water and oxygen.

$$2H_2O_2 \rightarrow 2H_2O + O_2$$

The reaction is very slow but becomes faster if manganese(IV) oxide is added. The manganese(IV) oxide does not get used up during the reaction.

a) What is the role of the manganese(IV) oxide in this reaction? [1]

b) The graph below shows how the volume of oxygen collected changed with time when 1 g of small lumps of manganese(IV) oxide were added to $10\,cm^3$ of hydrogen peroxide.

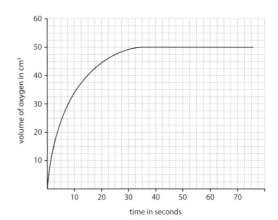

Copy the graph and sketch on it the results obtained when:

i) the experiment is repeated using 1 g of powdered manganese(IV) oxide. Label this sketch A. [2]

ii) the same volume of hydrogen peroxide is used but $5\,cm^3$ of water is added to it before the manganese(IV) oxide is added. Label this sketch B. [2]

c) Describe a test for oxygen gas and the positive result. [1]

4 A student investigated the effect of temperature on the rate of reaction between hydrochloric acid and sodium thiosulfate.

- The student added 5 cm³ of hydrochloric acid acid to 50 cm³ of a sodium thiosulphate solution in a flask.

- The flask was placed over a cross.

- The student timed how long after mixing it took for the cross to disappear.

a) i) Copy and balance the chemical equation for this reaction.

$$Na_2S_2O_3(aq) + HCl(aq) \rightarrow NaCl(aq) + H_2O(l) + SO_2(g) + S(s)$$ [1]

ii) What causes the cross to disappear? [1]

b) A graph of the results is shown.

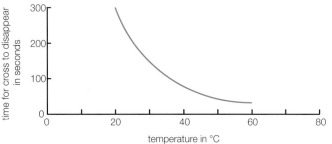

i) What effect does temperature have on the rate of this reaction? [2]

ii) Explain why temperature has this effect on the rate of reaction. [2]

c) Using a reaction profile diagram, explain how catalysts can increase the rates of reactions. [3]

5 Two students were investigating the effect of concentration on the rate of a reaction. They used the reaction between zinc metal and dilute hydrochloric acid. The hydrochloric acid was in excess in each trial. They did the experiment using three different concentrations of the acid. Here are their results:

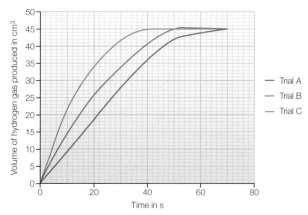

a) What does the term excess mean? [1]

b) Which trial had the most concentrated acid? Explain your answer. [2]

c) What was the volume of gas produced after 30 seconds in trial B? [1]

d) Explain why all three trials had the same final gas volume. [1]

e) Explain, using collision theory, why trial A produced less gas after 40 seconds than trial B. [3]

6 Sulfur dioxide is reacted with oxygen in the presence of a vanadium oxide catalyst to make sulfur trioxide. The reaction is exothermic. Here is the equation.

$$2SO_2(g) + O_2(g) \rightleftharpoons 2SO_3(g)$$

a) What does the symbol $\rightleftharpoons$ mean? [1]

b) The reaction can reach a position of dynamic equilibrium. State what is meant by the term 'dynamic equilibrium'. [1]

c) The percentage of sulfur trioxide at equilibrium can be altered by changing the conditions in the reaction vessel. What effect will the following changes have on the percentage of sulfur trioxide at equilibrium? Explain your answers.

i) Carrying out the reaction at a higher temperature but at the same pressure. [2]

ii) Carrying out the reaction at a higher pressure but at the same temperature. [2]

d) What is the effect of the catalyst on the equilibrium? [2]

EXTEND AND CHALLENGE

Measuring enthalpy changes really accurately

When you try to measure enthalpy changes in the laboratory by measuring the increase or decrease in temperature of the reactants and products, there are all sorts of problems. Heat energy is transferred to and from the environment and the apparatus used. So how do chemists obtain results that are both reproducible and accurate?

The answer is the bomb calorimeter. Originally made from a bomb casing, which gives the apparatus its name, it is an ingenious device to ensure that virtually all the heat energy released by a burning fuel can be measured. How is it done?

The sample is burned in a crucible inside the calorimeter (Figure 1) and the temperature of the water is monitored and a graph produced. The crucible is then replaced with a heating coil, and the water allowed to cool to its original starting temperature. The current is then switched on, and sufficient current is supplied to produce a graph curve identical to the original curve. By measuring the current used during the heating by the coil it is possible to find the exact same amount of energy that heated the water as the fuel did. This must be the heat energy that was produced.

1 Describe the differences between the bomb calorimeter and the apparatus for measuring enthalpy change shown in Figure 2.2 in Chapter 3.2.

2 Suggest what the purpose is of the following parts of the bomb calorimeter:
   a) the stirrer
   b) the air jacket
   c) the data logger.

3 Suggest why there is no need to know the specific heat capacity of the water or the apparatus.

4 Explain how the differences you have given in question 1 could improve the reproducibility of the results obtained in the bomb calorimeter.

5 Explain why the results from the bomb calorimeter will be more accurate.

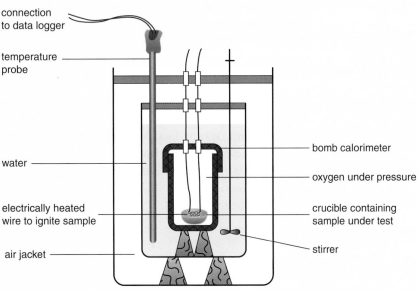

Figure 1 A bomb calorimeter.

4 Organic chemistry

In the early 19th century organic chemistry was the study of the chemicals found inside the organs of dead bodies, and it is from this that it gets its name. Analysis of crude oil in the mid-19th century showed great similarities between the chemicals from corpses and the chemicals in crude oil. This is not surprising, since crude oil is made from the fossilised remains of living things.

Today organic chemistry is concerned with all compounds containing carbon, except carbon dioxide, carbon monoxide and carbonates. The photo of a living room shows just how dependent we are on making items from the chemicals in crude oil. Every item in the picture has at some stage been dependent on organic chemicals for its material or manufacture. Many of these come from crude oil.

DISCUSS · PRESENT

1 Think about everything you've touched since you woke up this morning. Make a table to show those items that need chemicals from oil to be made, and those that you think didn't. Compare your list with a friend's. See if you agree about your classification.

2 There are predictions made about when crude oil will run out. In the 1950s it was thought it would run out by the 1990s. Today we think it may last until 2050. Suggest some reasons why these predictions are so different.

3 Some people think these predictions are little more than guesses. Make a list of as many variables as you can that will affect how long crude oil supplies will last. There are more than you think!

By the end of this section you should:
- know that organic chemistry is the study of chemicals that are found in living things, and of substances such as crude oil that were once living things
- know the effects of burning carbon based fuels
- know that organic compounds can be grouped together according to their structure in homologous series
- know that hydrocarbons have only carbon and hydrogen in their molecules
- know the difference between saturated and unsaturated compounds
- understand the differences between general, molecular and displayed formulae, and how the same general formulae can have several different molecular or displayed formulae known as isomers
- Know how addition and condensation polymers are made.

4.1 Crude oil

Figure 1.1 An oil field in the Middle East.

Figure 1.2 Crude oil has formed over millions of years from the effects of temperature, pressure and bacteria on dead sea creatures. This fossil of a prehistoric fish was left when the rest of it became crude oil.

Crude oil is a major source of fuels and industrial chemicals throughout the world. It is a sticky, smelly, dark-brown liquid. Crude oil is a mixture containing hundreds of different compounds. These vary from simple hydrocarbons like methane (Chapter 4.4) to complicated substances with long chains and rings of carbon atoms. Nearly all the substances in crude oil contain carbon. These carbon compounds are often called organic compounds. Coal, natural gas, wood and all living things also contain organic compounds. Crude oil is a non-renewable resource.

■ Separating crude oil into fractions

The carbon compounds in crude oil have different boiling points. This means that crude oil can be separated by boiling off portions over different temperature ranges.

> These portions are called **fractions** and the process of boiling off fractions is called **fractional distillation**.

Most of the fractions from crude oil are used as fuel.

Crude oil is far too toxic to distil in an open laboratory. Instead, the process is often demonstrated using an artificial crude oil.

Figure 1.3 shows the small-scale fractional distillation of artificial crude oil. The ceramic wool, soaked in artificial crude oil, is heated very gently at first and then more strongly so that the distillate slowly drips into the collecting tube. Three fractions are collected, with the boiling ranges and properties shown in Table 1.

Table 1 also shows the industrial names of the fractions. Notice how the properties of the fractions – colour, viscosity (runniness) and flammability – gradually change as the boiling range gets higher.

The fractions from crude oil contain mixtures of similar substances. Each fraction contains compounds with roughly the same number of carbon atoms. As the number of carbon atoms increases, the molecules get larger and they have higher boiling ranges.

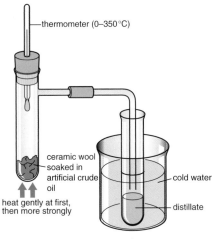

thermometer (0–350°C)

ceramic wool soaked in artificial crude oil

cold water

heat gently at first, then more strongly

distillate

Figure 1.3 The small-scale fractional distillation of artificial crude oil may have been demonstrated to you. **Wear eye protection.**

231

Table 1 The properties of fractions obtained by the small-scale fractional distillation of crude oil.

Boiling range in °C	Name of fraction	Colour	Viscosity (runniness)	How does it burn? (flammability)
20–70	gasoline (petrol)	pale yellow	runny	easily with a clean yellow flame
120–170	kerosene (paraffin)	dark yellow	fairly viscous	harder to burn, quite smoky flame
170–270	diesel	brown	viscous	hard to burn, very smoky flame

From Table 1 we can see that as the boiling range gets higher, and the molecules get larger, the fractions are:

- less volatile
- darker in colour
- more viscous (less runny)
- less flammable and less easy to ignite.

The difficulty in igniting the higher fractions with larger molecules limits their use as fuels.

■ Separating crude oil for industry

Figure 1.4 shows the products and their boiling ranges at different heights in an industrial fractionating tower. Inside the tower there are horizontal trays at different levels.

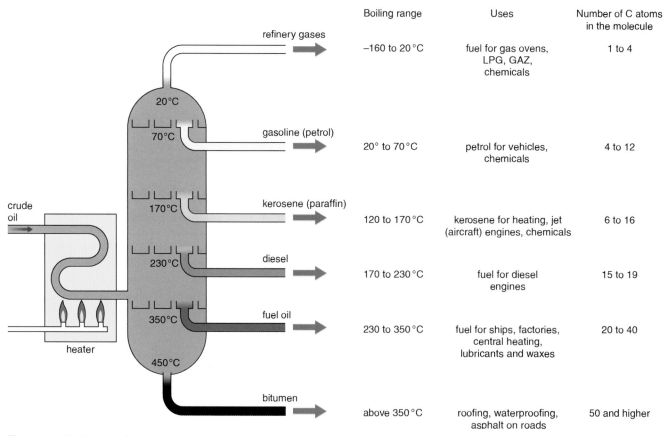

Figure 1.4 The fractions from crude oil and their uses.

The crude oil is heated in a furnace and the vapours pass into the lower part of the tower. As the vapours rise up the tower, the temperature falls. Different vapours condense at different heights in the tower, collect on the horizontal trays and are then tapped off.

Liquids like gasoline, which boil at low temperatures, condense high up in the tower. Liquids like fuel oil, which boil at higher temperatures, condense low down in the tower.

The fractions from crude oil contain mixtures of similar substances with roughly the same number of carbon atoms. Figure 1.4 also shows the number of carbon atoms in the constituents and the uses of each fraction. The uses of the various fractions depend on their properties.

Uses of some fractions

- Gasoline vaporises easily and is very flammable, so it is ideal for use in car engines.
- Fuel oil is very viscous and does not ignite easily. It is used as fuel in central heating systems.
- Bitumen is solid, but easy to melt. It is used for waterproofing and mixed with stone chippings for road surfacing.

STUDY QUESTIONS

1 a) Why is crude oil important?
   b) Why should we try to conserve our reserves of crude oil?
   c) How is crude oil separated into various fractions at a refinery?
2 a) List the main fractions obtained from crude oil.
   b) Give the main uses of each fraction.

3 a) What does the word 'organic' mean in everyday use?
   b) Why do you think the study of carbon compounds is called 'organic chemistry'?
   c) To a chemist, organic compounds are simple molecular compounds. What physical properties would you expect them to have?

4.2 How pure is our air?

People have worried about the purity of their air ever since our ancestors could make fires. Smoke from fires made their eyes water and the smells were unbearable. So, air pollution isn't new, but the concerns about air purity have increased. This is because there are now many more people on Earth, and more people means more homes, more industries, more vehicles and therefore more air pollution.

Figure 2.1 In rush hour in Japan, air pollution is a serious problem. Some people wear face masks to help prevent breathing in pollution that could trigger an asthma attack.

■ What substances cause air pollution?

Air pollution is caused by the release of poisonous and harmful gases and particles into the air. These harm living things. Most air pollution is caused by burning fossil fuels in our homes, in our vehicles and in power stations (Figure 2.2). The substances responsible for most air pollution are shown in Table 1. The table also shows their harmful effects and the possible methods of control. Most of these control methods have been adopted in the last decade, leading to a significant improvement in air quality.

Table 1 Substances causing most air pollution.

Air pollutant	Source	Effects	Methods of control
soot and smoke	burning fuels	• deposits of soot on buildings, etc. • smoke harms our lungs	• use of smokeless fuels • improve supply of air to burning fuels
carbon monoxide	burning fuels – especially in vehicles	• poisonous to humans and animals	• make vehicle engines which burn fuel more efficiently • fit catalytic converters
sulfur dioxide	burning coal and oil which contain small amounts of sulfur	sulfur dioxide and nitrogen oxides react with rainwater to form sulfurous acid, nitrous acid and nitric acid – 'acid rain', which: • harms plants • gets into rivers and lakes, harming fish and other aquatic species • reacts with limestone and marble.	• burn less coal and oil • remove sulfur dioxide from waste gases
nitrogen oxides	vehicle exhaust gases		• adjust engines so that nitrogen oxides don't form • fit catalytic converters
chlorofluorocarbons (CFCs)	refrigerators, aerosol sprays	CFCs destroy the protective ozone layer resulting in damage from UV radiation	reduce the use of CFCs by using other substances

Figure 2.2 Motor vehicles and power stations are the source of most air pollution.

Carbon dioxide, carbon monoxide and soot

When a fossil fuel such as methane (CH_4) in natural gas burns in plenty of air (oxygen) it produces two gases, water vapour and carbon dioxide.

methane+ oxygen → water vapour+ carbon dioxide
$$CH_4(g) + 2O_2(g) \rightarrow 2H_2O(g) + CO_2(g)$$

If there is not enough oxygen or air present then poisonous carbon monoxide is made. Every year people are killed by sitting or sleeping in rooms heated by natural gas where there is not enough oxygen, and carbon monoxide is made instead of carbon dioxide.

methane+ oxygen → water vapour+ carbon monoxide
$$CH_4(g) + 1\tfrac{1}{2}O_2(g) \rightarrow 2H_2O(g) + CO(g)$$

When very little oxygen is available then burning the hydrocarbon produces water vapour and pure carbon, or soot.

methane+ oxygen→ water vapour+ carbon (soot)
$$CH_4(g) + O_2(g) \rightarrow 2H_2O(g) + C(s)$$

Carbon monoxide is dangerous and can kill you. The carbon monoxide is absorbed by your red blood cells in preference to oxygen and is not released in your cells. This stops your blood from carrying oxygen to your organs and cells, leading to unconsciousness and death.

Nitrogen oxides and car engines

Car engines need large volumes of air to burn their gasoline or diesel fuels. When the fuel burns inside the engine a very high temperature is reached, and some nitrogen molecules in the air react with the oxygen in the air to make nitrogen oxides. These oxides are one cause of acid rain.

■ Acid rain

Many fuels, natural gas, crude oil, coal and coke, contain small amounts of sulfur. When these fuels burn, sulfur dioxide is produced. This is a colourless, toxic and choking gas which irritates our eyes and lungs. The sulfur dioxide reacts with rainwater to form sulfurous acid. This is further oxidised to sulfuric acid and this, together with sulfurous acid, causes acid rain.

sulfur dioxide + water → sulfurous acid

$$SO_2(g) + H_2O(l) \rightarrow H_2SO_3(aq)$$

sulfurous acid + oxygen → sulfuric acid

$$2H_2SO_3(aq) + O_2(g) \rightarrow 2H_2SO_4(aq)$$

Nitrogen oxides from vehicle exhaust gases also contribute to acid rain. These nitrogen oxides react with rainwater to form nitrous and nitric acids which also cause acid rain (Figure 2.3 on page 236).

Acid rain harms all living things. It has been blamed for the poor growth of trees in Scandinavia and the death of fish in rivers and lakes. It is thought that the sulfur dioxide produced in the industrial areas of Scotland and Northern England can be carried by prevailing winds across the North Sea to Scandinavia. Acid rain also attacks metals and the stonework of buildings.

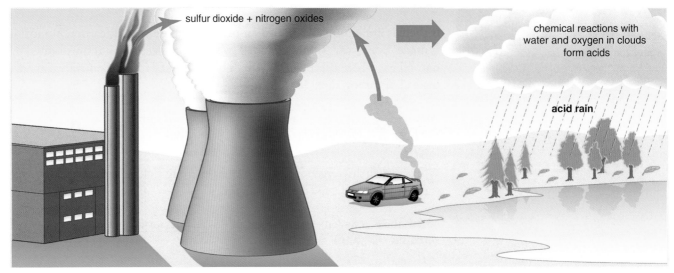

Figure 2.3 The formation of acid rain.

STUDY QUESTIONS

1 **a)** What are the main substances that cause air pollution?
   b) How do they get into the air?
   c) Suggest three ways in which air pollution causes harm or damage.

2 **a)** What is acid rain and how is it caused?
   b) How does acid rain affect:
   i) lakes
   ii) forests?

3 **a)** What further steps could be taken to reduce air pollution in heavily industrialised areas?
   b) What problems are there with stricter controls over air pollution?

4.3 Cracking – more petrol from crude oil

During the 1930s, the demand for gasoline increased much faster than the demand for heavier fractions containing long-chain hydrocarbons which make up two-thirds of crude oil (Table 1). This meant that refineries were left with large unwanted amounts of the heavier fractions. Fortunately, chemists found ways of converting the heavier long-chain hydrocarbons into shorter-chain hydrocarbons, such as those in gasoline and other useful products.

Figure 3.1 Oil refineries work 24/7 to give us all the gasoline and diesel we need.

Table 1 Relative amounts of the different fractions in crude oil and the everyday demand for each fraction.

Fraction	Percentage in	
	Crude oil	Everyday demand
refinery gases	2	4
gasoline	6	22
kerosene	13	8
diesel	19	23
fuel oil and bitumen	50	38

■ Cracking heavier fractions into useful lighter fractions

The main method of converting the heavier long-chain hydrocarbons from crude oil into gasoline, with shorter-chain alkanes, is **catalytic cracking**.

Catalytic cracking involves the thermal decomposition of long-chain hydrocarbon molecules into short-chain hydrocarbons using a catalyst at high temperature.

Figure 3.2 shows the apparatus needed to crack liquid paraffin, which contains a hydrocarbon called decane (see Figure 3.3), into octane and ethene (see Figure 3.4). Octane is one of the molecules in petrol. Ethene is useful as a chemical feedstock from which to make many polymers and pharmaceutical chemicals.

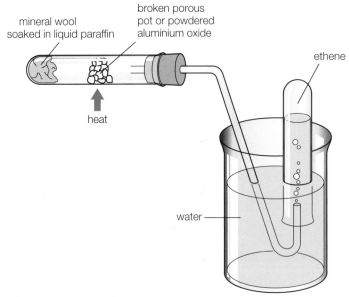

Figure 3.2 Cracking **liquid paraffin** to obtain octane and ethene.

What are the products of cracking?

Figure 3.3 The displayed formula of decane.

Look at the long molecule of decane ($C_{10}H_{22}$) in Figure 3.3. Decane has a chain of 10 carbon atoms with 22 hydrogen atoms. Now, suppose decane is cracked (split) between two carbon atoms. This cannot produce two smaller alkane molecules because there are not enough hydrogen atoms to go round. But suppose one product of cracking decane is the alkane, octane (C_8H_{18}).

$$C_{10}H_{22} \longrightarrow C_8H_{18} + C_2H_4$$

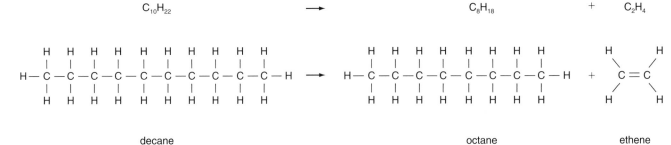

Figure 3.4 When decane undergoes catalytic cracking, it forms an alkane, like octane, and an alkene, like ethene.

If C_8H_{18} is split off from $C_{10}H_{22}$, the molecular formula of the remainder is C_2H_4 (Figure 3.4). This is ethene (Chapter 4.5). Notice in Figure 3.4 that ethene has a double bond between the two carbon atoms. This double bond allows all the carbon atoms in the molecule to have four bonds.

Hydrocarbons such as ethene, which contain a carbon–carbon double bond (C=C) are known as **alkenes**.

■ How are molecules cracked?

Unlike distillation, cracking is a chemical process. It involves breaking a strong covalent bond between two carbon atoms. This requires high temperatures in the range of 600–700 °C and a catalyst of finely powdered aluminium oxide (alumina) or silicon(IV) oxide (silica). The catalyst does not react with the crude oil fractions but it does provide a very hot surface that speeds up cracking. At high temperatures, the longer alkane molecules have more energy and they break apart, forming two or more smaller molecules.

Cracking is important because it is used to produce more gasoline (petrol) and important alkenes such as ethene. Larger alkanes in crude oil are cracked to produce alkanes with about eight carbon atoms like octane. These are the main constituents in gasoline. The gasoline obtained in this way is better quality than that obtained by the straightforward distillation of crude oil. Cracked gasoline is therefore blended with other petrols to improve their quality.

Figure 3.5 The catalytic cracking plant at an oil refinery.

STUDY QUESTIONS

1 Explain these words:
   cracking; catalytic; alkene; unsaturated.
2 **a)** Why is cracking important?
   b) What conditions are used for cracking?
   c) Write an equation for the cracking of octane (C_8H_{18}) in which one of the products is pentane (C_5H_{12}).
   d) Draw the displayed formulae of the products in part **c)**.
   e) Cracking can produce hydrogen. Write an equation for the cracking of butane (C_4H_{10}) in which one of the products is hydrogen.
3 What changes do you think there will be in our lives when crude oil begins to run out?

4.4 Alkanes

■ Crude oil and hydrocarbons

The developed countries of the world consume large quantities of hydrocarbons from crude oil and natural gas. Developing nations need progressively more crude oil and natural gas to develop their economies. Just what is it about crude oil and natural gas that makes their molecules so useful to us all?

Figure 4.1 Crude oil and natural gas are vital sources of carbon compounds we call hydrocarbons.

Most of the substances in crude oil and natural gas are made from just two elements, hydrogen and carbon. Substances that contain only hydrogen and carbon are called **hydrocarbons**.

Crude oil contains dozens of different hydrocarbons. These vary from methane (CH_4) with just one carbon atom per molecule to very complex hydrocarbons with more than 30 carbon atoms per molecule.

All these different hydrocarbons exist because carbon atoms can form strong covalent bonds with each other. Atoms of other elements cannot do this.

Because of these strong C—C bonds, carbon forms molecules containing straight chains, branched chains and even rings of carbon atoms. There are thousands of different hydrocarbons and millions of different carbon compounds.

■ Alkanes

The four simplest straight-chain hydrocarbons are methane, ethane, propane and butane. Table 1 shows the molecular formulae, displayed formulae, dot and cross diagrams and molecular models for these four hydrocarbons. The displayed formulae show which atoms are attached to each other. But they cannot show the three-dimensional structures of the molecules which you can see from the molecular models.

Table 1 The first four alkanes.

Name	Methane	Ethane	Propane	Butane
Molecular formula	CH_4	C_2H_6	C_3H_8	C_4H_{10}
Structural formula	CH_4	CH_3CH_3	$CH_3CH_2CH_3$	$CH_3CH_2CH_2CH_3$
Displayed formula	H | H—C—H | H	H H | | H—C—C—H | | H H	H H H | | | H—C—C—C—H | | | H H H	H H H H | | | | H—C—C—C—C—H | | | | H H H H
Dot and cross diagram	H H C H H	H H H C C H H H	H H H H C C C H H H H	H H H H H C C C C H H H H H
Molecular model (black balls for carbon, white for hydrogen)				

There are four covalent bonds to each carbon atom. Each of these bonds consists of a pair of shared electrons. The four pairs of electrons around a carbon atom repel each other as far as possible. So, the bonds around each carbon atom spread out tetrahedrally, as in methane (Figure 4.2).

Methane, ethane, propane and butane are members of a series of compounds called **alkanes**. All other alkanes are named from the number of carbon atoms in their chain. So C_5H_{12} with five carbon atoms in its chain is *pentane*; C_6H_{14} is *hexane*; C_7H_{16} is *heptane*; and so on. The names of all alkanes end in **–ane**.

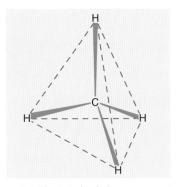

Figure 4.2 The tetrahedral arrangement of bonds in methane.

■ Alkanes are a homologous series

Look at the formulae of methane, CH_4; ethane, C_2H_6; propane, C_3H_8; and butane C_4H_{10}. Notice that the difference in carbon and hydrogen atoms between methane and ethane is CH_2. The difference between ethane and propane is CH_2 and the difference between propane and butane is also CH_2. This is an example of a **homologous series**.

A homologous series is a family of compounds with similar chemical properties and in which the formulae differ by CH_2.

Can you see from the displayed formulae in Table 1 that if an alkane has n carbon atoms, it will have $2n + 2$ hydrogen atoms? (Every carbon atom in the chain has two hydrogen atoms, except the two C atoms at the ends of the chain, both of which have an extra H atom.)

This allows us to write a **general formula** for alkanes as $C_nH_{2n + 2}$.

Figure 4.3 A small blue butane cylinder used to fuel a camping cooker.

Isomerism

We mentioned in Chapter 1.23 that carbon could form a large number of compounds. There are even more compounds than you might expect, because it is sometimes possible to join the same set of atoms in different ways. For example, take the formula C_4H_{10}. We know already from Table 1 that butane has the formula C_4H_{10}. But there is another compound which also has this formula, called methylpropane (Table 2). Notice that each carbon atom in butane and in methylpropane has four bonds and each H atom has one bond. Butane and methylpropane are two distinct compounds with different properties as shown in Table 2.

Compounds like this with the same molecular formula, but different displayed formulae and different properties are called **isomers**.

Table 2 Isomers with the formula C_4H_{10}.

Name	Butane	Methylpropane
Molecular formula	C_4H_{10}	C_4H_{10}
Displayed formula	(displayed structure of butane)	(displayed structure of methylpropane)
Melting point / °C	−138	−159
Boiling point / °C	0	−12
Density / g / cm³	0.58	0.56

Empirical and molecular formulae

The empirical formula of any compound can be calculated provided we know the actual masses of the different elements in a sample of the compound and the relative atomic masses of the elements. For example, when ethane is analysed, it is found to contain 80% carbon and 20% hydrogen.

	C		**H**
reacting masses	80 g	:	20 g
mass of 1 mol	12 g	:	1 g
∴ reacting moles	$\dfrac{80}{12}$	:	$\dfrac{20}{1}$
	6.67	:	20
ratio of moles	1	:	3
∴ ratio of atoms	1	:	3

$\Rightarrow$ empirical formula $= CH_3$

This formula for ethane shows only the simplest ratio of carbon atoms to hydrogen atoms. The actual formula showing the correct number of carbon atoms and hydrogen atoms in one molecule of ethane could be CH_3, C_2H_6, C_3H_9, etc., since all of these formulae give CH_3 as the simplest ratio of atoms.

The simplest formula for a substance, such as CH_3 for ethane, is called the **empirical formula**. This shows the simplest whole-number ratio for the atoms of different elements in the compound.

In the case of simple molecular compounds such as ethane, it is usually more helpful to use the **molecular formula**. This shows the actual number of atoms of the different elements in one molecule of the compound.

Experiments show that the relative molecular mass of ethane is 30. But the relative molecular mass of CH_3 is only 15, so the molecular formula of ethane is C_2H_6.

In ionic compounds, such as sodium chloride, Na^+Cl^-, it is meaningless to talk of molecules and molecular formulae. In this case, the formulae we use are empirical formulae showing the simplest ratio for atoms of different elements in the compound.

The word 'empirical' comes from a Greek word meaning 'experimental' and an empirical formula is the simplest formula obtained from experimental results.

■ The properties of alkanes

Low melting points and low boiling points

Alkanes are typical molecular (non-metal) compounds. They have low melting points and low boiling points. Alkanes with one to four carbon atoms per molecule are gases at room temperature. Methane (CH_4) and ethane (C_2H_6) make up about 95% of natural gas. Propane (C_3H_8) and butane (C_4H_{10}) are the main constituents of 'liquefied petroleum gas' (LPG). The best known uses of LPG are as 'Calor Gas' and 'GAZ' for camping, caravans and boats.

Alkanes with 5 to 17 carbon atoms are liquids at room temperature. Mixtures of these liquids are used in gasoline (petrol), kerosene, diesel and engine oil. Alkanes with 18 or more carbon atoms per molecule, such as bitumen (tar), are solids at room temperature. Even so, they begin to melt on very hot days.

Notice that alkanes become less volatile and change from gases to liquids and then to solids as their molecules get larger down the series.

Insoluble in water

Alkanes are insoluble in water, but they dissolve in solvents like petrol.

Poor reactivity

Alkanes do not contain ions and their C—C and C—H bonds are strong. So they have very few reactions. They do not react with metals, acids or alkalis. It may surprise you, but gasoline (which contains mainly alkanes) will not react with sodium, concentrated sulfuric acid or sodium hydroxide. You **must not try any experiments** with gasoline. It is highly flammable.

Figure 4.4 Two red propane cylinders, stored outside.

Reaction with oxygen (combustion)

The most important reactions of alkanes involve burning. In a plentiful supply of air or oxygen, alkanes are completely oxidised to carbon dioxide and water when they burn.

$$C_4H_{10} + 6\tfrac{1}{2}O_2 \rightarrow 4CO_2 + 5H_2O$$
(butane in camping gas)

Burning reactions are very **exothermic**: they release heat energy. Because of this, natural gas and crude oil, which contain mainly alkanes, are used as fuels.

When a carbon-based fuel burns, if it has lots of oxygen it produces only carbon dioxide and water vapour. If it hasn't got enough oxygen it produces some carbon monoxide instead of some of the carbon dioxide as well as the water vapour.

If there is too little air or oxygen, alkanes are only partially oxidised during burning and combustion is incomplete. In this case, soot (carbon) and carbon monoxide are formed as well as carbon dioxide and water.

Carbon monoxide has no smell and it is very poisonous (toxic). It reacts with **haemoglobin** in the blood forming carboxyhaemoglobin and this reduces the capacity of the blood to carry oxygen. Because of this, it is dangerous to burn carbon compounds in a poor supply of air or in faulty gas appliances.

Reaction with halogens

Chlorine and bromine are very reactive non-metals. It is not surprising that these halogens react with alkanes on exposure to ultraviolet (UV) radiation.

During the reaction, hydrogen atoms in the alkane molecules are replaced (substituted) by halogen atoms. For example, when methane and bromine vapour are mixed together in strong sunlight, a steady reaction takes place forming bromomethane and hydrogen bromide.

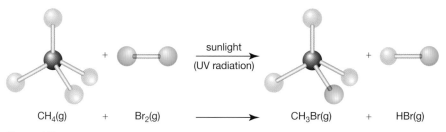

$$CH_4(g) \quad + \quad Br_2(g) \quad \longrightarrow \quad CH_3Br(g) \quad + \quad HBr(g)$$

Figure 4.5

One of the H atoms in methane is substituted by a Br atom, forming bromomethane. Chlorine reacts in a similar way to bromine, initially forming chloromethane and hydrogen chloride.

The reaction is started by breaking bonds in the halogen molecules, which requires energy. This energy is provided by UV radiation. The energy splits the halogen molecules into highly reactive free atoms.

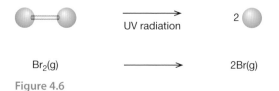

Figure 4.6

These highly reactive free atoms can now react with the relatively unreactive methane molecules. In a similar way, the heat from a spark or from a burning match is required to initiate the reaction of methane and other alkanes with oxygen. If methane is mixed with oxygen or with bromine in the dark at room temperature, there is no reaction.

STUDY QUESTIONS

1 Explain the meaning of the following:
   hydrocarbon, alkane, homologous series, isomerism,
   empirical formula.

2 **a)** Why is C_8H_{18} called octane?
   b) Draw a displayed formula for C_8H_{18}.
   c) How many H atoms will the alkane with 10 carbon atoms have?

3 Why can a homologous series of compounds be compared to a group of elements in the Periodic Table?

4 **a)** Draw the displayed formula for the alkane pentane.
   b) Write the molecular formula of pentane.
   c) There are two isomers of pentane. Draw the displayed formulae of these two isomers.

5 **a)** Write a balanced equation for the complete combustion in oxygen of octane (one of the alkanes in gasoline).

   b) What are the products when octane burns in a poor supply of oxygen?
   c) Why is it dangerous to allow a car engine to run in a garage with the door closed?

6 Why do the different alkanes change from gases to liquids and then to solids as their molecular size increases?

7 **a)** Use molecular models to build a molecule of hexane.
   b) Write the empirical, molecular and displayed formulae of hexane.
   c) Draw two other displayed formulae with the same molecular formulae as hexane.
   d) Build molecular models of your structures in part (c).

4.5 Alkenes

Ethene is a 'wonder' molecule. All the items in the photo can be made from ethene, as well as thousands of other ones. It is a very special molecule because it is highly reactive, and can be easily converted into a wide range of products. It is a by-product of the manufacture of petrol and diesel to keep transport moving. It is the simplest molecule of the group of hydrocarbons called alkenes.

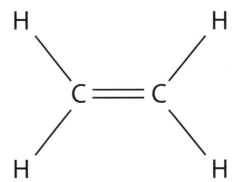

Figure 5.1 Just some of the items that can be made from ethene.

Figure 5.2 In nature, ethene acts as a trigger for the ripening of fruit, particularly bananas.

Alkenes

Ethene is the first member of a homologous series called the alkenes. It has the molecular formula C_2H_4. The two carbon atoms are joined together by a double bond like this:

The >C=C< part of the formula is an example of a functional group, as it determines the properties and reactions of the molecule. You will see more functional groups later in the chapter. Displayed formula can take a long time to write, particularly for large molecules, so we can use a shorter formula.

This shows the atoms joined to each carbon atom and is known as a structural formula. The structural formua for ethane is $CH_2=CH_2$. Notice that the double bond is shown in the structural formula.

Table 1 shows the molecular, structural and displayed formula for the first three alkenes. If an alkene has n number of carbon atoms it will need $2n$ number of hydrogen atoms, so the general formula for alkenes is C_nH_{2n}.

Table 1 The first three alkenes.

Name	Ethene	Propene	Butene
Molecular formula	C_2H_4	C_3H_6	C_4H_8
Structural formula	$CH_2=CH_2$	$CH_2=CHCH_3$	$CH_2=CHCH_2CH_3$
Displayed formula			

Testing for ethene

Some molecules can 'add across' the double bond in ethene (and other molecules with C = C bonds) to make two single bonds. Alkenes readily undergo such **addition reactions**.

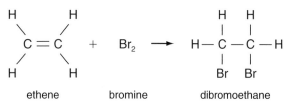

This explains why orange bromine water becomes colourless (decolorises) on shaking with an alkene, like ethene. The bromine molecules add across the double bond in ethene, forming dibromoethane.

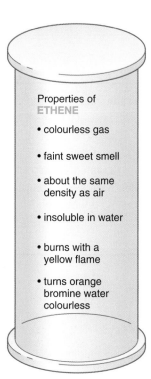

Properties of
ETHENE

• colourless gas

• faint sweet smell

• about the same density as air

• insoluble in water

• burns with a yellow flame

• turns orange bromine water colourless

Figure 5.3 Properties of ethene.

Comparing alkanes with alkenes

Ethane and other alkanes are fairly unreactive. They have substitution reactions with chlorine and bromine in ultraviolet radiation, but they do *not* react with bromine water.

In comparison, ethene and other alkenes are very reactive. They have addition reactions with chlorine and bromine at room temperature and they readily decolorise orange bromine water.

Saturated or unsaturated

The reaction between ethene and bromine water shows that the double bond of ethene can be broken and more atoms added to the molecule. We say that any molecule that has carbon double bonds is **unsaturated**. Ethane, which has only single bonds, is **saturated**.

Figure 5.4 The relative amounts of double bonds in polyunsaturated vegetable oils, such as sunflower oil, can be measured by timing how long it takes to decolorise bromine water.

STUDY QUESTIONS

1 The displayed formula of propene is shown below.

$$\begin{array}{ccccc} & H & & H & H \\ & | & & | & | \\ H - & C & - & C & = C \\ & | & & | & | \\ & H & & H & H \end{array}$$

  a) Write equations for the reactions of propene with:
  i) hydrogen, ii) bromine.
  b) Draw the displayed formulae of the products in part a).

2 Look at the structures of alkanes and alkenes in Chapter 4.4 and this chapter. Why is the general formula for alkenes C_nH_{2n}?
3 When you are caught out in the rain and your clothes are soaking in water you are saturated. Explain why the same term is used to describe carbon compounds where the molecules contain no double bonds.

4.6 Alcohols

When people talk about alcohol, they really mean *ethanol*. Ethanol is the substance which makes alcoholic drinks intoxicating. It is also the major constituent in methylated spirits (meths). After water, ethanol is the most widely used industrial solvent.

Figure 6.1 Foam in a copper brewery tank. What causes the foam?

■ Alcohols are a homologous series

In the last two chapters we looked at alkanes and alkenes as examples of two homologous series of hydrocarbons. Alcohols are another homologous series, but they are not hydrocarbons. An oxygen atom has been introduced into the molecule to provide the functional group –OH.

Methanol is the simplest alcohol; it has the formula CH_3OH. Table 1 shows the structural and displayed formulae of the first four alcohols.

Table 1 Methanol, ethanol, propanol and butanol.

Name	Methanol	Ethanol	Propanol (propan-1-ol)	Butanol (butan-1-ol)
Molecular formula	CH_3OH	C_2H_5OH	C_3H_7OH	C_4H_9OH
Structural formula	CH_3OH	CH_3CH_2OH	$CH_3CH_2CH_2OH$	$CH_3CH_2CH_2CH_2OH$
Displayed formula	(displayed structure of methanol)	(displayed structure of ethanol)	(displayed structure of propanol)	(displayed structure of butanol)

■ Manufacturing ethanol

At one time, all ethanol, including methylated spirits, was produced by fermentation of sugars. Today, fermentation is still important in brewing and wine making, but most industrial ethanol and methylated spirits is manufactured from ethene.

Manufacturing ethanol by fermentation

The starting material for fermentation is a glucose solution. In countries where sugar beet and sugar cane grow well and are readily available, industrial alcohol is manufactured from sugar extracted from these plants. The starting material in wine making is a sugary solution of grape juice and in beer making it is a sugary solution of malted barley.

Natural yeasts in the plant materials and, in some cases, added yeast, contain enzymes that break down the sugar. The first product is glucose, which is then broken down to ethanol and carbon dioxide (Figure 6.2). The process takes place at about 30 °C.

$$C_6H_{12}O_6 \rightarrow 2CH_3CH_2OH + 2CO_2$$
$$\text{glucose} \qquad \text{ethanol}$$

The glucose must be fermented with the yeast in the absence of air. If oxygen is present then the ethanol made is rapidly oxidised on to ethanoic acid. Yeast is a living organism and uses enzymes to ferment glucose to ethanol. If the temperature is too low the enzymes work very slowly. If the temperature is too high then the enzymes are denatured (usually above 45 °C). The optimum temperature is where the fermentation takes place quickly without damaging the yeast.

Fermentation can only produce a dilute solution of ethanol in water because the yeasts are killed if the solution is more than 15% ethanol. But fermentation is ideal for wine making (about 12% ethanol) and beer (about 3% ethanol). Fractional distillation is used to obtain higher concentrations of ethanol for industrial use and for producing whisky, gin and vodka. These drinks contain about 40% ethanol.

limewater

5 g glucose dissolved in 50 cm³ water + 1 spatula measure of yeast

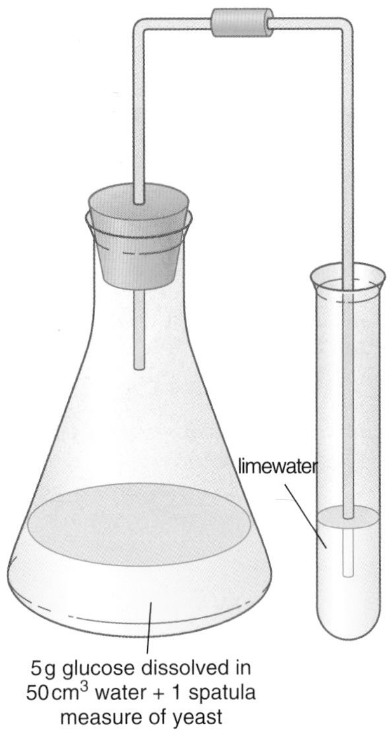

Figure 6.2 Making ethanol by fermentation on a small scale. Leave the apparatus in a warm place for five days. Why does the limewater go milky? Then filter the solution in the conical flask and separate ethanol from the filtrate by fractional distillation. **Wear eye protection** and be aware it is likely to froth considerably because of dissolved carbon dioxide. The first few drops of distillate will burn like ethanol. Do not taste the distillate.

Manufacturing ethanol from ethene

Most industrial ethanol and methylated spirits is manufactured by an addition reaction between ethene and steam (water). The ethene is obtained from crude oil by cracking (Chapter 4.3). Ethene and steam are passed over a catalyst of phosphoric acid at 300 °C and a pressure of 60–70 atm.

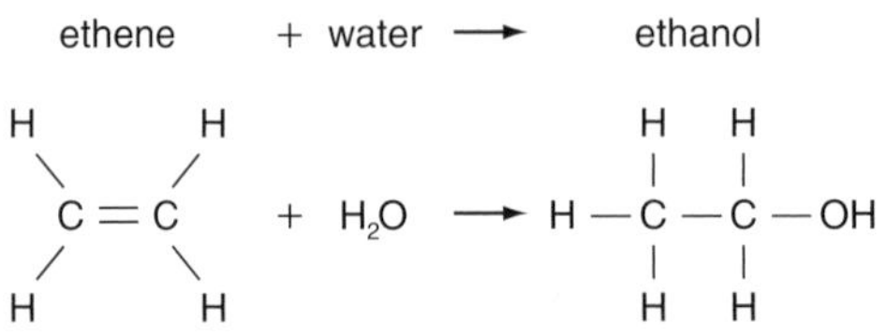

A reaction like this, which involves the addition of water, is described as **hydration**.

Figure 6.3 Methylated spirits is used as a solvent in table polishes to spread the polish and obtain a smooth, shiny surface.

Large quantities of ethanol are used in industry as solvents for paints, dyes, glues and soaps. Ethanol is miscible with both oils and water so it can be used with a wide range of solutes. It also evaporates quickly which makes it useful as a solvent for perfumes and aftershave lotions.

Most of the ethanol used in industry and in our homes is sold as methylated spirits (meths). This contains about 90% ethanol, 5% water and 5% methanol. The methanol gives the meths a bitter taste and makes it unfit to drink.

■ Oxidations of ethanol

Burning in air

All alcohols burn easily in air. Ethanol burns with a blue flame to produce water vapour and carbon dioxide:

$$\text{ethanol} + \text{oxygen} \rightarrow \text{carbon dioxide} + \text{water}$$

$$2CH_3CH_2OH \text{ (l)} + 6O_2 \text{ (g)} \rightarrow 4CO_2\text{(g)} + 6H_2O \text{ (l)}$$

Reaction with air to form ethanoic acid (CH_3COOH)

If the fermentation of glucose is done in the presence of air or oxygen, then the ethanol formed oxidises to ethanoic acid (CH_3COOH):

$$CH_3CH_2OH\text{(l)} + O_2\text{(g)} \rightarrow CH_3COOH\text{(l)} + H_2O\text{(l)}$$

The change is caused by **microbial oxidation.**

Heating with potassium dichromate

If a mixture of orange potassium dichromate(VI) solution and dilute sulfuric acid is added to some ethanol and warmed then ethanoic acid is formed. The orange potassium dichromate(VI) solution turns green as chromium(III) ions are formed. It is this change that provides oxygen [O] for the oxidation. This is the basis for chemical breathalyser tests used to determine the amount of ethanol (alcohol) a driver has drunk. The warmed mixture gives off the typical vinegary smell of ethanoic acid.

$$CH_3CH_2OH\text{(l)} + \text{[O]} \rightarrow CH_3COOH\text{(l)}$$

STUDY QUESTIONS

1 Explain the words:
   fermentation, enzyme, alcohol.

2 **a)** Why is fermentation important?
   b) What are the main products of the fermentation of glucose with yeast?
   c) What causes the fermentation process?
   d) Why are there two important and viable methods for the production of ethanol?

3 **a)** If an alcohol has *n* carbon atoms, how many hydrogen atoms will it have?
   b) Write a general formula for the family of alcohols.

4 Look at the formula of butanol in Table 2. One isomer of butanol (C_4H_9OH) has the structural formula of $CH_3CH_2CH_2CH_2OH$.
   a) Draw the structural formula of another isomer of butanol which is also an alcohol.
   b) Use molecular models to construct butanol and its isomer from part **a)**.

5 **a)** Write a balanced chemical equation for the burning of ethanol with oxygen.
   b) Describe two ways that ethanol may be converted into ethanoic acid.

4.7 Carboxylic acids

In many countries pickling is used as a method of preserving foods. The cabbage, beetroot, onions, vegetables, fish and meat are covered in vinegar and the container is sealed. The vinegar is a solution of a weak acid called ethanoic acid (or acetic acid). The acid kills microbes and so prevents the food rotting. It also gives the food a sharp acid taste. Why is it safe to eat foods pickled in ethanoic acid, but not in a strong acid such as sulfuric acid?

Figure 7.1 Onions will not decay if pickled in vinegar (ethanoic acid).

■ Carboxylic acids

The active ingredient in vinegar is ethanoic acid. It is one of a group of organic compounds called carboxylic acids.

Carboxylic acids have a –COOH **functional group** attached to a carbon chain. They are named like other organic molecules using the longest chain of carbon atoms to give the 'methan-', or 'ethan-' number of carbon atoms. The name is completed by '-oic acid'.

Table 1 The first four carboxylic acids.

Name	Methanoic acid	Ethanoic acid	Propanoic acid	Butanoic acid
Molecular formula	HCO_2H	CH_3CO_2H	$C_2H_5CO_2H$	$C_3H_7CO_2H$
Structural formula	HCOOH	CH_3COOH	CH_3CH_2COOH	$CH_3CH_2CH_2COOH$
Displayed formula				

Table 1 shows the molecular and displayed formulae of the first four carboxylic acids. Each carbon atom has four covalent bonds attached to it. Note that the carbon atom which is part of the carboxylic acid functional group has one bond to the carbon chain, a double bond to one oxygen atom, and then a single bond to an oxygen atom that has a hydrogen atom attached to it.

Like alkanes, alkenes and alcohols, the carboxylic acids are a homologous series. They have the general formula $C_nH_{2n}O_2$. The formula is often expanded to show that the carboxylic acid functional group is present, like this: CH_3CO_2H or CH_3COOH.

■ Why is the carboxylic acid group an acid?

The hydrogen atom attached to the oxygen atom in the carboxylic acid group can be easily detached from the molecule as a hydrogen ion.

$$CH_3COOH(aq) \rightleftharpoons CH_3COO^-(aq) + H^+(aq)$$

The hydrogen ion is the particle that gives solutions of molecules containing the carboxylic acid group their acidic properties. It is not as easy to remove the hydrogen ion from a carboxylic acid as it is to remove it from an acid such as sulfuric acid, so carboxylic acids are weak acids (see Section 2.14).

Reaction of carboxylic acids with metals

Carboxylic acids are weak acids. They have the same reactions as strong acids but they do not react as vigorously. When reacted with reactive metals, such as sodium and iron, carboxylic acids produce hydrogen gas. This reaction is far slower than the reaction of reactive metals with hydrochloric acid.

sodium + ethanoic acid → sodium ethanoate + hydrogen gas

$$2Na(s) + 2CH_3COOH(aq) \rightarrow 2CH_3COO^-Na^+(aq) + H_2(g)$$

The salt produced by the reaction of ethanoic acid is called an ethanoate.

Table 2 Naming the salts made from carboxylic acids.

Carboxylic acid	Carboxylate salt
methanoic acid	methanoate
ethanoic acid	ethanoate
propanoic acid	propanoate
butanoic acid	butanoate
pentanoic acid	pentanoate

Reaction of carboxylic acids with metals carbonates

Metal carbonates react vigorously with acids such as sulfuric acid. They produce carbon dioxide gas, water and the salt of the acid used. The same applies to carboxylic acids. They react with metal carbonates to produce the carboxylic acid salt, carbon dioxide and water. This is the reaction of sodium carbonate with propanoic acid:

$$\text{sodium carbonate} + \text{propanoic acid} \rightarrow \text{sodium propanoate} + \text{carbon dioxide gas} + \text{water}$$

$$Na_2CO_3(s) + 2C_2H_5COOH(aq) \rightarrow 2C_2H_5COO^-Na^+(aq) + CO_2(g) + H_2O(l)$$

Copper(II) carbonate also reacts with carboxylic acids:

copper(II) carbonate + ethanoic acid → copper(II) ethanoate + carbon dioxide gas + water

$$CuCO_3(s) + 2CH_3COOH(aq) \rightarrow (CH_3COO^-)_2Cu^{2+}(aq) + CO_2(g) + H_2O(l)$$

Each copper ion needs two ethanoate ions to balance copper's two positive charges.

STUDY QUESTIONS

1 Draw the displayed formula of pentanoic acid ($C_4H_9CO_2H$).
2 Write a chemical equation to show how propanoic acid can produce a hydrogen ion in water?
3 Explain why butanoic acid is an acid.
4 Suggest the name of the salt formed by pentanoic acid.
5 Describe the reaction of propanoic acid with lithium metal. Write a balanced chemical equation and name the products. Describe a test to identify the gas given off.
6 Describe the reaction of potassium carbonate with methanoic acid. Write a balanced chemical equation and name the products. Describe a test to identify the gas given off.

4.8 Esters

Figure 8.1 Where does perfume get its smell from?

In earlier times perfumes were made from two sources; either plant extracts or from the scent glands of animals. Today, the large quantities of perfumes manufactured mean that for all but the most expensive perfumes these sources are unable to produce enough to meet demand. Instead, manufacturers use a range of compounds, many of them known as esters. Esters are made from alcohols and carboxylic acids. Esters are also used as artificial flavours in foods.

■ Making an ester from an alcohol and a carboxylic acid

Mix $1\,cm^3$ of ethanol and $1\,cm^3$ of anhydrous ethanoic acid in a test tube. Add 3 drops of concentrated sulfuric acid to the test tube and warm the mixture for 10 minutes in a water bath. The test tube will now contain some of the ester ethyl ethanoate. Pour the reaction mixture into $10\,cm^3$ of sodium carbonate solution to neutralise any unused ethanoic acid. Carefully smell the solution. It should have a fruity aroma from the ethyl ethanoate.

$$\text{ethanoic acid} + \text{ethanol} \rightleftharpoons \text{ethyl ethanoate} + \text{water}$$

$$CH_3COOH(l) + C_2H_5OH\,(l) \rightleftharpoons CH_3COOC_2H_5(l) + H_2O(l)$$

The reaction is an equilibrium and can be easily reversed. The concentrated sulfuric acid is used as a catalyst for the reaction and is not included in the equation.

REQUIRED PRACTICAL

This required practical relates to specification point 4.43C.
When warming the mixture of ethanol and ethanoic acid you should remember that both liquids are flammable and keep them away from flames. Wear goggles rather than safety spectacles: concentrated sulfuric acid must be handled with great care.

■ Esterification

This type of reaction is called an esterification. The following equations show how the two molecules react:

ethanoic acid + ethanol ⇌ ethyl ethanoate + water

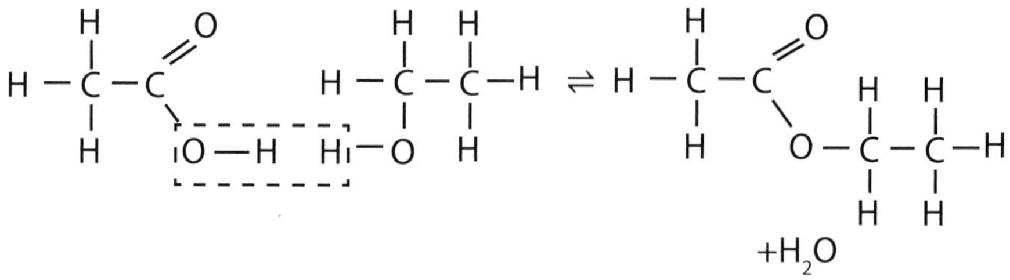

The carboxylic acid loses its –OH group and the alcohol loses the hydrogen from its –OH group to produce the molecule of water. The two molecules join together linked by the oxygen atom from the alcohol. As the reaction produces water, often as steam this is known as a **condensation reaction**.

This linkage is the functional group of esters:

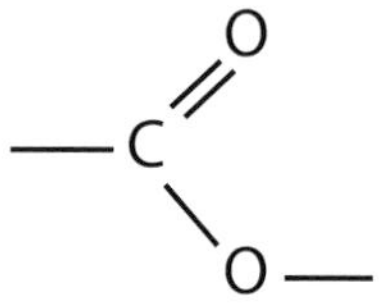

■ Naming esters

Most alcohols and carboxylic acids can react together in an esterification reaction. The first part of the name of the ester formed is always based on the name of the alcohol used, and the second part of the name is based on the salt produced from the carboxylic acid (see Chapter 4.7, Table 2). If ethanol is used, then the alcohol's name is changed to 'ethyl' in the name of the ester. Table 1 shows how the first part of the ester's name is based on the alcohol used.

Table 1 Naming an ester.

	Number of carbon atoms in alcohol	First part of ester's name from the alcohol
methanol	1	methyl
ethanol	2	ethyl
propanol	3	propyl
butanol	4	butyl
pentanol	5	pentyl
hexanol	6	hexyl

Figure 8.2 The pear flavour in pear drops is produced by the esters ethyl ethanoate and butyl propanoate.

Esters are volatile compounds that easily vaporise. Their distinctive smells can easily travel through the air to our noses. Inside our mouths they readily stimulate our taste buds. This is why esters are used as artificial flavourings in foods and are also used as perfumes. Ripening fruits produce these esters to attract animals to the fruit and encourage them to eat the fruit, so dispersing the seeds of the plant widely.

STUDY QUESTIONS

1　Draw the functional group of an ester.
2　Draw the structural formula of the ester ethyl methanoate.
3　Draw the displayed formula of the ester propyl ethanoate.
4　Draw the displayed structure of $CH_3COOCH_2CH_2CH_2CH_3$. Name the ester.
5　Name the ester formed by each of these reactions.
　　a) ethanol and pentanoic acid
　　b) propanol and ethanoic acid
　　c) butanol and methanoic acid
　　d) pentanol and propanoic acid.

4.9 Addition polymers

Figure 9.1 Clingfilm is made from PVC (polyvinylchloride).

Ethene is a very valuable substance for the chemical industry. Ethene, propene and other alkenes are used to make important polymers because they are so reactive. These important polymers include polythene, polypropene, polyvinylchloride (PVC), polystyrene and perspex.

■ Poly(ethene)

Ethene and other alkenes contain reactive carbon-to-carbon double bonds (C = C).

If the conditions are right, molecules of ethene will undergo **addition reactions** with each other to form **poly(ethene)** (sometimes shortened to polythene). Double bonds break, leaving single bonds as the molecules join together (Figure 9.2).

'Poly' means 'many'. So, poly(ethene) means 'many ethenes' joined together.

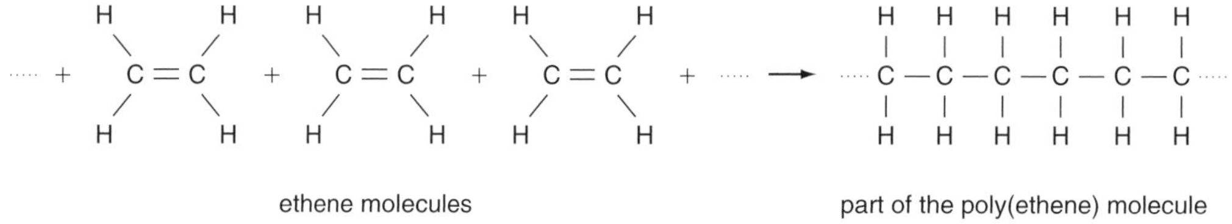

$$ \cdots + \underset{\substack{H \\ \diagdown \\ C = C \\ \diagup \\ H}}{\overset{\substack{H \\ \diagup \\ \diagdown \\ H}}{}} + \underset{\substack{H \\ \diagdown \\ C = C \\ \diagup \\ H}}{\overset{\substack{H \\ \diagup \\ \diagdown \\ H}}{}} + \underset{\substack{H \\ \diagdown \\ C = C \\ \diagup \\ H}}{\overset{\substack{H \\ \diagup \\ \diagdown \\ H}}{}} + \cdots \longrightarrow \cdots C - C - C - C - C - C \cdots $$

ethene molecules | part of the poly(ethene) molecule

Figure 9.2 Molecules of ethene can undergo addition reactions with each other.

Making poly(ethene)

Poly(ethene) is an addition polymer. It is manufactured by heating ethene at high pressure with special substances called **initiators**. Initiators start (initiate) the reaction by helping one of the double bonds to break. Carbon atoms in separate ethene molecules can then join together to form poly(ethene).

When ethene forms poly(ethene), very long chains are produced containing between 1000 and 5000 carbon atoms. The equation for this is usually summarised as:

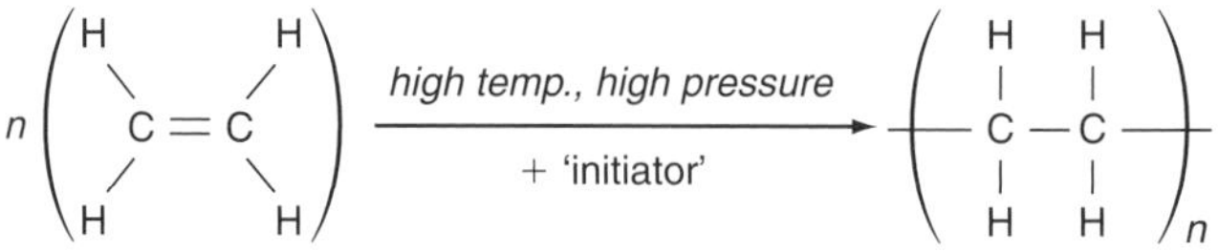

$$ n \left(\underset{\substack{H \\ | \\ H}}{\overset{\substack{H \\ | \\ }}{C = C}} \right) \xrightarrow[\text{+ 'initiator'}]{\text{high temp., high pressure}} \left(\underset{\substack{| \\ H}}{\overset{\substack{H \\ | \\ }}{C}} - \underset{\substack{| \\ H}}{\overset{\substack{H \\ | \\ }}{C}} \right)_n $$

In the structure of polythene, n is between 500 and 2500.

Addition polymerisation

Processes like this are called **addition polymerisations**.

During addition polymerisation, small molecules, like ethene, add to each other to form a giant long-chain molecule.

The giant long-chain molecule is called a **polymer**.

The small molecules, like ethene, which add to each other are called **monomers**.

Figure 9.3 lists the properties of poly(ethene). These have led to many different uses. Poly(ethene) is the most important plastic at present. It is used as thin sheets in plastic bags and boxes. It is moulded into beakers, buckets and plastic bottles. It is used to insulate underwater cables.

■ Other addition polymers

The two most useful and most commonly used polymers after poly(ethene) are **poly(propene)** and **poly(chloroethene)**, better known as **PVC**. These are also manufactured by addition polymerisation. The structure and uses of these two polymers are shown in Table 1.

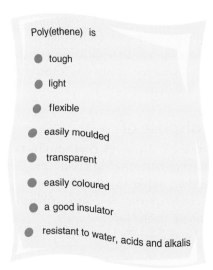

Poly(ethene) is

- tough
- light
- flexible
- easily moulded
- transparent
- easily coloured
- a good insulator
- resistant to water, acids and alkalis

Figure 9.3 The properties of poly(ethene).

Table 1 The structure and uses of poly(propene) and poly(chloroethene), PVC.

	Poly(propene)	Poly(chloroethene) (or polyvinylchoride, PVC)
Name and displayed formula of monomer	propene	chloroethene (vinyl chloride)
Section of polymer structure showing two repeat units		
Major uses	tough, easily moulded and easily coloured – used for crates and ropes	tough, rigid, water resistant – used in rainwear, insulation on electric cables, guttering, drain pipes and clingfilm

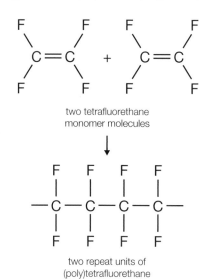

Figure 9.4 Two monomer units and a section of polymer chain of (poly) tetrafluoroethane.

PTFE, (poly)tetrafluoroethene is the polymer used to coat non-stick frying pans and sauce pans. It is used in many other applications such as plumbing where a slippery and reduced friction surface is required. The monomer is tetrafluoroethene and its polymerisation is shown in figure 9.4.

■ Making things from polymers

Polythene, polypropene and PVC are soft, flexible and slightly elastic. They are often called **plastics**. Once a plastic has been produced, it is then turned into a useful article.

This is usually done by:

- **moulding** the warm, soft plastic under pressure, or
- **extruding** (pushing out) the warm, soft plastic into different shapes by forcing it through nozzles or between rollers.

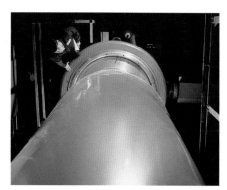

Figure 9.5 Polythene tubing emerging from an extrusion machine. The plastic is extruded from the container in which it is formed by hot pressurised air.

Figure 9.6 A biodegradable plastic bag.

Most plastics consist of molecules with very long, thin chains. Sometimes, however, the long polymer molecules can form bonds with each other at points along the chain. This produces cross-linked three-dimensional structures which are harder and more rigid. Melamine, resins and superglues (epoxyglues) are examples of these cross-linked plastics.

Addition polymers are hard to dispose of

The main raw material for all plastics is crude oil. Although these products have provided us with many new materials, they have one big disadvantage. They are **non-biodegradable**. This means that, unlike wood and paper, they are not decomposed by micro-organisms (bacteria). So plastic rubbish lies around for years, littering the environment. In the last few years, biodegradable plastics have been developed and used for bags, wrappings, bottles and other containers (Figure 9.6).

When addition polymers are burnt they can produce toxic gases. This is caused by the polymer chains reacting with other molecules that are being burnt at the same time, or because the monomer unit contains other elements or groups of atoms that when burnt produce toxic substances. In 2011 the Welsh Assembly introduced a 5p charge for plastic bags. In 2014 Scotland introduced the charge, and in 2015 so too did England. This has led to a dramatic 85% reduction in the number of plastic carrier bags being used.

STUDY QUESTIONS

1 Explain the following:
   polymer, addition polymerisation, non-biodegradable.
2 **a)** How is ethene manufactured?
   b) Why is ethene important in industry?
3 **a)** Give one use of plastic rubbish.
   b) Give one disadvantage of plastic rubbish.
4 An addition polymer has a repeat unit with this structure:

$$-\overset{\displaystyle H}{\underset{\displaystyle OH}{\overset{|}{\underset{|}{C}}}}-\overset{\displaystyle H}{\underset{\displaystyle H}{\overset{|}{\underset{|}{C}}}}-$$

   Draw the displayed structure of its monomer.

5 Look at the displayed formulae of the monomers in Table 1.
   a) Which part of their displayed formulae do they have in common?
   b) What happens when these monomers polymerise to form polymers?
   c) Polystyrene is made from the following monomer.

   Draw a section of polystyrene showing six carbon atoms in the chain.

4.10 Condensation polymers

Most common plastics are addition polymers formed by addition reactions. However, monomers can also be joined together by condensation reactions, and polymers produced in this way are called condensation polymers. The best known examples of synthetic condensation polymers are polyester and nylon.

■ Condensation reactions

In a **condensation reaction**, two larger molecules join together with the release of a small molecule from between them (Figure 10.2). The small molecule is usually water.

This is what happens when an ester is made (see Chapter 4.8). The ester is made from an alcohol and a carboxylic acid. The –OH group of the alcohol reacts with the –COOH group of the carboxylic acid to produce the ester link.

Making polyesters

If the carboxylic acid has a –COOH group at each end of the molecule, as shown in Figure 10.2, it could form ester links at both ends of the molecule and join with two alcohols. A carboxylic acid with two –COOH groups is called a **dicarboxylic acid**.

If the alcohol molecule has –OH groups in two places in the molecule, as is also shown in Figure 10.2, it too could form two ester links and join with two carboxylic acids. An alcohol with two –OH groups is called a **diol**.

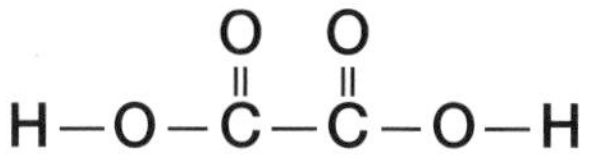

Figure 10.1 A polyester drinks bottle is an example of a synthetic condensation polymer.

ethanedioc acid

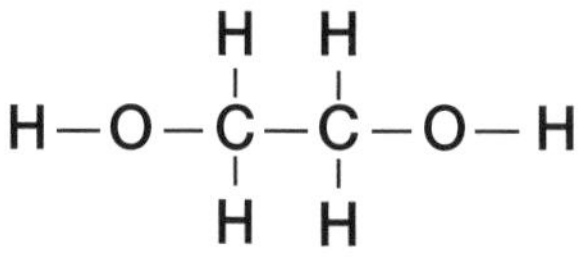

ethanediol

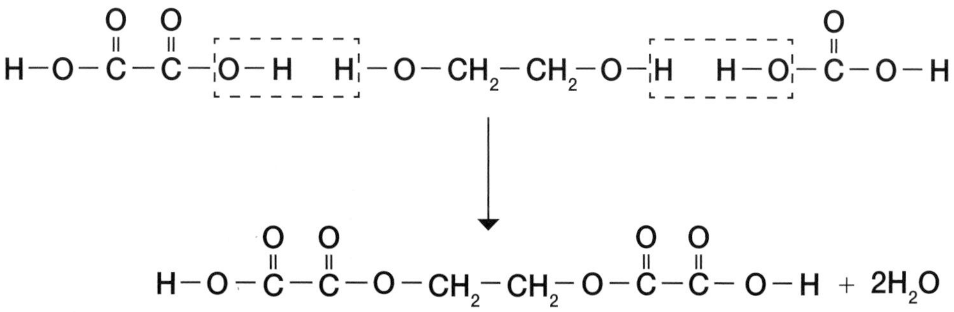

Figure 10.2 Ethanedioic acid and ethanediol taking part in a condensation reaction.

The type of polymer made is called a polyester. A molecule of water is released at each ester linkage, and so it is an example of a **condensation polymer**. This type of polymer is much tougher than most addition polymers, and are even harder to breakdown than addition polymers.

molecule of water
taken out from between
two larger molecules ...

... joining them together

Figure 10.3 A condensation reaction in block diagram format.

The reaction of the hundreds of ethanediol and ethanedioc acid molecules needed to make a single fibre of polyester can be represented by this equation:

$$ n \ \text{H-O-C-C-O-H} \ + \ n \ \text{H-O-C-C-O-H} \ \rightarrow \ \left[\text{C-C-O-C-C-O} \right]_n \ + 2n \, H_2O $$

Uses of polyesters

Polyesters are incredibly strong and are resistant to most chemicals. They make hard wearing clothes and fabrics, and are used to make plastic bottles for a variety of uses including bottled waters, soft drinks and beers.

Figure 10.4 Some uses of polyesters.

Biopolyesters

Polyesters are very resistant to chemical and microbial attack. This means that they can pose a significant environmental hazard as they are hard to biodegrade. To overcome this problem chemists have designed biopolyesters. These are polyesters that on prolonged contact with oxygen break down into carbon dioxide, water, sometimes methane, and biomass. This means that the residue from the polyester is non-toxic and can be subject to natural decay processes.

STUDY QUESTIONS

1 Describe the difference between ethanol and ethanediol.
2 Ethanedioc acid is the first of the homologous series of di-carboxylic acids. Explain why methanedioc acid cannot exist.
3 Describe how a polyester can be made from ethanedioc acid (HOOCCOOH) and propanediol (HOCH$_2$CH$_2$CH$_2$OH).
4 Evaluate the benefits of using a biopolyester thread against an ordinary polyester thread for making surgical stitches inside a person's body.

Summary

I am confident that:

✓ **I can describe how the mixture of hydrocarbons in crude oil is separated using fractional distillation, and can name the main fractions and state the number of carbon atoms in each fraction**

✓ **I can describe the trend in boiling points and viscosity of the main fractions of crude oil**
- As the number of carbon atoms increases, the boiling point increases.
- As the number of carbon atoms increases, the viscosity increases.

✓ **I know that fractional distillation of crude oil provides insufficient short-chain hydrocarbons such as gasoline.**
- The process of cracking makes long-chain hydrocarbons into alkenes and useful shorter-chain hydrocarbons.

✓ **I understand the complete and incomplete combustion of carbon-based fuels**
- Incomplete combustion produces carbon monoxide.
- Inhalation of carbon monoxide is dangerous as it reduces the capacity of blood to transport oxygen.

✓ **I know that nitrogen in the air at high temperatures inside car engines can be converted to nitrogen oxides**
- Nitrogen oxides as well sulfur oxides contribute to acid rain.

✓ **I know the products of complete and incomplete combustion of hydrocarbons**
- Complete combustion produces only water and carbon dioxide.
- Incomplete combustion produces water and carbon monoxide.
- Incomplete combustion produces water and carbon (soot).

✓ **I can explain the terms:**
- homologous series
- hydrocarbon
- saturated
- unsaturated
- general formula
- structural formula
- displayed formula
- isomerism
- functional group.

✓ **I know that alkanes are compounds containing only carbon and hydrogen**
- Alkanes have the general formula C_nH_{2n+2}.
- They have only single bonds.
- They are fairly unreactive.

✓ **I know that alkenes are compounds containing only carbon and hydrogen**
- Alkenes have the general formula C_nH_{2n}.
- Their molecules contain one carbon-to-carbon double bond.
- They are very reactive.

✓ **I can draw displayed formulae for straight-chain alkanes with up to six carbon atoms and name them**
- These are named according to the longest straight chain of carbon atoms, methane (1C), ethane (2C), propane (3C), butane (4C), pentane (5C) and hexane (6C).

✓ **I can draw displayed formulae for the alkenes ethene, propene and butene**

✓ **I can describe the UV radiation-initiated substitution reaction of methane with bromine**
- I can write a balanced equation using displayed formulae.

✓ **I can describe the addition reaction of alkenes with bromine**
- The decolorisation of bromine water is a test for alkenes.

✓ **I can describe how ethanol can be manufactured, by:**
- the reaction of ethene with steam
- the fermentation of sugars such as glucose by yeast.

✓ **I can describe how ethanol may be oxidised by**
- air in combustion
- microbial oxidation
- potassium dichromate(VI).

✓ **I can draw displayed formulae for molecules with up to four carbon atoms with these functional groups and name them**
- alcohols
- carboxylic acids
- diols
- dicarboxylic acid.

✓ **I know that an addition polymer is made up of many identical monomer units, and can deduce from a repeat unit the monomer from which the addition polymer was made**
- There are many useful addition polymers.
- Their disposal poses difficulties.

✓ **I know that some polymers such as polyesters are made from two different monomers**
- This is known as condensation polymerisation, because a small molecule such as water is produced when the two different monomers bond together.
- Biopolyesters degrade easily and safely in the environment.

Sample answers and expert's comments

1 Methane is the simplest hydrocarbon. The table below shows some information about methane molecules.

	methane	ethane
molecular formula	CH_4	
displayed formula	H | H—C—H | H	
dot and cross diagram of bonding	(dot and cross diagram of methane)	
state at room temperature	gas	

a) Copy and complete the table to show the same information for ethane as is shown for methane. (4)

b) What is a hydrocarbon? (1)

c) Methane and ethane are part of a homologous series. What is a homologous series? (1)

d) Methane burns to produce water vapour. Name the other three possible products of the combustion of methane, and state the conditions necessary for each product to be made. (3)

(Total for question = 9 marks)

Student response Total 7/9	Expert comments and tips for success
a) |	Ethane
molecular formula	C_2H_6 ✔
displayed formula	H H | | H—C—C—H ✔ | | H H
dot and cross diagram of bonding	(ethane dot and cross diagram) ✔
state at room temperature	gas ✔		Full marks. The formula is correct and so are the displayed formula and dot and cross diagram. The answer shows a clear understanding of carbon's need for four bonds, and hydrogen's one bond.
b) A compound containing only carbon and hydrogen ✔	Correctly explains the elements present in a hydrocarbon.

c) A group of compounds where each compound is different to the next by the same amount. In this case CH_2. ✔	Gives the correct definition, for 1 mark.
d) Carbon dioxide when there is lots of oxygen.✔ Carbon monoxide when there is no oxygen. O	Only 1 mark out of 3. Read the question carefully to find the number of answers wanted. Carbon dioxide and the conditions are right, but the conditions for carbon monoxide are wrong. There has to be some oxygen present for the methane to burn to make carbon monoxide and carbon.

2 Crude oil is separated by fractional distillation into hydrocarbon fractions.
A hydrocarbon is a compound that contains only hydrogen and carbon.
A fraction is a mixture of hydrocarbons that contains molecules with a similar boiling point range. The table gives some information about four fractions.

Common name of fraction	Average number of carbon atoms in the molecules	Average boiling point of fraction in °C	Time for ignition after flame applied in s
refinery gases	3	40	0
gasoline	8	110	1
kerosene	10	180	3
diesel	14	250	5

a) Explain why the table uses the average number to describe the number of carbon atoms in the molecules of a fraction. (2)

b) Describe the relationship between the average number of carbon atoms in a fraction and the average boiling point of the fraction. (1)

c) Explain why diesel is the most viscous of the fractions in the table. Use information from the table and your knowledge of hydrocarbons in your answer. (2)

d) Fuel oil and bitumen are two more fractions. Bitumen has more than 50 carbon atoms in its molecules and fuel oil has on average 35 carbon atoms. Explain which of the six fractions will be hardest to ignite. (2)

(Total for question = 7 marks)

Student response Total 7/7	Expert comments and tips for success
a) Each fraction is made up of lots of different molecules.✔ The molecules have similar boiling points as they have similar numbers of carbon atoms ✔, so it's best to use the mean value for the carbon atoms.	A good answer using information from the table and question with a clear explanation of why is it useful to give the average number of carbon atoms for a fraction.
b) The higher the number of carbon atoms, the higher the boiling point. ✔	This answer clearly relates the boiling point to the number of carbon atoms.
c) Diesel has the highest boiling point which means the molecules are most strongly attracted to each other ✔. So the molecules will find it harder to slip past each other ✔ making it more viscous.	You should use the data in this way. Refer to the data, then use your knowledge to explain the information and its relevance to the question.
d) Bitumen. ✔ The trend from the table shows increasing difficulty to ignite with more carbon atoms, so as it is the largest ✔, bitumen is hard to light.	1 mark for the correct choice. The trend from the table is given and then used to support the answer.

Exam-style questions

1 Crude oil is an important resource. It was formed over millions of years from the remains of dead plants and animals that were buried in sediments.

   a) The oil industry uses fractionating towers to split crude oil into more useful fractions.

   i)   How does the boiling point change as the number of carbon atoms in these fractions increases? [1]

   ii) Explain how the process of fractional distillation separates crude oil into more useful fractions. [2]

   b) Octadecane, $C_{18}H_{38}$, is found in the diesel oil fraction.

   i)   Octadecane can be **cracked** into smaller molecules. One way is shown in the equation.

   $$C_{18}H_{38} \rightarrow C_8H_{16} + C_8H_{18} + C_2H_4$$

   octadecane → octene + _____ + _____

   Copy and finish the word equation for this reaction. [1]

   ii) Explain why cracking long-chain compounds such as octadecane enables oil companies to make more profit. Use the equation in part (b) i) to help you with your answer. [2]

   c) The refinery gases fraction from crude oil contains propene and propane.

   propene   propane

   i)   Describe a chemical test which you could use to distinguish between propene and propane. [2]

   ii) Explain why propene can be polymerised, but propane cannot. [2]

   iii) Write an equation to summarise the polymerisation of propene. [2]

2 In some countries the exhaust gases from older cars must be tested each year. These exhaust gases contain carbon monoxide, unburned hydrocarbons and smoke.

   a) Look at the results below from an exhaust test.

   Use these results to answer the questions.

Item	Test result	Maximum limit
carbon monoxide	4.0%	3.5%
unburned hydrocarbons	297 ppm	1200 ppm
idle speed	pass	
smoke level	pass	

   i)   What is the maximum limit of carbon monoxide allowed? [1]

   ii) This car failed its test. Why? [1]

   b) Why is carbon monoxide dangerous? [2]

   c) As well as carbon monoxide, unburned hydrocarbons, smoke and water, car exhausts contain other gases. One of these gases may cause a change in the Earth's climate.

   Name this gas and explain why it can affect the climate. [3]

3 Ethene, C_2H_4, and methane, CH_4, are the first members of two different homologous series.

   a) One characteristic of a homologous series is that all its members have the same general formula.

   i)   State **two** other characteristics of a homologous series. [2]

   ii) What is the name of the homologous series to which methane belongs? [1]

   iii) What is the general formula of this homologous series? [1]

b) i) Use the Periodic Table on page 273 to help you copy and complete the diagrams to show the electronic configuration of hydrogen and of carbon.

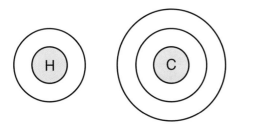

[2]

ii) Draw a dot and cross diagram to show the covalent bonding in a methane molecule. [2]

c) The alkane C_4H_{10} exists as two isomers.

i) What are isomers? [2]

ii) Draw the displayed formula of each isomer. [2]

4 Alkenes are unsaturated hydrocarbons.

a) State the general formula of all alkenes. [1]

b) Draw the displayed formula of ethene. [1]

c) Alkenes can be shown to be unsaturated using bromine water. Describe the colour change that occurs when an alkene reacts with bromine water.

5 Ethanol is manufactured in two ways.

a) By the fermentation of a carbohydrate.

i) What must be present in the solution of carbohydrate to make fermentation occur? [1]

ii) What process is used to separate ethanol from the fermentation mixture? [1]

b) By the hydration of ethene.

i) Write a balanced chemical equation, including state symbols, for the hydration of ethene to produce ethanol. [2]

ii) State the conditions for this reaction. [2]

c) Ethene can be prepared by dehydrating ethanol using aluminium oxide.

i) Copy and complete the equation for this process.

$$C_2H_5OH \rightarrow C_2H_4 + [\ \ ]$$ [1]

ii) Calculate the maximum volume of ethene, at room temperature and atmospheric pressure, that can be obtained from 2.30 g of ethanol. (C = 12, H = 1, O = 16)

(1 mol of gas occupies 24.0 dm³ at room temperature and pressure) [3]

6 Many useful substances are produced by the fractional distillation of crude oil.

a) Bitumen, fuel oil and gasoline are three fractions obtained from crude oil. There are several differences between these fractions. Which of these three fractions has:

i) the highest boiling point range [1]

ii) molecules with the fewest carbon atoms [1]

iii) the darkest colour? [1]

b) Some long-chain hydrocarbons are converted into more useful products by a chemical process. Name this process and describe how it is carried out. [3]

c) Some hydrocarbons, such as methane, are used as fuels. When methane undergoes incomplete combustion, carbon monoxide is formed.

i) Write a chemical equation for this reaction. [2]

ii) Explain why it is dangerous to breathe air containing carbon monoxide. [1]

7 Sugar can be converted into poly(ethene) as follows:

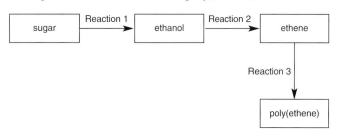

a) State the type of reaction occurring in:

    i)   Reaction 1 [1]

    ii) What type of polymerisation occurs in Reaction 3? [1]

b) State **two** conditions used in the conversion of sugar to ethanol in Reaction 1. [2]

c) Draw the displayed formula of ethanol. [1]

d) Many thousands of ethene molecules combine to form a poly(ethene) molecule. Draw that part of the structure of a poly(ethene) molecule that forms from **three** ethene molecules. [2]

e) Polyester is made by a different type of polymerisation. Name this type of polymerisation and describe how it is different from the type of polymerisation used to make poly(ethene). [3]

8 **a)** Describe briefly how crude oil was formed. [3]

b) Propene and propane can be produced from crude oil.

    i)   A propene molecule (C_3H_6) can be represented by the display formula below.

$$
\begin{array}{c}
H \\
\diagdown \\
C = C - C - H \\
\diagup \\
H
\end{array}
\quad
\begin{array}{c}
H \quad H \\
| \quad | \\
\\
| \\
H
\end{array}
$$

    Draw a similar displayed formula for the structure of a propane molecule (C_3H_8). [1]

    ii) Which molecule, propene or propane, is unsaturated? Explain your answer. [2]

c) The equation below summarises the polymerisation of propene.

$$
n\left(
\begin{array}{c}
H \quad H \\
| \quad | \\
C = C \\
| \quad | \\
H \quad CH_3
\end{array}
\right)
\longrightarrow
\left(
\begin{array}{c}
H \quad H \\
| \quad | \\
C - C \\
| \quad | \\
H \quad CH_3
\end{array}
\right)_n
$$

    i)   Name the polymer produced by this reaction. [1]

    ii) Explain the meaning of the term **polymerisation**. [1]

9 Ethanoic acid is a carboxylic acid. It has the molecular formula $C_2H_4O_2$.

a) Draw the structural formula of ethanoic acid. [1]

b) Ethanoic acid is a weak acid. The equation shows how it reacts with sodium carbonate.

$$2CH_3COOH(aq) + Na_2CO_3(aq) \rightarrow$$
$$2CH_3COO^-Na^+(aq) + H_2O(l) + CO_2(g)$$

    Name the sodium salt made. [1]

c) Ethanoic acid can also react with an alcohol such as ethanol (CH_3CH_2OH) to make an ester.

    Draw and name the ester made by ethanoic acid and ethanol. [2]

d) Explain why esters are used in the food industry. [2]

10 Polyesters are polymers that are very tough and hardwearing. They are highly resistant to chemical and bacterial attack. A polyester can be made from these two monomers.

$$H-O-\overset{\overset{O}{\|}}{C}-\overset{\overset{O}{\|}}{C}-O-H \qquad H-O-\overset{\overset{H}{|}}{\underset{\underset{H}{|}}{C}}-\overset{\overset{H}{|}}{\underset{\underset{H}{|}}{C}}-O-H$$

   monomer A   monomer B

a) What is a monomer? [1]

b) Monomer A is called ethanedioc acid. What is monomer B called? [1]

c) When monomer A and monomer B polymerise they make this repeat unit of polymer.

$$\left[-\overset{\overset{O}{\|}}{C}-\overset{\overset{O}{\|}}{C}-O-\overset{\overset{H}{|}}{\underset{\underset{H}{|}}{C}}-\overset{\overset{H}{|}}{\underset{\underset{H}{|}}{C}}-O- \right]_n$$

Explain why this type of polymerisation is known as condensation polymerisation. [2]

d) Some scientists have developed a type of polyesters known as biopolyesters. Suggest why these biopolyesters have been developed. [2]

EXTEND AND CHALLENGE

Fracking for gas

All across the world oil companies are starting a hunt for more natural gas using a technique called 'fracking'. This involves injecting high-pressure water and chemicals into rocks known as shales in order to release trapped methane (CH_4) or natural gas. The methane is trapped in the structure of the shale, and the rock needs to be broken up to release the gas.

One area where fracking has been carried out is in the Fylde part of Lancashire, UK, near Blackpool. Here a rock formation known as the Bowland Basin is estimated to contain as much as 20 trillion cubic metres of gas.

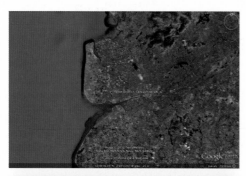

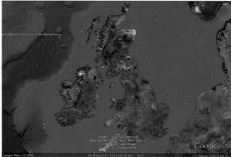

Figure 1 A fracking site in the UK.

In 2011 fracking was suspended after two minor earthquakes of magnitudes 2.3 and 1.5 on the Richter scale hit the Fylde which the British Geological Survey concluded had been caused by the fracking. By 2012 over 50 minor earth tremors had been recorded in the area since fracking began.

1 Why do we need to recover methane from shale rocks?
2 Describe the process of fracking.
3 Suggest how fracking might cause earthquakes.

In response to concerns expressed by those living nearby, the company's scientists suggested that they would cease fracking should an earthquake of scale 1.7 or greater occur, while investigations as to the cause are carried out. This was described by the company as being well below the threshold for damage to buildings.

Table 1 The Richter scale.

Richter scale	Description	Effect
less than 2.0	micro	not felt
2.0–2.9	minor	often not felt, but recorded
3.0–3.9	minor	often felt, but rarely causes damage
4.0–4.9	light	noticeable shaking of indoor items, rattling noises, little damage
5.0–5.9	moderate	major damage to poorly constructed buildings over small regions
6.0–6.9	strong	major damage in areas up to about 160 km across in populated areas
7.0–7.9	major	major damage over wider areas
8.0–8.9	great	major damage in areas several hundred kilometres across
9.0–9.9		devastating in areas several thousand kilometres across

The UK's Department of Energy and Climate Change (DECC) recommended that the threshold be set at 0.5 on the Richter scale, as small earthquakes often occur before much larger ones.

Friends of the Earth are strongly opposed to fracking, on several grounds. They are concerned about the risk of man-induced earthquakes, but also water and air pollution. Additionally they are concerned that burning the methane produced will increase greenhouse gases in the air. Friends of the Earth think that using wind and wave power are more environmentally friendly methods of obtaining energy for our needs in both the short and long term.

4 Use the Richter scale in Table 1 to determine how much damage was caused by the earthquakes.
5 Suggest why the company recommended a limit of 1.7 on the Richter scale, but the DECC recommended a much lower value of 0.5 at which to stop fracking.
6 An oil company has proposed to carry out fracking near to your home. Write a letter or email for your local paper explaining why you are in favour of fracking, or against it. You should mention both the risks to the area and the benefits.

Periodic Table

I	II												III	IV	V	VI	VII	0
1	2												3	4	5	6	7	
							1 **H** Hydrogen 1											4 **He** Helium 2
7 **Li** Lithium 3	9 **Be** Beryllium 4												11 **B** Boron 5	12 **C** Carbon 6	14 **N** Nitrogen 7	16 **O** Oxygen 8	19 **F** Fluorine 9	20 **Ne** Neon 10
23 **Na** Sodium 11	24 **Mg** Magnesium 12												27 **Al** Aluminium 13	28 **Si** Silicon 14	31 **P** Phosphorous 15	32 **S** Sulfur 16	35.5 **Cl** Chlorine 17	40 **Ar** Argon 18
39 **K** Potassium 19	40 **Ca** Calcium 20	45 **Sc** Scandium 21	48 **Ti** Titanium 22	51 **V** Vanadium 23	52 **Cr** Chromium 24	55 **Mn** Manganese 25	56 **Fe** Iron 26	59 **Co** Cobalt 27	59 **Ni** Nickel 28	63.5 **Cu** Copper 29	65 **Zn** Zinc 30		70 **Ga** Gallium 31	73 **Ge** Germanium 32	75 **As** Arsenic 33	79 **Se** Selenium 34	80 **Br** Bromine 35	84 **Kr** Krypton 36
85 **Rb** Rubidium 37	88 **Sr** Strontium 38	89 **Y** Yttrium 39	91 **Zr** Zirconium 40	93 **Nb** Niobium 41	95 **Mo** Molybdenum 42	99 **Tc** Technetium 43	101 **Ru** Ruthenium 44	103 **Rh** Rhodium 45	106 **Pd** Palladium 46	108 **Ag** Silver 47	112 **Cd** Cadmium 48		115 **In** Indium 49	119 **Sn** Tin 50	122 **Sb** Antimony 51	128 **Te** Tellurium 52	127 **I** Iodine 53	131 **Xe** Xenon 54
133 **Cs** Caesium 55	137 **Ba** Barium 56	139 **La** Lanthanum 57 *	178 **Hf** Hafnium 72	181 **Ta** Tantalum 73	184 **W** Tungsten 74	186 **Re** Rhenium 75	190 **Os** Osmium 76	192 **Ir** Iridium 77	195 **Pt** Platinum 78	197 **Au** Gold 79	201 **Hg** Mercuy 80		204 **Tl** Thallium 81	207 **Pb** Lead 82	209 **Bi** Bismuth 83	210 **Po** Polonium 84	210 **At** Astatine 85	222 **Rn** Radon 86
223 **Fr** Francium 87	226 **Ra** Radium 88	227 **Ac** Actinium 89 †																

*58–71 Lanthanum series
†90–103 Actinium series

140 **Ce** Cerium 58	141 **Pr** Praseodymium 59	144 **Nd** Neodymium 60	147 **Pm** Promethium 61	150 **Sm** Samarium 62	152 **Eu** Europium 63	157 **Gd** Gadolinium 64	159 **Tb** Terbium 65	162 **Dy** Dysprosium 66	165 **Ho** Holmium 67	167 **Er** Erbium 68	169 **Tm** Thulium 69	173 **Yb** Ytterbium 70	175 **Lu** Lutetium 71
232 **Th** Thorium 90	231 **Pa** Protactinium 91	238 **U** Uranium 92	237 **Np** Neptunium 93	242 **Pu** Plutonium 94	243 **Am** Americium 95	247 **Cm** Curium 96	245 **Bk** Berkelium 97	251 **Cf** Californium 98	254 **Es** Einsteinium 99	253 **Fm** Fermium 100	256 **Md** Mendelevium 101	254 **No** Nobelium 102	257 **Lr** Lawrencium 103

a = relative atomic mass
X = atomic symbol
b = atomic number

Relative atomic masses

Element	Symbol	A_r
aluminium	Al	27
antimony	Sb	122
argon	Ar	40
arsenic	As	75
barium	Ba	137
beryllium	Be	9
bismuth	Bi	209
boron	B	11
bromine	Br	80
cadmium	Cd	112
caesium	Cs	133
calcium	Ca	40
carbon	C	12
chlorine	Cl	35.5
chromium	Cr	52
cobalt	Co	59
copper	Cu	63.5
fluorine	F	19
gallium	Ga	70
germanium	Ge	73
gold	Au	197
helium	He	4
hydrogen	H	1
iodine	I	127
iridium	Ir	192
iron	Fe	56
krypton	Kr	84
lead	Pb	207
lithium	Li	7

Element	Symbol	A_r
magnesium	Mg	24
manganese	Mn	55
mercury	Hg	201
molybdenum	Mo	96
neon	Ne	20
nickel	Ni	59
nitrogen	N	14
oxygen	O	16
phosphorus	P	31
platinum	Pt	195
potassium	K	39
rubidium	Rb	85
scandium	Sc	45
selenium	Se	79
silicon	Si	28
silver	Ag	108
sodium	Na	23
strontium	Sr	88
sulfur	S	32
tellurium	Te	128
thorium	Th	232
tin	Sn	119
titanium	Ti	48
tungsten	W	184
uranium	U	238
vanadium	V	51
xenon	Xe	131
zinc	Zn	65

Index